THE RICH

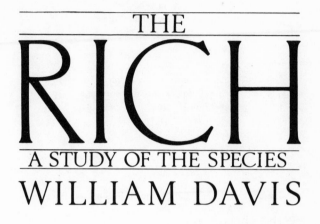

THE
RICH
A STUDY OF THE SPECIES
WILLIAM DAVIS

A GROLIER COMPANY

FRANKLIN WATTS
New York ● 1983

Other books by William Davis

Three Years Hard Labour
Merger Mania
Money Talks
Have Expenses, Will Travel
It's No Sin to be Rich
The Best of Everything (editor)
Money in the 1980s

The author is grateful to Malcolm S. Forbes
for permission to reprint extracts from
"The Forbes Four Hundred" from *Forbes Magazine*,
September 13, 1982.

Library of Congress Cataloging in Publication Data

Davis, William, 1933–
    The Rich: A Study of the Species.

    Reprint. Originally published: London: Sidgwick &
Jackson, 1982.
    Bibliography: p.
    Includes index.
        1. Wealth.   2. Millionaires.   I. Title.
HC79.W4D38   1983   305.5'234   82-23880
              ISBN 0-531-09893-1

First published in Great Britain in 1982
by Sidgwick & Jackson Limited
First published in the United States in 1983
by Franklin Watts

To my partners, Peter and Bob

Let me tell you about the very rich. They are different from you and me.
They possess and enjoy early, and it does something to them, makes them
soft where we are hard, and cynical where we are trustful, in a way that,
unless you were born rich, it is difficult to understand. They think, deep
in their hearts, that they are better than we are because we had to discover
the compensations and refuges of life for ourselves. Even when they enter
deep into our world or sink below us, they still think that they are better
than we are. They are different.

F. Scott Fitzgerald

CONTENTS

INTRODUCTION

Friends sometimes accuse me of being "obsessed" with the rich. As far as they are concerned the rich are an unappealing lot: greedy, unscrupulous, and indifferent to the problems of their fellow men. "Why," they ask, "do you want to write about them?"

The short answer is that I find them fascinating—and society's attitude toward them no less so. The drive to get rich is one of the most powerful known to man, and the use of wealth is an enormously important factor in human behavior. It has always been so, and it will always be so. Even societies that claim to have abolished the rich, such as the Soviet Union and China, continue to respect the power of money.

"Rich," for most people, is a term that encompasses all those who are better off than they are. To the average man living in India, even the poorest working-class Englishman is rich. To the Soviet peasant the Kremlin bureaucrat, with his chauffeur-driven car and country dacha, is rich. To the executive earning $100,000 a year the controlling shareholder whose stake is worth millions is rich. One's ideas change at each rung of the ladder. The late Paul Getty once said that no one is really rich if he can count his money, which I suppose is the ultimate. (Nelson Bunker Hunt, one of the Texas twins who tried to corner the silver market a few years ago, put it another way. Asked by a Senate Committee how much he was worth, he replied, "If I knew, I wouldn't be worth very much.")

Freud, who had a theory for everything, tried to establish a link between "anal eroticism" and the hoarding of money. He said it begins in early childhood: the act of defecation affords a pleasure of the sphincter which infants store up by postponing the motion. His theory was hotly debated at the time, as it was no doubt meant to be, but it is hardly an adequate explanation. The classic "anal character," as described by Freud, has three main characteristics that go together: excessive orderliness, parsimoniousness and obstinacy. There certainly are people who fit that description but there are also a great many self-made millionaires who don't. If there are any anal connections they are more likely to be the opposite to that postulated by Freud: just as a baby wants to win the approval of its mother by producing stool ("Look what I've done"), so the adult wants to win the approval of the world by making a fortune.

Childhood experiences undoubtedly have a strong bearing on the desire to get rich. Many tycoons are driven on by memories of what it was like to be poor—they have never quite managed to shake off their phobia. Others remain deeply influenced by their schooldays. The system aroused their competitive drive and it has been kept in high gear ever since. Money has taken the place of marks, prizes and degrees: it is the symbolic equivalent of the awards they tried so hard to get. Those who did badly have a great urge to prove to their parents, their former teachers and fellow pupils, and to the world at large that they were misjudged. "I'll show them," they resolved at sixteen, and they spend the rest of their lives doing just that.

As men—and women—grow wealthy, other motives play an increasingly important role. One is the compulsion to use the power of money to revenge themselves on people who have slighted them in the past. Then there is the desire for a luxurious and impressive life-style—the accumulation of expensive status symbols like yachts and villas in the South of France. And last, but certainly not least, is the thrill of the chase—the pleasure to be had from outsmarting rivals, acquiring the treasured possessions of others, and having one's judgment vindicated. Money as such ceases to be important; it is merely the yardstick by which the world judges their success.

Introduction

People who have built up a business empire, and make a fortune in the process, often make the quite serious claim that they have just as much right to be called creative as any artist. It may strike you as an outrageous argument, but that is how they like to see themselves. It gives them a satisfaction which those who have simply inherited millions often conspicuously lack.

Society has always taken a somewhat ambivalent view of the rich. On the one hand, they command attention and respect; a rich man or woman is never short of flattery. On the other hand, there is a widespread tendency to portray them as grasping parasites. Much of the criticism is based on resentment and envy rather than on a rational assessment of what they do. The most vehement critics are those who know that they are unlikely ever to join their ranks.

Academics and writers have never had much time for big business, and this is reflected in their interpretation of, and comments on, economic history. The businessman has rarely been depicted as a hero by those most influential in forming public opinion, however much his efforts may have contributed to economic progress. The public at large tends to take its cue from authors of racy novels such as Harold Robbins, who have become rich themselves through vivid descriptions of a jungle populated by power-mad tycoons who cut each other to pieces—when, that is, they are not busy hopping from one bed to another. We like to believe that this is how things really are.

Some people long to become part of that jungle, and avidly read every "how to" book that comes onto the market. This is particularly true of countries like the United States, where financial success is very much part of the American Dream. But the vast majority of people around the world, resigned to the fact that they will never be rich themselves, prefer to think that the battles and sacrifices needed to get there are not worthwhile. Life is short, they say, and there are more laudable objectives. "Money doesn't buy happiness," they intone, and for good measure add that much-used quote from the Bible: "It is easier for a camel to go through the eye of a needle than for a rich man to enter the Kingdom of God."

The rich often come to the same conclusion. It is by no means unusual for a billionaire to give away much of his fortune during his lifetime (cynics would say that he would rather endow a college or museum bearing his name than leave it to the taxman), or for a self-made man to change the whole course of his life at forty-five or fifty. Many self-made men reach the point where the game is no longer fun, and they use their money to chase some other rainbow with equal vigor. They may decide to paint, or become goldsmiths, or write poems. Most rich people are almost childishly pleased if you tell them that they are good at something else besides making money.

One of the key stages for a self-made man is the moment when he pauses just long enough to ask himself (often at the instigation of his family) where he is going. He suddenly realizes that he is more than halfway through his allotted span and could not possibly hope to spend all the money he has made. Some charge on because it is the only way of life they know and the only one that gives them the excitement they need. Others break off abruptly, sell their shares in the business, and do something else.

Heirs and heiresses either try to emulate the dynamos who built their fortunes (the "I'll show them" motive all over again), or decide early on that they cannot possibly hope to do as well and devote their lives to some other pursuit—the arts, perhaps, or luxurious idleness.

A few years ago I wrote a book called *It's No Sin to be Rich*, in which I argued that individuals should be allowed to do their own thing. I was promptly accused of being an apologist for the capitalist system. I am nothing of the sort. I believe in free enterprise because I believe it is the only system that can uphold and protect individual rights—and that, to me, matters more than anything else.

My purpose, in this book, is to take a much broader look at the rich—what money means to them and how they use it, their pleasures and ego trips, their fears and hang-ups, their involvement in the arts, their battles with the tax collector and other enemies (real or imagined), and their attitudes toward the rest of us. It is not an enthusiastic and indiscriminate attempt to justify all they do, or indeed a paean of praise to wealth itself. I fully recognize that it has its ugly side. *The Rich* is a highly personal view of people who, despite all today's political, social and economic pressures, still have an influential role in the world in which we live.

In more than thirty years as a financial journalist I have had ample opportunity to study the rich in many different countries. I have admired some and detested others; it is clearly absurd to pretend, as the left tends to do, that they are all the same. I have met millionaires who are stingy and others who are madly generous; millionaires who are totally indifferent to their fellow men and millionaires who have a strong sense of obligation toward the society in which they live; millionaires who enjoy their money and millionaires who have never quite learned to handle it; millionaires who lead happy lives and millionaires who are miserable.

Few have actually had a million in the bank. The self-made rich believe in putting their cash to good use, which means investing it. Many are heavy borrowers: one of Britain's most successful entrepreneurs once told me that he had *always* had an overdraft. When I asked the late Lord Thomson, on his eightieth birthday, how much cash he had on him, he turned out his pockets and produced a single five pound note. "But," he said, "I have a credit card." This may explain why the rich are often bad tippers, though I suspect that their apparent meanness has more to do with the fact that they resent being ripped off. A rich man knows that everyone around him thinks he is an easy mark. It makes him angry because, as he sees it, it means that people take him for a fool.

Like the rest of us, the rich also have their own perception of *need*. A hundred thousand dollars seems a fortune to the lowly office clerk struggling to make ends meet; to the rich, it seems a modest sum. Some millionaires will tell you, earnestly, that they need an income of a hundred thousand a year "just to stay alive." And I well remember one self-made man's description of how he felt when his accountant informed him that he was "down to the last million." He was so shattered that he locked himself up in his lavatory for several hours and had a good cry; he even (or so he said) considered suicide. His reaction may strike you as ridiculous, but I am sure that many of the rich would regard it as perfectly natural.

It is all too easy to envy the rich; it is also easy to pity them. I hope, though, that the species will survive. The rich make life more interesting: they are a luxury a civilized society should be able to afford. My thanks are due to the many men and women who have talked to me so freely over the years. This book will no doubt upset some and please others; we are all entitled to our own opinions. I have had the good fortune to travel widely and I have tried to inject a strong international flavor because I don't think one should take a narrow national view. *The Rich* is, essentially, intended to be a contribution to a debate that is likely to continue worldwide for a long time to come.

THE RICH

CHAPTER 1

THE SPECIES

No one is really rich if he can count his money.

PAUL GETTY

The cliché image of the wealthy businessman is that of a middle-aged, overweight tycoon sitting behind an imposing desk and barking out orders to terrified subordinates—when, that is, he is not talking into three telephones at once. There certainly are people like that, but the mere fact that a man has a big job and a desk to match does not necessarily mean that he is rich. He is likely to be a manager rather than an owner, a steward for a plurality of economic interests rather than a wealthy entrepreneur. He will, of course, have some of the customary status symbols of the rich—a Cadillac or Rolls Royce, and perhaps even the use of a company plane—and he will usually earn a salary that is large enough to qualify him for most people's definition of rich. But he may well lack the real basis of wealth—capital. This is particularly true of countries where the tax system makes it much more difficult for a salaried man to accumulate a fortune than his published income tends to suggest.

The chief executive of a large corporation wields considerable power (see pages 189–190) but he is ultimately dependent on the people who are the real owners of the business—big financial institutions, wealthy individual shareholders, and so on. He can sign a check for a million dollars without giving it more than a passing

3

thought, but it isn't *his* money. If he fails to give satisfaction, the rug may be unceremoniously pulled out from under him.

There are, of course, many chief executives who are themselves shareholders in the company. Some were given shares in the early days of the enterprise, when it was still struggling to make its mark, and have seen their value increase to such an extent over the years that they are worth a fortune. Some have acquired shares along the way. Others actually started the business, and behave as if they own it. But even founders can be vulnerable. Some of the best-known companies on both sides of the Atlantic, ostensibly the personal property of the individual who heads the board, are in reality owned by a large number of people who take no active part in the running of the business.

There may be all kinds of reasons for this. As a company grows, the founder often parts with shares in order to raise more funds or to cash in on his success. Acquisitions frequently dilute the share capital. The remaining shares may still be worth millions—even billions—but they no longer carry voting control. The founder continues to run the business mainly because the other shareholders think he is the best man for the job, or because his friends and associates have pledged themselves to use their own holdings to keep him at the helm.

Any attempt to compile a list of a country's richest men and women invariably hits a number of formidable snags. Most people are reluctant to talk about their wealth; they feel, not unreasonably, that it is entirely their own affair. One can try to use published figures to make some sort of estimate, but they probably tell only half the story. Many personal fortunes are tied up in a dozen different assets—not only shares in the family firm but also international investment portfolios, land, property at home and abroad, art collections. Even their owners may have no more than a general idea of what it all adds up to: who can really tell what a country mansion or Old Master is worth until one sells it?

Another complication is that, as they grow older, the rich go to increasing lengths to prevent the tax collector from getting his hands on their money after they are gone. A man or woman who fails to do this, and allows the Internal Revenue to collect millions, is held in low regard. The aim must be to reduce the liability of one's estate to the smallest possible amount; ideally one should be able to show that one is not wealthy at all. Properly speaking, therefore, any list should concentrate on the fortunes of families rather than those of individuals.

But before we go any further let us try to define what we actually mean by "rich." I said in my Introduction that, for most people, the term encompasses all those who are better off than they are. Let us try to be a little more specific. We have already noted that many of the executives whose photographs adorn the pages of *Forbes* or the *Wall Street Journal* do not really merit the label. But what is "rich?" Thirty years ago, a man whose net worth was a few hundred thousand dollars was generally regarded as rich and, of course, to a bricklayer struggling to pay off his mortgage he still is. But people with that kind of money are, nowadays, very much bottom of the league. Even a millionaire is not what he used to be, because of inflation. The term, moreover, means different things to different countries: a dollar millionaire is only half as well off as a sterling millionaire, and in Italy a million lire is only a few hundred dollars.

A recent survey showed that in the U.S. one in 427 people can nowadays call himself a millionaire. Even Britain, with its endless economic crises, is reckoned to have four thousand millionaires. It seems to me, therefore, that for the purpose of this book we ought to narrow the field. I propose to take $3 million as the starting point for my definition, and establish four main categories:

Rich: $3 million to $15 million.
Very Rich: Over $15 million to $50 million.
Super Rich: Over $50 million to $100 million.
Can't Count (the Getty definition): any family worth more than $100 million.

I realize that even this classification will strike some of the rich as unduly modest, (especially in Texas, where they talk in terms of "units"—a unit being a hundred million dollars) but one has to draw the line somewhere.

So who are the rich? A surprisingly large number of people come into the first category. It doesn't mean that they can lay their hands on $3 million; many are still so busy building up their companies that they are actually short of cash. It is a well-known maxim that the best way to acquire wealth is to use other people's money. As Onassis was once reported to have said: "Show me a millionaire and I'll show you a heavy borrower." But on paper, at least, they are worth $3 million or more. They include shopkeepers, publishers, restaurateurs, jewelers, and manufacturers of everything from shoes to ladies' underwear. Some of these occupations are also represented in the higher categories, together with a sprinkling of real estate men, financiers, and landowners. One hesitates to mention names because it is quite possible that those persons will either hotly deny that they deserve inclusion or accuse me of understating their worth. Some, no doubt, will complain that I didn't print their names large enough. There is also an obvious risk that in today's economic climate, any rating will be overtaken by events. Paper values can, and do, fluctuate a great deal, and today's high-fliers are sometimes tomorrow's dead ducks. Still, let us be bold and list some of the super-rich and can't counts. I am indebted to *Forbes* magazine for permission to quote from what is, without doubt, the most extensive inquiry ever made.

The magazine adopted a number of rules, mostly based on common sense. Blocks of publicly traded stocks were priced at the market in August 1982 for consistency. Privately held companies were valued according to estimated earnings, where estimable, based on multiples then prevailing for publicly traded companies in similar businesses. In some cases, *Forbes* had to settle for estimates of book value, particularly among private oil producers. In every case it went out of its way to be ultraconservative: it wanted to be sure that everyone on its list belonged there. Then came trusts. The inquiry had to proceed on an almost case-by-case basis, applying common sense. Most trusts are plainly set up to carry out a normal pattern of inheritance (to wives, husbands, or offspring) and exist mainly to minimize inheritance taxes. These trusts were generally attributed to the person who created the wealth, where still alive and in control, or else to the principal controlling family member where he was not. Similar treatment was given to certain special arrangements aimed at keeping control of valuable assets in the family. Irrevocable charity trusts were not counted in, nor were foundations.

6

Henry Ford II. He led a coup which forced his famous grandfather out of the driver's seat. (*Ford Motors*)

Edsel Bryant Ford II, son of Henry. "The crown prince thing is too stupid." (*Ford Motors*)

Above: Terence Conran. "It doesn't make any difference whether you have 10,000 in the bank or 10 million." (*Habitat*)

Above right: Prolific inventor Clive Sinclair with his highly successful ZX 81 personal computer. (*Sinclair Research*)

Right: Nigel Broackes was bored with life as an insurance clerk so he went into the property business. He heads the huge Trafalgar House conglomerate. (*Financial Times*)

Above left: Hugh Hefner (center) with the author (left) at a Playboy party. (*Playboy*)

Far left: Ray Kroc, high school dropout and one-time piano player who has made millions out of hamburgers. (*McDonald's*)

Left: The tiny colony of Hong Kong has produced an impressive list of millionaires. Y.K. Pao, seen here with Princess Margaret, started his working life as a bank clerk and went on to make a fortune in shipping. (*John McCulley*)

Ex-Beatle Paul McCartney, here with his wife Linda, is reputed to have an income of $40 million a year.

Arnold Weinstock—the brilliant tailor's son who saved Britain's GEC (*GEC*).

The Species

When the findings were published in September 1982, it was stressed that the list was tentative rather than authoritative: a well-informed estimate, not an audited report. Predictably, some readers complained that it was inaccurate; others angrily accused *Forbes* of producing a "kidnappers' hit list." But it *is* the most careful inquiry to date, and my table (see pages 31–35) of the richest Americans is based on it.

Heading it is Daniel K. Ludwig, who began his business career at the age of nine when he bought a sunken boat for $75, repaired it, and chartered it for twice the price. He later pioneered the buy-now-pay-later plan in shipbuilding, and at forty was the world's largest fleet-owner. In 1967, at the age of sixty-nine, he embarked on the most ambitious project of his career: he bought a chunk of Brazilian land the size of Belgium and set in motion a bold plan for developing the area to meet anticipated world shortages of food, lumber and wood pulp for papermaking. In vast stretches of virtually unpopulated jungle he built a string of airstrips, thousands of miles of roads, a private railroad to haul freight, a deep-water port, a hospital, a school and a giant service depot stocked with spare parts and equipment. He hoped that some of the profits would go to cancer research. But even billionaires cannot always get what they want. Plagued by soaring costs, low pulp prices, and endless wrangling with the Brazilian government, Ludwig decided in early 1982 that he had had enough and, after pouring more than $1 billion into the scheme, sold out to a consortium of Brazilian companies. He will be paid nothing for the next five years, and it is doubtful if he still merits the title of "the world's richest man." But the title never meant much to him, anyway. The project did, and the collapse of his dream must have been a shattering blow to a man in his eighties. If and when the venture starts to make profits the consortium will pay dividends to his Switzerland-based cancer research center.

Others in the first dozen, who are nearly all connected with the oil business, include Gordon Peter Getty (fourth son of the late Paul Getty), Perry and Sid Richardson Bass, Philip Anshutz, Marvin Davis, and several members of the Hunt family—Nelson Bunker Hunt, William Herbert Hunt, Lamar Hunt, Margaret Hunt Hill, and Caroline Hunt Schoellkopf.

11

Inevitably, business tycoons and their offspring dominate the ratings. It may surprise you to hear that the Rockefellers are no longer in the first dozen and that none of the Kennedys even makes the top hundred. It may also surprise you to hear that at least one entertainer, Bob Hope, is reckoned to be worth more than $200 million.

Many entertainers earn large and well-publicized sums of money. We live in an age of mass entertainment, and the man or woman who hits the jackpot in America can make millions in a relatively short time. The Beatles made a fortune; the Rolling Stones are still busy adding to theirs. (Sweden's pop supergroup, Abba, is another moneymaking phenomenon. In 1980 it earned more than $15 million; despite high taxation, each member is wealthier than the king.) But entertainers are often reckless spenders or put their earnings into disastrous ventures. To reach the super-rich you not only have to remain a star for a very long time but must also invest wisely. Bob Hope put his money into real estate and Texas oil wells.

Forbes also reckons that Yoko Ono, the widow of John Lennon, is worth around $150 million. But other well-known names have to be content with much lower placings. I doubt if it bothers them: you don't, after all, *need* hundreds of millions to live well.

Lucille Ball, the one-time chorus girl who made a big hit as the dizzy blond star of "I Love Lucy," made the kind of fortune most of us would be more than content with. She and Desi Arnaz, her ex-husband, had the good sense to retain ownership of the "I Love Lucy" taped shows. They later sold their company, Desilu, to Gulf and Western for $17 million in stock. Lucille married someone else, started another company, and went on to make more money. A year or two ago she and her family were reported to be worth more than $50 million. Johnny Carson, the smooth and swift-witted host of the "Tonight" show, has also made millions out of television. He is said to earn $5 million a year. Now fifty-six, athletic and gray-haired, he has killed off many programs shown at the same time as his by rival networks. He lives high on a hill in the most coveted part of Beverly Hills, in an all-glass house behind a high stone wall, and although he is skillful at getting people on his show to talk about themselves he zealously guards his own privacy.

Sport, too, has been good to many people. Tennis star Bjorn

Borg is reckoned to have made at least $20 million from the game, and Jimmy Connors could end up with substantially more.

Authors, alas, are a *very* long way behind the oilmen and even behind people like Bob Hope. Harold Robbins, Arthur Hailey, the British author Frederick Forsyth (*The Dogs of War, The Odessa File, The Day of the Jackal*) are all millionaires, but compared with the Hunts they are paupers.

Enough, though, of lists and ratings. Let us now take a closer look at some of the more interesting families and individuals, past and present. I intend, first, to consider the inheritors and then to examine, briefly, the careers of some of the self-made men who are still on the way up. We shall also look at some of Europe's royal families and wealthy aristocrats, because you might like to compare the life-styles (and problems) of the old and the new. Last, but certainly not least, we shall focus on some of the people who are the richest of all—the rulers of the Middle East oil-producing nations. The names of some of these men and women will turn up again in other parts of the book. People are not, after all, interesting just because they know how to make fortunes: how they spend it is often just as fascinating.

CHAPTER 2

THE INHERITORS

The larger a man's roof, the more snow it collects.

PERSIAN PROVERB

To people whose prospects of inheriting millions are nil—which means most of us—the sons and daughters of the rich seem very fortunate indeed. Their wealth protects them from the tiresome financial facts of life: they can do what they like, when they like, without worrying about the cost. If the idea of work doesn't appeal to them they can devote their lives to the pursuit of pleasure; the choice is theirs and theirs alone. That, at least, is how we tend to see the inheritors, and of course there is a good deal of truth in it. But it is not, by any means, the whole story.

Men who have built up fortunes are often much harder on their offspring than is generally realized. Many do not care at all for the idea that their children should be allowed to dissipate the assets they have built up so painstakingly over the years. They are much more likely to insist that they take over the business and run it with the same hardheaded determination. Daughters may be permitted some self-indulgence, though once they are of marriageable age their fathers keep a wary eye on suitors who appear to be playboy opportunists. Sons are expected to be chips off the old block. They are sent to the best schools ("My son is going to get the education I never had") and God help them if they don't come out top of the class. They are then given a desk in the office, and although they can generally count on progressing through the ranks with enviable speed they also face some awkward hurdles. Their colleagues are likely to be suspicious and cynical: they will naturally assume that anything the new boy may achieve will be the result of his family connections rather than his own abilities. The Old Man will watch every step (or his spies will do it for him) and mistakes will be punished with long parental lectures.

David Rockefeller once told me that, as a child, he was taught that hard work was to be valued rather than despised and that "excess of any kind was intolerable for a Rockefeller." It was a message which the first John D., founder of the family's fortunes, had drummed into his only son, David's father, and which he had, in turn, passed on to his own children. The second John D. had been left $450 million (an even more formidable sum in those days than it is now), but David's allowance during his early years of grade school was a mere 25 cents a week—and he had to spend eight hours raking leaves to get that. He could earn extra pulling weeds, so much for each weed pulled, and had to keep a written account of every cent he spent. The youngest of five brothers, David was sent to Harvard and the London School of Economics. He then took a Ph.D. at the University of Chicago. His thesis was entitled *Unused Resources and Economic Waste,* and it included this revealing statement: "From our earliest days we are told not to leave food on our plates, not to allow electric lights to remain burning when we are not using them, and not to squander our money thoughtlessly, because these things are wasteful . . . of all forms of waste, however, that which is most abhorrent is idleness."

David was prepared to work hard but was reluctant to work in the family enterprises. He did a variety of other jobs—assistant to New York's Mayor La Guardia, file clerk on Governor's Island, and so on—and when America joined the war he went into the army. But in 1946 he agreed to go into the family bank (the Chase National Bank, as it then was named). He became an assistant manager in the foreign department, lowest of the junior executive positions. Everyone knew that he wouldn't be in it for long; a Rockefeller isn't expected to be an assistant manager all his life. But the old cartoon cliché about the millionaire's son—beginner one day, managing director the next—did not apply either. It was three years

15

before he joined the ranks of vice-presidents (which were larger than the title may suggest) and another three years before he was named a senior vice-president. He became president in 1960 and chairman of the board in 1969. He has since retired from the chairmanship, but colleagues say that he put in long hours throughout his years as an executive.

Like his father before him, David did his best to persuade his children that money (and the desires it represented) was an urge that had to be controlled. If it was not, then it could be destructive—not only of self, but of the family. He, too, insisted that they should keep account books. He was fairly successful with his oldest son, but his daughters rebelled against the idea, considering it absurdly old-fashioned. They did, however, accept his views on the destructive power of millions. Indeed, some of them said they felt that the burden of such tremendous wealth (and of the Rockefeller name) outweighed the advantages.

Abby Rockefeller recalls the difficult conversation she had with her father when he informed her that one day she would inherit $25 million. "When he was finished, I said that I thought that I would prefer not to have it. I said that what I did not like was the idea of it hanging over me, affecting my future and my present, affecting my relations with people, and affecting my relations with him. I said that it was just bad for relations. I thought we had enough to deal with between us without this sort of thing."

David, according to Abby, looked "stunned and upset." He said: "Well, I'm terribly sorry to tell you, but there's nothing I can do about it." The money was in a trust fund set up by his father, and what she did with it after he was gone was her affair.

There may have been a certain amount of bravado in Abby's statement (it is easy to reject millions when you have never known what it is like to be poor), but Abby was not the only Rockefeller of her generation who genuinely questioned the value of all that wealth. Most of the children of the five brothers went through the same process; some even enlisted the help of psychiatrists. They were disturbed by the envy and hostility so often engendered by the mere mention of their name (some were moved to declare that they were "ashamed" of their name and connections), and they resented the notion that they had special obligations toward the clan. They wanted to establish their own identity, to do their own thing. Some became social workers, some went into medicine and the arts. Laurence Rockefeller's daughter Marion went to live on a farm and told an interviewer that she wanted the Rockefeller identity totally behind her. "The fortune should be made extinct," she said. "I hope the social revolution will come soon and take away from us the necessity of having to deal with it."

It would be wrong to suggest that the Rockefeller experience is typical but it is certainly not unusual. The young do not, on the whole, object to being rich but they don't want to be tied down. Nelson Rockefeller, who later became governor of New York and vice-president of the United States, summed it up very well in his younger days: "Just to work my way up in a business that another man has built, stepping from the shoes of one to those of another, making a few minor changes here and there and then, finally, perhaps at the age of sixty, getting to the top where I would have control for a few years—no, that isn't my idea of living a real life."

It is a comment which many inheritors have echoed since. Some have tried to reach the top in other, more congenial, fields. Others have done what the public tends to assume most of the scions of wealthy families do: they have led a life of leisure. "Inherited wealth," William K. Vanderbilt was quoted as saying many years ago, "is as certain death to ambition as cocaine is to morality." But by no means has everyone taken the easy way out. Some inheritors have not only accepted the challenge but have gone on to build a much bigger business than their fathers or grandfathers did. Far from quietly accepting that they could never hope to match the founder's achievements they have devoted their lives to proving that they can do better still.

Paul Getty's father was a highly successful attorney who became an equally successful oilman. (When he died, he left an estate worth more than $15 million.) Paul was twenty-two before he took any particular interest in business; until then, his ambitions alternated between a desire to become a writer and a wish to enter the U.S. diplomatic service. But once he had made up his mind to follow in his father's footsteps he tackled the task with fierce determination, and by the age of twenty-four he too was a millionaire.

His interest had been aroused at sixteen when he was taken along to one of the exploration sites. It wasn't the prospect of riches that excited him but, as he wrote later, "... the challenge and the adventure in field operations, in the hunt for oil." He asked his father for permission to spend his summer vacations from school working in the field and was told: "It's all right with me—if you are willing to start at the bottom." It meant that he would be employed as a roustabout—an oilfield laborer whose job it was to perform the heaviest (and usually the dirtiest) work on a drilling site. He was paid the roustabout's going wage, $3 a day for a twelve-day tour, and his father warned him that he could expect no special treatment because he was the boss's son. He would have to hold his own with the other men, take his share of the orders, and do his share of the work.

During the next three years his time was divided between college terms in California and summer vacations working on the site. But at this stage he was still bent on taking up some other career. He went to England where he studied political science and economics at Oxford, and by the time he left there at the age of twenty-one he had more or less decided on the diplomatic service. But on his return to the United States his father presented what he frankly admitted was "his side of the case." He said that he had built up what he hoped would be a family business. Would Paul be willing to consider a year-long detour before joining the service? Paul said he might, depending on the nature of the detour. "Try your hand as an independent operator in the fields," his father urged. "If the experiment doesn't work out or you're unhappy when the year is over, you can do whatever you wish. I won't say another word."

It was a shrewd move. Paul was not being asked to join the firm (he would almost certainly have refused) but was being offered the chance to do his own thing, with the old man's financial help. He accepted and started to look around for leases. Long months went by without result, but he did eventually manage to pick up a lease for $500 and started drilling. He was lucky: the well came in for 700 barrels a day initial production. A rapid succession of profitable lease transactions and additional oil strikes followed.

Paul then did what many other young men would have done in the same circumstances—he stopped working. For the next two years he took what he described, in his autobiography, as "a total

immersion course in practical application of the pleasure principle."
But the lure of oil proved to be stronger than he thought, and he
went back into the prospecting business for good. He later became
president of the family business, as well as his own company, and
went on to make far more money than his father had ever dreamed
of.

Getty told me, at a party not long before his death, that those
early days were the most exciting of his long life, and that he had
no time for the negative attitude of so many modern young people.
He had always been an optimist. I didn't have the nerve to ask him
about his own sons. Two of them, I knew, had dropped out of the
firm after relatively brief periods and the oldest, who had been
marked out as Getty's successor, had died of barbiturate poisoning
in 1973. It didn't seem right, somehow, to remind him of his
darker moments.

Some months later I met another prominent tycoon, Henry Ford
II, then still boss of Ford Motors. We talked at length about his
involvement in the company started by his famous grandfather, and
about his attitude toward the job.

He was twenty-five when the Old Man's only son, Edsel, died
prematurely in 1943. As the eldest grandson, young Henry found
himself hastily spirited out of the wartime navy, where he was an
ensign, and installed as a director and executive vice-president. His
brothers Benson and William trailed him into the company later.
It was a classic riches-to-riches story, but the atmosphere in the
Ford boardroom was not a happy one. The autocratic founder had
lost his touch; under his heavy-handed administration the business
was losing $10 million a month. The Old Man followed a stubborn
anti-union policy that was effectively and brutally carried out by
Harry Bennett, his long-time lieutenant, and which led to much
bitterness (with occasional violence) and sagging productivity. Young
Henry decided that something had to be done. Backed by his mother
and his brothers, he led a coup which forced the Old Man out of
the driver's seat. One of his first acts as president was to fire Bennett
and make peace with the United Auto Workers. In little more than
ten years he sextupled the value of the company, and in the two
decades that followed he brought it to new heights of wealth and
public esteem. When we met, he was fifty-eight and still very much

in charge. Why, I asked him, did he do it? Why work hours when he could so easily spend his days on some sunny beach in the Bahamas?

"I have," he said, "a responsibility to the company. I wouldn't be happy with myself if I didn't fulfill that responsibility." It was the kind of remark one felt compelled to take with a large pinch of salt, but his record suggested that he meant it. Colleagues later told me that he was a workaholic who pushed himself hard and expected everyone else to do the same.

Ford clearly enjoyed the power and the prestige that went with the job—the power to hire and fire, the personal control over new products, the attention of the press, the easy access to presidents and prime ministers. These are things that money alone cannot buy. For an energetic and self-confident man they tend to be as necessary as a hammer is to a carpenter.

His only son, Edsel Bryant II, has a personal fortune estimated at $20 million (with the prospect of more to come) but also works long hours. He joined the company in 1974 as a product analyst and now earns close to $100,000 a year as marketing plans manager. Inevitably, it is widely assumed that he is being groomed for the top. Comparisons are made with Prince Charles (the two men were born in the same year, 1948) but Edsel himself insists: "The crown prince thing is so stupid. There is no crown prince; I'm not the heir apparent. Ford is not a private company like it was when my dad took it over. The board of directors is responsible for running the company. If I get to the top, it will be because I worked to get there, not because I was born into it." His current job involves talking to dealers and customers about features they want in future models. "I really enjoy my weekly visits to the Design Center," he says. "Giving input into the development of new products is very exciting, like a woman giving birth to a baby." He shares his father's passion for cars. "As a little kid," he recalls, "I used to collect small plastic replicas and trade them like baseball cards. Later my father would bring home a new car every weekend. I used to drive them up and down the driveway long before I had my license." As a teenager he visited racetracks all over the world and he spent one summer in California with a company-sponsored team. Even today

Edsel drives laps at Ford's Dearborn Proving Ground at least once a week. "I'll take any car I can get my hands on," he says.

Howard Hughes is chiefly remembered for his eccentric behavior in old age, but he was also a formidable businessman who turned his inheritance—estimated at around $500,000—into billions. Hughes Senior was an oil wildcatter, like Getty's father, who developed a new kind of oil-drilling bit, one which could cut through hard rock far beneath the earth's surface and thus open up huge reservoirs of oil that had so far been unattainable. He died when Howard was eighteen, and left his son three-quarters of the oil company's stock. The boy had been a mediocre student at school, and his relatives thought that he would let his stock be handled by some kind of voting trust until he was twenty-one. But Howard, it soon appeared, was in a hurry. He went to court and argued that he was competent to vote his own shares. The judge found in his favor, but felt that he had to add a word of warning. "I would like to suggest," he said, "that you find older men to help you carry the burden of your new responsibility for a few years. Your education should not stop here. You should go on to college." Hughes nodded politely, but he had no intention of going back into any classroom. He was impatient to try himself against the real world.

During the next few years he not only expanded his father's company, and bought out his relatives' shares, but also went into the movie business. By the time he was twenty-five his net worth was conservatively estimated at $20 million. It wasn't enough; his next move was to establish an aircraft service and repair shop which eventually grew into the Hughes Aircraft Company. He also started to take flying lessons and before long he was entering and winning air races. He went on to buy his own airline—which everyone thought was a crazy thing to do—and made it into one of the great names in civil aviation, TWA (When he finally sold his TWA stock in 1966 he received more than half a billion dollars.) He later launched an electronics company and, as if that wasn't enough, bought up hotels and real estate in Las Vegas.

There are many other examples of heirs who have outperformed the original fortune builders. They have usually done so with the help of able associates, but that does not detract from their achievements—the ability to pick good management is, after all, one of the most valuable talents in business. Some have taken over the family firm and turned it into a much larger enterprise, as Ford did. Others have used their inheritance as seed money for new ventures in entirely different fields. Others still have gone their own way and, after proving their worth, have returned to assume control of the family firm. Getty did just that; so did Forrest E. Mars, who was given a check for $50,000 in the 1930s, plus some of the foreign rights to his father's trademarks, and told to try his luck in some other country. He went to Britain, set up his own successful confectionery business, and went back in 1964 to take over the running of Mars Inc.

Malcolm Forbes, one of America's most flamboyant tycoons, built his father's business magazine, *Forbes*, into a kind of millionaire's house journal. It gives him an annual income that has been estimated at $10 million and finances a luxurious life-style: he runs a yacht the size of a small liner and owns eight major residences in various parts of the world, including exotic places like Bali and Tahiti. Ask him how he came to be so rich and he invariably replies with a grin and a practiced one-liner: "Sheer industry and ability—you spell those words i-n-h-e-r-i-t-a-n-c-e." But the magazine's astonishing success (it has a paid circulation of 700,000 and is crammed with lucrative advertising) has been largely due to his own energetic efforts. He became its editor and publisher in 1954, and turned it into a mildly eccentric, staunchly pro-business fortnightly which he proudly labeled a "Capitalist Tool." He writes leading articles that tell other rich Americans what they want to hear; his style—crisp, outspoken, controversial—is very much like the late Lord Beaverbrook's.

But it isn't necessary to outdo one's father or grandfather; the business world has just as much respect for those who carry on where the founders left off. The du Ponts in America, the Agnellis in Italy, and the Sainsburys in Britain are among the numerous other families who have done a remarkable job without the razz-matazz of a Getty or a Hughes.

Harry Oppenheimer, the richest man in South Africa (and one of the richest men in the world), was his father's closest associate for many years and, after his death, continued to run the business.

He may not be as well known outside his country as America's more flamboyant types, but he has had an interesting and extremely successful career.

His father was born in Germany; at the age of sixteen he went to England to work for a firm of diamond merchants, and was later sent to South Africa. By the time Harry came along his father was a highly regarded diamond expert and in the decades that followed he became one of the biggest names in the mining industry. Harry went to school in England and won a scholarship to Oxford. During his university days he toyed with the idea of becoming a diplomat (as Getty did), but he knew that he was expected to join the company and didn't have the heart to say no. Once back in South Africa he soon settled down. The diamond industry was going through difficult times in the 1920s, and one of his tasks was to boost sales through advertising campaigns. He went to New York, where an agency persuaded him to accept a slogan that was to become world-famous—Diamonds Are Forever. Harry could see the merits of establishing diamonds as the eternal symbol of love, and he extended the effort from America to Europe, with a new angle: a bid to show that diamonds were not necessarily the preserve of the rich, but that the man in the street could buy them too. The most important market, not surprisingly, turned out to be the engagement ring.

As the Oppenheimer empire grew, Harry found himself increasingly involved in his father's many complex manipulations. He was a quick learner, and the two men got on well together. In 1940 Harry went off to fight in the war (he spent most of it in the desert), but returned to the business when it was over. His father urged him to play some role in public life, and he became a member of Parliament. He vigorously opposed the concept of apartheid, arguing that it would have disastrous consequences for South Africa—a warning he has repeated on countless occasions since. When the old man died at the age of seventy-eight, it was quietly announced that Harry would become the new chairman of an empire which, by then, was so large that it controlled 40 percent of the country's gold, 80 percent of the world's diamonds, half of Southern Africa's coal, and almost one-sixth of the world's copper. He expanded it still further: by 1970 there were more than a hundred companies, with interests in six continents, and Harry's personal influence extended to its furthest extremities—prospecting operations in the Yukon and the Amazon basin, nickel in Australia, potash in Yorkshire, tin in Malaysia, oil in Canada, diamond sales in London, the bullion market in Zurich, beer-brewing in Zambia, hotel management in Natal.

When I interviewed him a few years ago he told me that the idea of making money through the stock exchange bored him: he preferred to do something creative, even if the inherent risks were greater and the return took longer to materialize. "In the long run," he said, "you make more from starting something new." He also said that he liked to do things which were "big and difficult." Getty and Hughes would no doubt have agreed with him—and so, I imagine, would Ford.

At the risk of being branded a male chauvinist (it wouldn't be for the first time), let me point out that all the people in this gallery of business stars are men. There have been, and still are, some highly successful women but they are very much in a minority. It is much more common for widows and daughters of the rich to take up some interest outside business. They may sit on the boards of companies, but it is comparatively rare for them to play an active role.

One obvious reason is that business has always been a male-oriented concern, and to a large extent still is. Most of today's better-known enterprises have been founded by men, and there is much greater pressure on sons to follow their lead than there is on daughters. Men are urged, as a matter of course, to make their careers in business; women are generally discouraged from doing so. It is an old-fashioned attitude and I like to think that it is changing, but it remains deeply entrenched. The female offspring of empire builders are expected to marry and produce more heirs; they are not expected to stage boardroom coups and build even bigger empires.

If a founder has no sons, he will usually try to persuade his daughter—or daughters—to marry someone who seems capable of taking over. Aristotle Onassis, who was shattered when his only son died in a plane crash at the age of twenty-four, extracted a promise from his daughter Christina (when he was close to death himself), that she would marry Peter Goulandris, the thirty-year-old heir to another shipping fortune. He loved Christina, but felt that the business would fare better if it were directed by a man.

Deprived of an appropriate training, and made to feel that any woman who attempts to run a business will be regarded as a freak, many business heiresses lead empty, aimless lives. They become an easy target for fortune hunters and often go through marriage after marriage, searching for elusive happiness. Barbara Hutton, granddaughter of the founder of the Woolworth store chain, inherited $42 million when she was twenty-one. She was a bright, assertive girl who might have made a competent businesswoman, but the possibility clearly never occurred to anyone; wealthy young ladies did not dirty their hands with trade. She was introduced to New York society, rushed from party to party, and married a succession of men, most of whom were only too willing to help her spend her money during the short period they were around. Seven times a bride, she was a lonely and miserable figure at sixty—still enormously rich but thoroughly disillusioned. It was Barbara Hutton who was first dubbed the "poor little rich girl" by the press; there have been countless others since.

But not all rich women have such a sad experience. Just as many—if not more—settle down to the routine mapped out for them. They marry men who gladly take on responsible positions in daddy's company, run great houses, entertain on a lavish scale, and involve themselves in charitable work.

Sons-in-law quite often do prove themselves to be eminently successful substitutes for sons. In Britain, Arnold Weinstock is one of the most outstanding examples. Weinstock was born in North London, the son of a tailor who had arrived from Poland in 1906. He went to the London School of Economics and Cambridge, and then joined a firm which specialized in property development and the renovation of small companies. During his seven years as the chairman's personal assistant he learned about balance sheets and profit and loss accounts, and about dealing with the problems of sick companies. He also married Netta, the daughter of Michael Sobell.

Sobell, a manufacturer of radio and television sets, brought in Weinstock as manager, and he rapidly made an impact on the business. In 1958 the company went public and three years later it was bought by GEC for $17 million; he and his father-in-law moved on to the GEC board and collected a sizable chunk of the equity. But the group was doing badly and Weinstock increasingly found himself involved in management rows. Eventually a palace revolution ended with his appointment as managing director. By that time GEC was, in his own words, "on the brink of ruin." He sold off many of its properties, cut the staff, closed some of the factories, and reorganized the whole structure of the company. His strategy paid off: bank borrowings were sharply reduced and profits doubled within a year. The improvement continued and the value of the shares rose dramatically: Sobell had every reason to be pleased with his daughter's brilliant young husband.

Another family-run company that has benefited from marriage is Marks & Spencer. Simon Marks, the founder's son, married the sister of Israel Sieff, who in turn married Simon's sister. Together the two men transformed the business. It was the Sieffs, not the Marks, whose main line provided the management succession.

Sons-in-law don't always work out that well, but the same is true of sons—or, for that matter, nephews. The ability to make big money is not something which is passed on by some immutable law of nature, from one generation to the next. All rich families produce at least some offspring who have no talent whatever for business. The sad thing is that proud fathers so often do not recognize the obvious or, if they do, refuse to accept it. They are so eager to create a dynasty that they make demands which their children cannot possibly cope with. Instead of encouraging them to develop their own talents they insist on trying to turn them into faint carbon copies of themselves. When they find that it doesn't work they leave no doubt about their disappointment. They cannot, or will not, acknowledge that business success isn't everything— that there are many other fields which are no less important. They would be disappointed even if their sons or daughters walked off with the Nobel Prize in literature or medicine. The frequent result, inevitably, is quite unnecessary alienation. Children give up trying to make their parents understand that they are different, and that there is nothing wrong with being different. Some become suicidal; some take to drugs; some seek psychiatric help. ("The best thing about money," one of the Rockefeller children was once quoted as saying, "is that it buys good analysis.") Many more simply leave home, to lead some other way of life well away from their parents. The angry father's response, in many cases, is to use the only weapon he knows: he cuts them out of his will. It all seems so foolish, so utterly pointless, but successful businessmen frequently lack two of the most important human qualities—compassion and common sense.

Heirs who do try to emulate their fathers, but lack the required talent, can easily end up with egg all over their prosperous faces. To be fair, it isn't always their fault. By the time they get their hands on the steering wheel the company may be on the skids, or the old man may have attached so many conditions to his will that the heir is like a driver trying to go uphill with the handbrake on. If the inheritance has been divided among four or five people there may be heated arguments about which direction the vehicle should take. (One sometimes suspects that many self-made businessmen secretly *want* their companies to fail after they have gone.) But clumsy heirs are more than capable of making their own mistakes. Some run into trouble because they wrongly assume that the formula which worked well for father will work just as well for them, even though conditions have changed. Some allow themselves to be talked into backing ventures they don't really understand. Some are, quite simply, incompetent.

If the heir accepts his limitations and allows professional managers to run the show he may be able to get by without doing any significant harm. Many a chairman or president has been saved by his subordinates, but he is on dangerous ground whenever he embarks on some swashbuckling enterprise. G. Huntington Hartford II, the heir to the A & P store fortune, came into his inheritance in the 1950s, and used it to finance all sorts of ill-starred projects: by 1973 he had managed to reduce his fortune from $100 million to $30 million. "My tragedy," he said in a recent interview, "was that I was not trained for anything. I knew nothing about business. When I got my capital I was suddenly rolling in so much money that I had a guilt complex about it. I didn't know what to do with all that stuff." Lamont du Pont Copeland, Jr., a scion of the du Pont family, went bankrupt after a series of disastrous investments in fields ranging from newspaper publishing to film distribution, real estate development, insurance, shopping centers, and (appropriately enough) toys. And then there is Nelson Bunker Hunt—ah yes, let us take a good look at the curious case of Nelson Bunker Hunt, the man behind the great silver caper.

The Hunts are part of Texas folklore: their story reads like a script for a television soap opera, and indeed Bunker has been compared to J. R. Ewing, the fictional villain of the popular television series "Dallas." The father, H. L. Hunt, was a gambler who is said to have won his first oil well in a game of poker and who, relying on a gambler's combination of luck and shrewdness, multiplied his stake by trading in oil leases. He was delighted when, in 1946, *Life* magazine named him as the richest man in America, but insisted that "Money doesn't mean anything to me, it's only the way you keep the score." He lived in a replica of George Washington's home at Mount Vernon, but wore cheap suits and carried his lunch to work in a brown paper bag. A great admirer of Senator Joseph McCarthy, he spent millions on a relentless propaganda campaign for the extreme right and wrote a Utopian novel called *Apalca* to spread his ideas. He also managed to run three families all at once: he fathered no fewer than fourteen children because, as he once confided to an associate, he thought he carried a genius gene and was doing the world a favor. (Two of his children in fact suffered from incapacitating mental illness.) His eccentricities flourished, the richer and older he got. One morning in 1972 he was giving health food tips to a young reporter from the Dallas *Morning News* when suddenly he dropped on the floor and began to crawl round and round the dining-room table, slowly at first, then faster and faster. "I'm a crank about creeping!" he shouted gleefully. Creeping, he explained, was far superior to other forms of exercise. "I have lots of money, so they call me the Billionaire Health Crank. Heh, heh, heh."

Nelson Bunker Hunt (no one ever seems to have called him anything but Bunker) was born in 1926. He dropped out of school and, after a spell in the navy, went to work for his father. He was like him in many ways; in particular, he had inherited his love of gambling. But H. L. was not easy to please—he kept finding fault with his second son, and eventually fired him. Bunker promptly went into oil exploration on his own. In 1955 he announced an ambitious drilling program in partnership with the Pakistani government; it produced $11 million worth of dry holes. He had more luck when he went after concessions in Libya; one of the concessions, in which he had a half share, turned out to be a winner. He had to borrow money from his father to get the oil out of the ground, and it was several years before he could get it to the market, but once he started pumping he made huge profits. Bunker bought real estate, horse farms, cattle stations, and oil leases in Canada, the U.S. and the North Sea. But he was still left with a great deal of cash, and a New York commodities broker persuaded him to try the silver market. Inflation, he said, was bound to grow worse and this, combined with the unsettled outlook for the world in general, was sure to boost the price of silver. Bunker's brother Herbert agreed to join him in the venture and they began to buy. They did quite well at first, and it encouraged them to step up their purchases.

Meanwhile, the operation in Libya was running into trouble. Colonel Ghadaffi, the country's young revolutionary leader, was threatening to nationalize the oilfields, and by May 1973 Bunker had lost the principal source of his wealth. He decided to plunge more deeply into silver. During the next few years the brothers built up by far the largest private hoard in the world. They failed in a bid to acquire a silver mine, but managed to convince a group of rich Arabs that they would stand to gain considerably by joining them in a silver-buying partnership. The price went up and up, and in January 1980 it hit an all-time peak of $50 an ounce. Bunker's judgment appeared to have been triumphantly vindicated. But profits remain paper profits until one sells, and the brothers did not sell. On the contrary, they went on buying. Silver started to fall, partly because so many people were selling their family silverware for scrap and partly because other speculators were getting out. By mid-March the price was down to $21 an ounce. The brothers were still showing a handsome profit on their earlier purchases, but they had taken a beating in the futures market and on the silver they had bought when prices were much higher.

Playing with futures — the buying and selling of commodities to be delivered in the future — has been compared to "climbing aboard a big dipper which has no brakes and no seat belts." You put down 10 or 15 percent with your order, and hope for the best.

If it comes off, the rewards are impressive, but if it doesn't, losses can mount rapidly. You also face further cash calls, to keep the margin at the same percentage. The brothers were getting margin calls for millions of dollars a day and they did not have the necessary cash. When the news leaked out, the silver price dropped still further, to just over $10 an ounce. The Hunts were bailed out by a consortium of banks who put together a massive loan, but they had to mortgage most of their possessions including their homes, cars, horses and paintings. And they were forced to appear before congressional committees to answer the charge that they had attempted to "corner, squeeze, or manipulate the silver market." The media, not surprisingly, gave them a rough ride. Bunker got the worst of it: there was general agreement that in trying to be like his father he had not only hurt his family but had done considerable harm to the image of American business.

THE RICHEST AMERICANS

Source: *Forbes* magazine, September 1982

$1 BILLION AND UP

Daniel Keith Ludwig	Shipping, real estate
Gordon Peter Getty	Oil
Perry Richardson Bass and Sid Richardson Bass	Father and son; oil, investments
Margaret Hunt Hill	Inheritance; eldest child of H. L. Hunt
Caroline Hunt Schoellkopf	Inheritance; daughter of H. L. Hunt
Philip Anschutz	Oil
Forrest Mars Sr.	World's largest confectioner
Lamar Hunt	Inheritance, oil; son of H. L. Hunt
William Herbert Hunt	Inheritance, oil; son of H. L. Hunt
Nelson Bunker Hunt	Inheritance, oil; son of H. L. Hunt
David Packard	Electronic equipment
Marvin Davis	Oil

$500 MILLION AND UP

David Rockefeller	Inheritance, real estate
Walter H. Annenberg	Publisher
Stephen Davidson Bechtel, Sr., and Stephen Davidson Bechtel, Jr.	Engineering and construction
Harry Brackmann Helmsley	Real estate
Sam M. Walton	Wal-Mart Stores
William R. Hewlett	Electronics
Edward J. deBartolo	Shopping centers
Samuel J. Newhouse, Jr., and Donald Newhouse	Newspapers, TV
Haroldson Lafayette Hunt III	Inheritance; son of H. L. Hunt
William Walter Caruth, Jr.	Real estate
Cyril Wagner, Jr., and Jack Brown	Partners; oil

Henry Lea Hillman	Industrialist
Paul Mellon	Inheritance
Roy H. Cullen and family	Inheritance, oil
A. Alfred Taubman	Shopping centers
Barbara Cox Anthony and Ann Cox Chambers	Sisters; Cox Enterprises
Leonard Norman Stern	Hartz Mountain Industries
Richard Mellon Scaife	Inheritance, investments
Robert O. Anderson	Oil, land
Curtis L. Carlson	Entrepreneur
Jack Kent Cooke	Publishing, cable TV
Trammell Crow	Real estate
Kenneth W. Ford	Timber
Samuel J. LeFrak	Real estate
J. R. Simplot	Potatoes

$200 MILLION AND UP

Samuel Curtis Johnson	Johnson Wax
Laurance Spelman Rockefeller	Inheritance, investments
Edwin L. Cox	Oil, Dallas
Charles Cassius Gates	Gates Corporation
Michel Fribourg	Grain trader
George P. Mitchell	Oil, real estate
Winthrop Paul Rockefeller	Inheritance
Malcolm Murcell McLean	Trucking, shipping
David H. Murdock	Real estate
Cordelia Scaife May	Inheritance
Lamont du Pont Copeland	Inheritance
Roger Milliken	Textiles
Carlton Beal	Oil
Albert B. Alkek	Oil
Donald L. Bren	Real estate
John L. Cox	Oil
A. N. Pritzker and family	Financiers
H. Ross Perot	Computer services

The Inheritors

Raymond A. Kroc	McDonalds
Arthur M. Wirtz	Real estate, sports
Lawrence A. Tisch and Preston R. Tisch	Loews Corporation; hotels
Robert Ruliph Carpenter, Jr., and family	Inheritance
Pierre Samuel du Pont III and relatives	Inheritance
Leonard Marx	Real estate
August A. Busch, Jr.	Anheuser-Busch
Marion du Pont	Inheritance
John T. Lupton	Coca-cola bottler
Georgia Rosenbloom Frontiere	Inheritance
John Jeffrey Louis, Jr.	Inheritance
Bob Hope	Entertainer, real estate
Charles G. Koch and brothers	Oil
Leon Hess	Oil
Henry Crown and Lester Crown	Father and son; financiers
Richard Marvin de Vos and Jay Van Andel	Partners, Amway Corporation
Philip H. Knight	Nike shoes
Clint W. Murchison, Jr.	Oil, investments
Clarence Scharbauer, Jr.	Inheritance
Walter Shorestein	Real estate
Joe Lewis Allbritton	Newspapers, TV
David B. Shakarian	Health food stores
Ted Arison	Shipping
Arthur B. Belfer	Oil, real estate
Jane Engelhard	Inheritance
Edward L. Gaylord	Newspapers, TV
Warren Buffett	Stock market
Larry Fisher and Zachary Fisher	Brothers; real estate
Jake Louis Hamon, Jr.	Oil, gas
O. Wayne Rollins	Rollins Inc.

Jack Rudin and Lewis Rudin	Brothers; real estate
Betsey Cushing Whitney	Inheritance
Harry Weinberg	Real estate
Kenneth W. Davis, Jr., and brothers	Inheritance
Melvin Simon	Shopping centers
Sylvan Nathan Goldman	Supermarkets, real estate
Henry John Heinz II	H. J. Heinz Co.
Dolly Green and sisters	Inheritance
Sol Goldman	Real estate
Charles B. Berenson	Real estate
Lila Acheson Wallace	*Readers' Digest*
Harold Farb	Real estate
Milton Petrie	Retailer
William B. Ziff, Jr.	Publisher
Robert Alfred Lurie	Real estate
R. E. (Ted) Turner	TV, cable
Arthur Charles Nielsen	A. C. Nielson Co.
Ray Lee Hunt and family	Inheritance, oil, real estate
John Willard Marriott, Sr.	Marriott Corporation
Stephen Muss	Real estate
Victor Posner	Financier
Eugene S. Pulliam	Newspapers
Chapman S. Root	Coca-cola bottler
Oakleigh Blakeman Thorne	Commerce Clearing House Inc.
Edwin C. Whitehead	Medical instruments
Vivian L. Smith	Inheritance
John Dempsey	Bulk containers
Abby Milton O'Neil	Inheritance
Hugh Rodney Sharp, Jr., and Bayard Sharp	Brothers; inheritance
Alexis Felix du Pont, Jr., and sister	Inheritance
Norton Winfred Simon	Industrialist
Seymour Cohn	Real estate
John Thompson Dorrance, Jr., and John Thompson Dorrance III	Father and son; Campbell Soup

Doris Duke	Inheritance
Edward Bradford du Pont and Margaret Lewis du Pont Smith	Brother and sister; inheritance
Charles B. Grant	Oil well supplies
Bob Guccione	Publisher
Joyce Clyde Hall and Donald J. Hall	Father and son; Hallmark Cards
William Randolph Hearst, Jr., and family	Inheritance
Oveta Culp Hobby	Newspapers
Howard Kaskel	Real estate
Howard B. Keck and William Keck, Jr.	Brothers; oil
Robert Adam Mosbacher	Oil
Jack Parker	Real estate
Donald Worthington Reynolds	Newspapers and media
Daniel Crow Searle and family	Inheritance
Athalie Irvine Smith	Inheritance
An Wang	Wang Laboratories

CHAPTER 3

THE MONEYMAKERS

The makers of fortunes have a second love of money as a creation of their own, resembling the affections of authors for their own poems, or of parents for their children, besides that natural love of it for the sake of use and profit.

PLATO, THE REPUBLIC

It has become fashionable in recent years to argue that the age of fortune building is over—that the conditions which enabled the Rockefellers, the Fords and the Gettys to amass great wealth have vanished for good. They operated in periods of rapid economic growth, they were comparatively free from government interference, and they were able to exploit the big discoveries and inventions which have played such a fundamental role in shaping modern life: oil, railroads, motor cars, airplanes, television and so on. Caught between state capitalism and the giant corporation, it is said, today's entrepreneur has little chance of making big money.

It would be foolish to deny that conditions have changed, but the same point could just as easily have been made (and no doubt was) at different stages in history. I dare say that an earlier generation thought that the days of fortune building were over when the inventor of the wheel had made his pile.

Conditions change all the time. The earliest source of wealth was political power, and we know what a fickle thing that is. A duke would have millions of acres of land one moment and then he would say or do something which offended the king and whoosh, his fortune was gone. During the Industrial Revolution—now hailed as the "golden age"—small businessmen constantly complained about the ruthlessness of bigger competitors. In Getty's day, independent operators were said to have little chance against the companies who dominated the industry. Countless people have, over the centuries, argued themselves out of fortunes by insisting that it made no sense to take risks because defeat was inevitable.

Nathan Rothschild, who founded the English branch of that remarkable family in the eighteenth century, once told an associate: "I always said to myself, what another man can do, I can do too." This is the attitude which has produced more success stories than anything else, and will continue to do so. There have, inevitably, been numerous casualties and I don't think anyone, including Nathan's descendants, would claim that making millions is easy. But if there is such a thing as the "millionaire mentality" (see Chapter 16) it is above all the willingness, indeed eagerness, to have a go.

It would obviously be difficult these days to build up a business in heavy chemicals or heavy engineering or, for that matter, railroads. Such ventures require a vast capital outlay, without any guarantee that it will pay off. But plenty of people have made sizable fortunes in a variety of other fields during the past few decades. This is particularly true in the United States, a huge market for all kinds of products and services, but it also applies to countries like Britain and West Germany, the Arab world, and the Far East.

Some have done well by taking over existing businesses: companies with weak managements have been acquired by strong personalities, often with borrowed funds. Men like Lord Forte, who started with a London milkbar in the 1940s and built up the world's largest hotel and catering group, did not sit back and wail about conditions. Others have done well, in industries dominated by huge corporations, by taking the specialist route. Masaru Ibuka, the co-founder of Sony, was not deterred by the fact that U.S. corporations ruled in his line of business. He went to America in 1952, found that American businessmen appeared to be unaware of the enormous commercial possibilities of transistors, and persuaded Japanese banks to back his own venture. Others still have spotted new market trends and made the most of them. Ray Kroc did not tell himself that America already had more than enough restaurants and certainly more than enough hamburgers: he saw that the "fast food" business had great potential and used every cent he had to buy his way into the McDonald's chain.

Some of the most successful entrepreneurs in the world today have their homes—and companies—in the Far East. Hong Kong, in particular, has produced an impressive crop of millionaires. This tiny colony comes closer to Adam Smith's concept of pure capitalism than anywhere else. It is a remarkably vigorous community—living evidence of what Chinese talent and energy can achieve under a free enterprise system. The Hong Kong rich may not be household names in the West, but they command the respect of those they do business with—which, to them, is probably all that matters.

Y. K. (for Ye-Kong) Pao began his working life in pre-Communist China as a bank clerk, rising to number two in a big Shanghai bank not long before the People's Republic came into being. When the Communists took over, Pao and his family escaped to Hong Kong with enough capital to start anew. In 1955, at the age of thirty-seven, he decided to plunge into shipping, a business in which he frankly concedes he had no experience and absolutely no expertise. He sent away to London for basic books on ship chartering and maritime banking and a set of manuals on how to run a ship. Armed with his new knowledge, he bought a twenty-seven-year-old secondhand coal-burning steamer, which he optimistically named *Golden Alpha*—and it was promptly chartered by Tokyo's Yamashika Line to carry coal from India to Japan. By 1975 he had built up a seagoing empire larger than the fleets of either of the legendary Golden Greeks, Stavros Niarchos and the late Aristotle Onassis. He is, of course, a multimillionaire, but says he can't remember when he made his first million or, indeed, how many millions he is worth today. "It's better," he says, "not to remember how much money you have so you still have to work hard."

Peking gets a lot of badly needed foreign currency through Hong Kong, but no one knows for sure what will happen when the lease on 90 percent of the land runs out in 1997. Will China annex the colony, or will it decide that Hong Kong can still play a useful role as a separate entity? The present Chinese leadership has told investors to "put their hearts at ease," but it is impossible to tell who will be in charge fifteen years from now. Many of the Hong

Kong rich have, therefore, built up interests elsewhere. Their sons have been sent to foreign universities and many have stayed to look after the local family business. Chinese ingenuity is at work in many different countries, notably America.

Like Y. K. Pao, Dr. An Wang was born in Shanghai. He went to the United States in 1945 and was educated at Harvard. He invented the core memory, which remained the standard for computer data storage until the semiconductor became popular in the 1970s. Wang sold the core memory patent to IBM after starting his own one-man company in Boston in 1951; last year it made a profit of $90 million, and Wang's 44 percent shareholding was estimated to be worth some $850 million. The company's current emphasis is on the so-called Office of the Future. His executives speak glowingly of work stations with electronic calendars, information filing and retrieval systems, instant mail, even audio and video messaging devices.

It would take half a dozen volumes to tell the story of all the entrepreneurs who have proved the pessimists wrong, but let us concentrate on some of the more interesting people in fields which remain open to all.

THE HAMBURGER KING

The franchise business must surely rate as one of the best money-making ideas of the post-war era. The principle is delightfully simple: you develop some product or service that is likely to have popular appeal, establish and publicize a trademark, and then rent it to people who are eager to run their own business. They become your franchises, or franchise-holders, and they work long hours to make profits for you. I don't know who first thought of this splendid wheeze, but that man (or woman) was clearly a financial genius.

Like so many things, the franchise game started in America. One of the earliest operators was a one-time insurance salesman who had opened a restaurant in Kentucky and found that people liked the way he prepared that ubiquitous dish, fried chicken. His name was

Harland Sanders, and during the 1950s he spent a great deal of time selling his recipe to other restaurants. It became the basis for a national, and later international, franchise network known as Colonel Sanders' Kentucky Fried Chicken. Since then the concept has been extended to many other areas — laundry and dry cleaning services, hotels and motels, equipment rental, magazines, car hire and even fashion. But it is the "fast food" business which continues to produce the most impressive results, and one of the most lucrative items is that American institution, the hamburger.

Ray Kroc, the "hamburger king," did all kinds of work after he dropped out of high school. He played piano with several traveling bands, chose the music for a Chicago radio station, sold real estate in Florida and paper cups in the Mid-West. In 1937 he started a small Chicago company that distributed multimixers — machines that could make a number of milkshakes at one time. The business did reasonably well, but it didn't make him rich. Then, in 1954, he discovered that a small restaurant in California, run by Mac and Dick McDonald, was using eight of his mixers — more than anyone else. Intrigued, he went to see the McDonald operation for himself: the brothers were doing a roaring trade in hamburgers and milk-shakes. When he asked why they didn't open more restaurants (he wanted to sell more mixers) they said that they were quite content to stick to the one they had. Kroc saw his chance and grabbed it. The McDonalds agreed to let him franchise their outlets anywhere in the country in exchange for one half of 1 percent of the gross receipts. He opened his first McDonald's, which he owned himself, in a Chicago suburb the following year and others quickly followed. In 1960 he decided to buy the name McDonald outright for $2.7 million. By the mid-1970s Kroc had franchise holders all over the world and the chain's annual turnover was several billion dollars a year. His personal fortune was estimated at $300 million.

THE PLAYBOY

Hugh Hefner has what most of the readers of his magazine regard as the ideal life-style. He holds court in his own Magic Kingdom—

a magnificent, well protected Californian mansion where he is surrounded by fawning acolytes and nubile creatures eager to make his fantasies (if there are any left) come true. He seldom goes out: why should he? The kind of world he cares about is always ready to come to him. He works when he feels like it, but most of the time he has his own brand of fun—watching movies; playing backgammon, poker, gin rummy and pinball machines; giving parties for Hollywood stars and people who hope to become stars; and—well, you know what. Hefner is said to have made love to more beautiful women than any other man in history. Neither he nor his public relations men bother to deny it; it is, after all, good for his image.

Friends who know that I have been his guest often ask me, with a leer, what his parties are like: they have visions of mad orgies. I hate to disappoint them, but I found the world of Hefner rather boring. Most of the people seemed to spend their entire time talking about their careers. The girls, young and empty-headed, chatted about their dreams of stardom; the men appeared to be mostly interested in money. The host, dressed in silk pajamas, walked among us, bottle of Pepsi in hand, and tried to show polite interest. If he had organized an orgy he neglected to tell us about it; the whole thing was about as exciting as an IBM convention.

Still, one has to hand it to the aging playboy: the magazine he launched almost three decades ago, and which he has guided ever since, has done phenomenally well. When Playboy Enterprises went public in 1971 his personal fortune was valued at $200 million. It is hard to say what he is worth today—ventures such as his involvement in casinos have come unstuck—but he is certainly very rich.

Hefner's father was an accountant who worked for a large corporation. He spent long hours at the office and had little time for his children. Hef, the older of two sons, produced his first "newspaper" at the age of eight: it consisted of news and cartoons, all written and drawn by himself. Each issue was painstakingly typed out on an old Royal typewriter on single sheets of white paper, then stapled together and sold by the young publisher, who knocked on doors in his neighborhood offering copies for a penny a piece. He followed this with a school journal called *The Pepper*, and at fifteen he launched *Shudder Magazine*—a periodical with a circulation of one copy (the original). It was passed around by hand for his subscribers to read. He then spent two years in the army, and afterward enrolled at the University of Illinois, where he promptly started another publication, a campus humor magazine called *The Shaft*.

But these were all amateur efforts, and Hefner was determined to have a proper magazine of his own. "The only thing wrong with that dream," he said later, "was money. I didn't have any." He nevertheless conceived the idea of a picture magazine for and about the people of Chicago, and placed an ad in the *Chicago Tribune* offering printers the opportunity to go into partnership with him. Only one responded, and he wanted Hefner to pay for the paper and ink. Hef couldn't afford to do so, so he reluctantly decided that the project would have to be temporarily shelved. He also decided that the only way to get any money at all was to look for a steady job. But editorial jobs in publishing were few and far between, and he eventually became a copywriter for a men's fashion store, at night drawing cartoons which he sent out to newspapers and magazines. He was later hired by *Esquire* to write direct mail subscription solicitations, but when the head of the department refused to give him a $5 increase he quit.

Hefner had $600 of borrowed money when he decided to have a go at the men's magazine market (he pledged his furniture as collateral), and he spent most of that on the rights to reproduce a color photo of Marilyn Monroe in the nude. He wrote a letter to the twenty-five largest newsstand wholesalers throughout the United States, outlining the contents of the magazine he had in mind, and the response encouraged him to press on. He formed a company, sold shares in it to relatives and friends, persuaded a printer to give him credit, bought second rights to articles, and put the first issue together on a card table in his living room. The total cost was $8000.

Hefner was lucky: *Playboy* (his original title was *Stag Party*) caught on at once. If it hadn't, he would almost certainly have been forced to give up. Recalling those days, he says, "The only reason I tried it was that I had no conception of the almost insurmountable difficulties and the odds against my success. If I had known what

I know now, I doubt if I would have even tried." *Playboy* worked, he reckons, because ". . . it was the right idea in the right place at the right time." Most of his imitators have been less fortunate, although Bob Guccione has made millions from *Penthouse*.

Hefner went on to create Playboy Clubs and moved into films, gambling and hotels. Gambling paid off handsomely for a while, but the company was dealt a sharp blow when it lost its London casino licenses. The magazine itself continues to attract a large readership and substantial advertising revenue; I am sure there are times when he wishes that he had stuck to the business he knows best.

THE SHOPKEEPER

Terence Conran will probably never forgive me for describing him as a shopkeeper. He is, after all, a talented designer who only went into retailing because he felt that Britain's furniture shops were doing a poor job and he is proud of the fact that his design agency, Conran Associates, is one of the most successful companies of it kind in Europe. But the public knows him best as the man who launched Habitat stores and, now that he has added the Mothercare chain to his group, he is stuck with the label of shopkeeper, whether he likes it or not.

The retail trade has always been a favorite hunting ground for would-be millionaires. In the U.S., Frank Winfield Woolworth started his world-famous chain of stores when he was twenty-six with money borrowed from relatives, and numerous other young men have followed him since. In Britain dozens of people have made considerable fortunes while everyone else has been busy talking about the "economic crisis." Lewis Cartier started at the age of twenty-two with $100 savings, a $1000 loan from his father, and a van bought on time payments. This mobile shop rapidly gave way to a supermarket and in 1979, at age thirty-three, he sold his Cartier superfoods chain to Tesco for $40 million, more than half

of which was all his own. Richard Northcott built up a group of
do-it-yourself stores, and at the age of thirty-five sold it to Woolworth for $35 million. Selim Zilkha, the scion of a wealthy Baghdad
banking family, bought a chain of chemists' shops when he was in
his early twenties, added others, and invented the name Mothercare,
together with a slogan, "Everything for the mother-to-be and her
baby and children under five." In the late 1970s he sold $60 million
worth of shares in the company, and when he agreed in 1981 to
hand over control to Terence Conran his remaining shares were
reckoned to be worth another $40 million.

Like most of his customers, Terence Conran comes from a middle-
class background. He studied textile design at the Central School
in London, and set up business in the 1950s as a designer and
manufacturer of furniture. He didn't think of retailing until the
year he took his team around the country to look at the way their
furniture was being displayed and sold in shops. Everywhere they
saw only "a sea of brown squares," recalls one colleague. (Conran
himself talks scathingly about that "great dull ditch of buyers, those
who totally controlled taste in the big shops.") It was clear that
they needed their own premises. Then they realized that they should
sell not just furniture, but everything that went with it, in an
ambiance of bustle, color, cheerfulness and light. The first Habitat
store opened in Fulham Road in 1964 and it quickly became apparent that Conran's approach fitted in with the mood of Londoners,
particularly the young (these were the days of "swinging London").
"Many of the first-time visitors," *The Times* commented, "thought
they must have gone to heaven."

Conran's aim was twofold: to produce good design for everything
people used in their homes, and to produce it inexpensively. His
dream was that quite ordinary families should share his vision of
what a home should look like—modern, practical, simple, fresh.
Other stores followed; when the company went public there were
more than fifty, of which thirty-two were in the U.K., fifteen in
France and Belgium, and six on the East Coast of America, trading
under the name of Conran. Net sales were in excess of $100 million
a year, and the flotation placed a paper value of more than $50
million on Conran's shares.

He says it hasn't been easy: it took four years to get Habitat profitable in France, and the U.S. operation also lost money in the early days. But he reckons that there is still plenty of scope. "The other day," he says, "I was walking down a street and looking in through front windows. It was absolutely predictable where people had put their furniture and what they'd got, like peas in a pod. I longed to march in and tell them that you can turn things around. You can have two sofas instead of a three-piece suite, you can take out the center light." He thinks that during the last five years there has been "a fairly massive change in the style of life in the U.S.," where he recently opened his eighth store. . . . "There are a great deal more single apartments, there is a boom in homosexuality and a boom in divorce. . . . These are all slightly depressing things but they all help our business. . . ."

He also seems confident that his flair for design and marketing will work wonders for the much larger Mothercare group. His critics say he may have taken on more than he can handle: they acknowledge that he is a talented designer, but question whether he is a good enough businessman. At fifty-one, Conran is determined to prove that he is both. He has already made a great deal of money, but says, "It doesn't make any difference whether you have $20,000 in the bank or $20 million. Money is actually of little importance to me personally. I'm interested in it from a business point of view. That's what is exciting."

THE POP MUSICIAN

I don't know what Beethoven would have made of the world of Paul McCartney, but I can guess. Like so many great artists of the past, he went through years of poverty. In the eighteenth and nineteenth centuries composers largely depended on wealthy patrons and not on their publishers, who often paid trifling sums for their works. "They feed on my lifeblood and, to me, they give nothing," Beethoven used to tell friends. There are, to be sure, modern composers who also feel hard done by, but the music business is not what it was. Paul McCartney enjoys an annual income that educated guesses put at more than $40 million a year—a pleasing sum by anybody's standards.

The story of Beatlemania is so well known that there is no point in going over it all again. The Beatles were the biggest money-spinners the music business has ever seen. There have been other winners, notably the Rolling Stones, and individual entertainers like Frank Sinatra (aptly known to his friends as "the chairman of the board") have made vast fortunes. But the Beatles were exceptional, not only because they had a new kind of music but also because John Lennon and Paul McCartney were uniquely talented songwriters. In the seven years before the group split up in 1970, they composed more than two hundred songs, most of which have retained their popularity. Bad financial judgments cost the group dearly in the early days, and Paul bitterly regrets that he and John parted with the copyright of most of those songs. He has tried to buy them back from ACC; his last offer was said to be in excess of $40 million. But he would be enormously rich even if he lost all the millions he made during the Beatle years. His own group, Wings, has also done remarkably well and his company, McCartney Productions, deals briskly in music publishing, films and records. It receives from EMI what is believed to be the highest royalty ever paid to any recording artist (so high, indeed, that EMI's ability to make a profit from the deal has often been doubted), and it owns a catalog of songs which includes the music to the shows, *Grease*, *Annie* and *A Chorus Line*, as well as its chairman's own output.

Yet, ironically, he cannot read or write music. "I tried when I was eight, and again when I was sixteen, and yet again when I was twenty-two," he says. "But I couldn't handle it because it was like school homework—it didn't associate with music to me." One of the reasons he originally got into songwriting, it seems, was the influence of old Hollywood musicals. "There's always this very nice character who sits at home and his life is a laugh. I always imagined myself as that. . . ." Occasionally, he says, he can fall out of bed and there is a new tune in his head and he doesn't know where it has come from. "They tend to be the best ones."

The Moneymakers

Paul and his American wife Linda, who is an accomplished photographer, shuttle between his farms in Sussex and Argyllshire and his houses in London and Liverpool. At home he composes songs and nonsense verses, walks and rides, and watches the television a great deal. In an interview on German radio some months ago he talked at length about his views on money, marriage and fatherhood. "My dream when I was seventeen or eighteen," he said, "was to have a guitar, a car and a house. I've got a car and a house now and I don't really need a lot of money for anything else. I don't live to extremes, you know. I don't have chauffeurs, and we don't have lots of servants. Money is really just security." In a world of rocky showbiz marriages, security is what Paul also seems to have found in his life with Linda. "She's great, I like her. I don't want to go on about it too much because it sounds too sloppy. But she's a good kid. She keeps me straight . . . and I like her legs too." Their children, he said, enjoyed a normal family life. (Asked to sum up his ideas of normality he replied that it was "the kind of household where everyone helps with the washing up.") It wasn't easy for them to cope with their father's fame, but he was determined to ensure that it didn't go to their heads. "Our kids are probably very talented—at least they can all sing in tune—and I could probably get them all a lot of work as Paul McCartney's kids. But I was from an ordinary background myself, and it seems to me it was one of the best. I don't think it does kids any harm to learn to be ordinary first." He wouldn't object if one of them wanted to go into showbusiness, but he wouldn't push them. "If they want to do it they would have to do it themselves."

At forty, Paul is the world's most successful pop musician and certainly the richest ex-Beatle. But he is very much aware that he has never been loved in the way John Lennon was. He reckons that his mistake was to seem invulnerable. "John showed his warts. I have only just realized, after all this time, that people like to see warts. It makes them sympathetic." Cynics would no doubt say that, with all those millions in the bank, he doesn't need sympathy. But Paul clearly feels that money isn't everything: it's nice to have friends as well as cash.

THE PROPERTY MAN

They call Chinn Ho "the Chinese Rockefeller of Hawaii." No one knows just how much he is worth, and he won't say, but by his own estimate he has bought and sold a billion dollars worth of real estate during the past fifty years and even among the wealthy he is considered one of the golden people.

Real estate has probably made fortunes for more Americans than anything else. It is a business in which, despite competition from powerful corporations, the individual can still do remarkably well. The risks are high, but so are the rewards.

"Buy land, they've stopped making it," Mark Twain once advised a friend. It isn't strictly true—in many parts of the world extra land has been created by filling in swamps and lakes—but the old boy had a point. I daresay his friend made a fortune, as so many of his contemporaries did. You don't have to be an economist to recognize that a static supply of land, accompanied by a rapidly growing demand, adds up to rising prices. If only those Indians who sold Manhattan to the whites had managed to resist the lure of beads they would have made the Rockefellers look like paupers.

One inevitable result of this immutable supply-demand situation has been a reappraisal of land which few people would have bothered with thirty or forty years ago. As cities have grown, areas that used to be unspoiled countryside have been turned into sprawling suburbs. They are even building condominiums in the Arizona desert, for dudes who want guaranteed sunshine all the year round. Who needs farmland when you can buy all the vegetables you can possibly want at the local supermarket?

When Chinn Ho was a young man, Hawaii was a tranquil haven for people who wanted to get away from it all. There are parts which have retained that tranquility, but Waikiki isn't one of them. Chinn Ho put up the first high-rise, and others followed. He went on to build hotels, office buildings, and condominiums. Makaha Valley, a failed sugar plantation forty-five minutes from downtown Honolulu which he bought for $1.25 million, is now reckoned to

Some entertainers are enormously rich. Bob Hope, seen here sharing a joke with Princess Margaret, is a multi-millionaire. (*Keystone Press*)

The world's best-known sheik, Ahmed Zaki-Yamani. "I'm just a simple bedouin," he says. He is not, but such modesty goes down well with the people who pay his salary. (*Keystone Press*)

Left: The Duke and Duchess of Westminster, posing outside the Guildhall after receiving the freedom the City of London. He is reputed to the richest man in Britain. (*Keystone Press*)

Below: Prince Rainier (left) with the author at the Palace of Monaco. (*Sylv Jouclas*)

Right: The traveling Queen and her Consort. Style is expensive. (*British Airways*)

Below right: The Aga Khan (right) chatting to friends at a party. He ow an estate outside Paris, a collection o racehorses, a yacht, and a lavish reso in Sardinia. (*Keystone Press*)

Press tycoon Rupert Murdoch—
admired, feared, hated, and ridiculed.
(*The Times*)

Diamond King Harry Oppenheimer,
the richest man in South Africa. (*Anglo-
American*)

be worth more than $25 million. He has had several battles with environmentalists, but has won most of them. "I am concerned about future land," he says, "but I am also concerned about future money. I have the corporation to think of."

One of six children, Ho turned to making money early, selling beans for 15 cents a bag as a child. His father raised ducks and fish to supplement his income as a clerk. "A palmist told me I would do all right," Ho recalls. "I don't believe in fortune tellers, but I've done all right." He sold pennants and pencils in high school for $150 a month, and invested his profits in penny stocks. Then he turned to property. His corporation, Capital Investments, was founded forty years ago and he remains chairman of the Board.

James Michener used Ho as the prototype for Hong Kong Wee, the wily money changer in his book *Hawaii*. Detractors call him an old pirate, which he finds amusing, but they say it with respect and out of earshot. "Money," he insists, "is only a game. You use it to prove something to yourself. I can live comfortably on $250,000 a year. A man doesn't need much more."

THE INVENTOR

Inventions have made money for so many people that they are still widely regarded as the key to riches — the obvious way for a talented individual to triumph in a world dominated by big corporations. Patent offices on both sides of the Atlantic get thousands of applications each week from people who are confident that they have found a winner. Many, of course, never make it. The London office has a fascinating record of ideas that didn't get to first base. There was, for example, the "apparatus for the prevention of snoring" which, like the dual-spouted teapot, made its debut in 1931 and was never heard of again. The same fate befell the musical toilet paper holder patented in 1912; William Mumford's reversible trousers, invented in 1907; and, more recently, Arthur Pedrick's golf balls with wings. But it is an encouraging fact that simple ideas are often the most successful. Wouldn't you like to have been the first to think of the zipper, the coat hanger, the mousetrap, the paper clip, and the ballpoint pen?

Unfortunately, inventors tend to be poor businessmen. They are preoccupied with the idea itself, and they usually lack the capital and marketing techniques needed to make the most of their inventions. Many end up selling to someone else for a relatively modest sum, but some have done remarkably well and it is worth taking a brief look at the career of one of them: Dr. Edwin Land, the inventor of the Polaroid camera.

Land's first product was a transparent sheet capable of polarizing light. His interest in the subject had begun while he was a seventeen-year-old freshman at Harvard; walking along Broadway at night, it suddenly struck him that polarizing filters could eliminate headlight glare and thus reduce the hazards of night driving. He took a leave of absence from college and spent day after day in the New York Public Library, reading everything which might be relevant. At night he carried out experiments in a small laboratory he had set up in a rented room nearby. For the next three years college was forgotten, but when he patented his sheet polarizers Harvard not only welcomed him back but offered him one of its own laboratories. He spent the following three years there, but never got around to taking his degree: the "Dr." attached to his name is strictly honorific.

In 1937, at the age of twenty-eight, he launched the Polaroid Corporation with the help of a group of Wall Street financiers who relished the prospect of putting his filters on every car headlight and windshield in the country. He retained a majority of the voting stock and was placed in complete control for the next ten years. But Detroit, it soon emerged, didn't want to know. Land had to find other uses for his invention, and he incorporated it in products like sunglasses. During World War II the company was kept busy manufacturing lenses and gunsights for the military, but Land also spent a great deal of time in his lab trying to invent an "instant camera." He later said that it was his small daughter who provided the inspiration: when he was taking pictures of her on a family holiday she asked impatiently how soon she could see them; he explained that it took time to get them developed, and then thought about what he had said. There was something basically wrong with photography if people had to wait hours, or even days, to see a picture. He started to experiment with ways of getting a finished picture directly out of the camera that took it. By 1947 he had come up with the answer, and his new sixty-second camera went on the market in the summer of 1948. The trade was skeptical, but the public liked it.

Land later developed a simple system for instant color photography and produced all kinds of other ideas; by 1980 he had more than four hundred patents in his own name. He played a key role in the development of cameras that can take pictures at high altitude; the cameras used in the famous U-2 espionage, and those which detected the Soviet missiles in Cuba, were his. He is immensely rich, but has always insisted that he is not interested in money as such: it is merely a useful by-product of worthwhile endeavor.

Land maintains that the ability to create and invent is not rare; in his opinion it is commonplace but generally uncultivated. "My whole life," he once said, "has been spent trying to teach people that intense concentration for hour after hour can bring out resources in people that they didn't know they had." He has never lacked followers; who would reject the opportunity to be taught by a man who has succeeded so brilliantly in proving his point?

THE NEW BOYS

When Land retired as head of the company in 1980 his Polaroid stock was valued at $75 million. It is a formidable sum, but some of America's young innovators seem poised to do even better. One who has already done so is a twenty-seven-year-old college dropout, Steven Jobs.

Jobs is one of the new breed of entrepreneurs in "Silicon Valley," a part of California that got its nickname when tiny semiconductors made with chips of silicon were first manufactured there at the end

55

of the 1960s. Nearly eight hundred electronics firms are now established in the region, and they have been joined by a range of other industries, notably genetic engineering.

Jobs started his company, Apple Computer, six years ago in a bedroom and garage of his parents' house. It went public four years ago and early in 1982 his personal share stake was estimated to be worth more than $100 million. It is an extraordinary achievement and, not surprisingly, many people question whether it can be sustained. Jobs himself is confident that it can, but he faces some formidable competition.

His good fortune began when he became friendly with a talented young designer, Stephen Wozniak. Together they built and sold so-called blue boxes, which were illegal electronic attachments for telephones that allowed users to make long-distance calls for free. In 1972 Jobs entered Oregon's Reed College, but left two years later to take a job designing video games. Wozniak, meanwhile, had dropped out of Berkeley to become a designer at Hewlett-Packard, a large electronics firm. After hours, Wozniak worked hard building a small, easy-to-use computer. In 1976 he succeeded. The machine was smaller than a portable typewriter, but it could perform the feats of much larger computers. The two raised $1300 to open a makeshift production line by selling Jobs' Volkswagen Microbus and Wozniak's Hewlett-Packard scientific calculator. Jobs, recalling a pleasant summer that he spent working in the orchards of Oregon, christened the new computer Apple. He looked around for capital and eventually agreed to take on another partner, a former marketing manager of a computer chip company who offered his expertise and $250,000 of his own money. It was a sensible decision: the newcomer helped to arrange a credit line with the Bank of America and persuaded two venture capital firms to invest in Apple.

Sales in 1977 were $2.7 million. By 1980 they had soared to $200 million and the target for 1982 was three times that figure, giving Apple almost a quarter of the worldwide market in personal computers. But I.B.M. has joined the fray with its first personal computer, and several other companies are equally determined to give the young man a run for his money. Jobs has greatly increased his spending on research and development in a bid to outpace his rivals; one result is a new and more powerful computer that he has code-named Lisa, after one of his ex-girlfriends. Wozniak, meanwhile, has gone back to Berkeley to finish his studies!

"Silicon Valley" has produced other success stories, but America is by no means the only country where big money is being made by thinking small. Japan led the way years ago and European countries are also cashing in on the new technology.

One of Apple's competitors is a shy, reserved forty-one-year-old Briton, Clive Sinclair. A prolific innovator, Sinclair pioneered the world's first pocket calculator before turning his attention to computers, Britain's first digital watch, and the world's smallest and cheapest television. His early ventures won critical acclaim but were not the financial success he had hoped for; he quit the company he had founded not long after it was bailed out by the National Enterprise Board. But Sinclair pressed on. Early in 1981 his new company, Sinclair Research, launched a tiny computer for just under $200 and sold more than one hundred thousand over the next eighteen months. Later in 1981 he produced a more sophisticated model, and sold a quarter of a million within a year. The company is making healthy profits and Sinclair has become a millionaire. He plans to launch other new products, including an electric city car, but concedes that he is an idea man rather than a manager and subcontracts practically everything except research and development. "I do the first stage of everything," he says. "I think about the systems and innovate, but after that I get involved only when I need to." His computers are being made by Timex, which is also marketing them in North America.

"Computermania" on both sides of the Atlantic has had one other interesting result: a rapidly growing cottage industry which turns out software—the programs that tell the machines what to do. School teachers, civil servants and technicians have set up small operations in their spare time to sell manuals, programs, extra memory, graphics boards and sound generators. Programs vary from games to critical path analysis, from Space Invaders to payrolls and a host of new industrial and commercial applications. Some of the brightest entrepreneurs are still in their teens. Too young to know the meaning of the word "impossible," these keyboard prodigies often make breakthroughs which have eluded their seniors.

In New York in 1981 three schoolboys teamed up to form a

company called Software Innovations. They persuaded their families to invest $1500 and sold teachers and schoolmates forty shares of stock at $5 each. With the money they published a catalog of fifty programs and mailed it to four thousand computer hobbyists. The boys grossed $15,000 and cleared about $1500 after reimbursing their parents and paying a dividend. In California another company, Plum Software, is owned by two twelve-year-old boys. A sixteen-year-old, Jeff Gold, is making $2000 a week from two of his programs—one which solves the puzzle of the Rubik Cube, and a program to prevent the theft of other programs. In Britain, nineteen-year-old Keith Purkiss from Ashby, near Workington in Cumbria, designs and produces computer attachments for a business which he started at eighteen.

They make me feel ancient.

THE BUILDER

Few people in the West have ever heard of Chung Yu Yung, for his name rarely appears in the financial columns of newspapers. Yet he is, at sixty-six, one of the world's richest men, an Oriental squarely in the mold of the rags-to-riches entrepreneurs who built Western industrial societies.

A slight, trim man, Chung came out of a farm on Korea's east coast in the early 1930s. He was, it is said, too poor to afford the three-hundred-mile train trip to Seoul, so he walked. Like numerous other young men, before and since, he took whatever work he could find. He eventually saved up enough money to set up his own truck and auto repair shop and, after the end of World War II, moved into the construction business. When the Korean War broke out Chung began building army camps and other military facilities. When that ended, leaving South Korea's economy in ruins, Chung was poised to make the most of the opportunity to rehabilitate his devastated country; on that base, he expanded into world markets. In the 1970s, when OPEC diverted enormous wealth into the oil-producing Gulf countries, Chung became a major builder in Iran,

Bahrain, Kuwait and Saudi Arabia. He built on a grandiose scale: ports, shipyards, military installations and housing projects, including the $930 million Saudi Industrial Harbour Project at Jubail. Today his company, the Hyundai Group, ranks as Korea's largest contractor and builder and is among the half dozen largest engineering and construction companies in the world. But construction provides no more than a third of Hyundai's turnover. Ten years ago Chung launched his most ambitious project—a massive $1 billion shipyard on Korea's southern coast. Hyundai Heavy Industries became the focus of all the group's industrial activities—not only ships but also marine engines, building materials and equipment, iron and steel, petrochemicals, and even nuclear power. Hyundai Motors, another offshoot, sells two hundred thousand cars and trucks a year.

Chung readily concedes that his phenomenal growth has been made possible by a compliant labor force. Koreans work with almost military precision and dedication, and at wages significantly lower than those in the industrial West or Japan. His critics regard him as the modern equivalent of America's Robber Barons—men like John D. Rockefeller and Andrew Carnegie—and there is clearly a lot of truth in the charge. But it is also true that his drive, enthusiasm and skillful leadership have brought considerable benefits to his country.

Like most entrepreneurs, Chung is a great believer in the merits of borrowing, especially in inflationary times. Much of the group's expansion has been financed by loans from banks around the world. It has enabled him to retain the bulk of the shares, but he claims that he doesn't know how much he is worth. "I've never added it up," he says. "I've never calculated it."

THE PLANNER

The cliché image of Australia is of a nation of square-jawed, uncultured extroverts who wear bush hats with immense brims, exercise a vocabulary restricted to expletives, and care about boozing and winning at sports. There *are* Australians who fit the description, but they are vastly outnumbered by those who do not. More Australians work in factories and offices than on sheep farms; on a per capita basis it is one of the most highly industrialized countries in the world. The men you see as you walk around cities like Sydney and Melbourne (85 percent of the population lives in urban centers) tend to be pink-cheeked and, like so many of us, a little paunchy. They wouldn't dream of wearing a bush hat.

One man who is in every way the opposite of the postcard Australian is Robert Holmes a'Court, who stepped into the spotlight in Britain when, early in 1982, he made a multi-million-pound takeover bid for ACC, the entertainment empire built up by the flamboyant Lord Grade. Reputed to be one of Australia's richest entrepreneurs, he is a quiet, enigmatic forty-four-year-old lawyer with an aristocratic bearing and a taste for Havana cigars, racehorses and expensive cars.

Robert Holmes a'Court inherited his chivalric name from a line of nineteenth-century British landowners. His father, the younger son of a younger son, went out to Rhodesia between the wars to farm near Bulawayo. In the 1950s, the family moved to New Zealand. Robert was sent to law school in Australia and later started a small law practice in Perth; he employed his mother to help out in the office. In 1970 he found himself acting as legal adviser in the affairs of an insolvent textile firm, Western Australian Worsted and Woollen Mills. He bought a 21 percent stake in the firm for $60,000, persuaded the state government to write off most of its loans, and turned it into a money spinner. Later he acquired two small-town papers and a radio station. As they grew, he used these assets in the classic manner to finance further expansion. In 1974, with a loan from Citibank, he paid $12 million for Bell Bros., a Perth engineering and road haulage company that was in trouble, and developed it as the base for his present operations. These now include transport, engineering, oil and minerals, textiles, hotels, television and newspapers.

When I first met him, in his Perth office toward the end of 1980, he had just decided to launch a new weekly paper, the *Perth Western Mail*. Knowing his track record, I had expected to find a strong, aggressive personality. The man who greeted me was a tall, languid intellectual who talked about his life and ambitions in a voice so soft that it was hard to catch some of the things he was saying. Behind his desk were the layouts of the paper, pasted up on boards, and he outlined the contents of the first issue. I thought he was just another millionaire with a new toy; I failed to recognize that the relaxed manner and soft voice concealed a sharp business brain and steely determination. Others made the same mistake when he quietly built up a stake in ACC and then used Lord Grade's financial difficulties—brought on chiefly by his involvement in disastrous film projects like *Raise the Titanic*—to take over the company.

Robert Holmes a'Court is a planner, a financial strategist (and keen chess player) who looks for openings, works out fallback positions for every contingency, and proceeds methodically from one stage to the next. He takes risks, but they are calculated risks. Sir William Rees-Mogg, who had some dealings with him when Holmes a'Court made a bid for *The Times*, says that he has "a very architectural view of business: you design a structure, and if the design doesn't make sense you simply walk away from the drawing board."

His basic technique has remained much the same over the years: he tries to find problem companies and restore them to profitability. He doesn't always win his takeover battles, but even his unsuccessful bids sometimes yield big profits. When, in 1979, he failed to win control of Ansett, one of Australia's two internal airlines, he sold his share stake to Rupert Murdoch and cleared a tax-free profit of $12 million. He repeated the feat in 1981, making $18 million from an unsuccessful bid for Elder's, the Adelaide finance group.

Critics say he is a ruthless operator, an opportunist who doesn't give a damn what happens to the victims of his crafty manipulations. Holmes a'Court counters that he has a respectable record of industrial development: "I'm no assets stripper." He thinks that British businessmen spend too much time wailing about the economy; Britain, he argues, has long suffered a crisis of confidence. Instead of wailing it ought to be getting on with the job of building successful enterprises.

Holmes a'Court has homes in London and Melbourne as well as Perth, two stud farms, a splendid collection of vintage cars, and collections of modern Australian and Aboriginal art. He clearly enjoys his luxurious life-style, but claims that he is not obsessed with making more and more money. "I've had an ample income for as long as I can remember," he says. "That's enough for me." It is the kind of statement one has learned to take with a large pinch of salt, but I have no doubt that the chase matters at least as much to him as the booty.

THE QUEEN OF COSMETICS

I have already noted that, when it comes to making millions, women are heavily outnumbered by men. But there is one woman who certainly merits a place in this gallery of money-makers: Estée Lauder.

Of the great entrepreneurs of the American beauty business, only Mrs. Lauder survives. Helena Rubinstein died in 1965; Elizabeth Nightingale Graham, the Canadian-born founder of the Elizabeth Arden group, died in 1966; Charles Revson, their arch-rival, departed in 1975. Others have tried to take their place, with varying degrees of success, but if anyone deserves the label of "the Queen of Cosmetics" it is the blonde, hazel-eyed woman, on no specified side of seventy, who started her company in 1946 and whose name has become a household word. "It is the General Motors of the cosmetics business," a French competitor was quoted as saying earlier this year. The company accounts for an estimated 50 percent of department store sales of fragrances in the U.S., and has around ten thousand employees worldwide.

Estée Lauder would be the first to admit that the credit must be shared with her husband and, more recently, her two sons. But the company got where it is largely through her considerable energy and creative talents. She not only founded the original business but was also responsible for its early diversification into other areas, notably Aramis (a line of men's toiletries) and Prescriptives, a high-tech skin-treatment line. She still has the last word on all creative matters—colors, fragrance, even advertisements. The beauty business was already overcrowded when she entered the field, but it is one of those areas where flair and skillful marketing can work wonders. Her strategy, from the start, was to sell top-of-the-line products through leading department stores rather than through drug stores and chains like Woolworth's. Over the years she has enhanced the company's appeal through a combination of line extensions, genuine new-product introductions, and clever positioning. The group's sales are reckoned to be close to the $1 billion mark, and although it works on modest profit margins the Lauder family, which still owns all the shares, is said to be worth at least $200 million. Her eldest son, Leonard, recently became president and chief executive officer, and her younger son Ronald heads the company's substantial overseas operations. Mrs. Lauder remains an active chairwoman. She frequently visits the group's district offices and retail outlets, and when she is in New York comes to work daily in the group's headquarters—where blue, her personal trademark, is the dominant color. When she retreated to Palm Beach last winter, she regularly summoned the group's researchers to her home. She claims to have an almost sixth sense in fashion, for seeing a future season's colors and a line of complementary cosmetics. "My mother," says Ronald, "is like a conductor of a great symphony orchestra. When she calls and makes a valid point—and 99 percent of the time it is a valid point—it's accepted."

Many people question whether the group can outlive its dynamic founder; the Helena Rubinstein and Elizabeth Arden companies were both sold to organizations after their creators had gone. Ronald is confident that it can; he sees great scope for expansion outside the U.S. But there is no doubt that she would be sorely missed.

CHAPTER 4

THE ROYALS

I never see any home cooking. All I get is fancy stuff.

PRINCE PHILIP

Royalty is in a class by itself. There are people who have far more money than some of the world's remaining royal families, but they don't have the inherited status which sets kings, queens and princes apart. The richest man in the world takes a back seat in the presence of royalty; the richest woman in the world is expected to curtsey when she meets her social superiors.

Monarchies are not what they used to be, but there are still some sixty royal families in business, not counting chiefs of small tribes. Many are hardly known outside their own countries. How many people, for example, have heard of the King of Swaziland? Several monarchs are enormously wealthy—the King of Saudi Arabia, who runs his country like a family firm, could buy up dozens of large Western companies and still have plenty of change left over for gold bathtubs—but a number of others have serious financial problems. All try to keep up appearances, with varying degrees of success.

Membership in the world's most exclusive club on earth has always carried dangers as well as privileges. Even Britain once beheaded one of its kings, Charles I. In Russia, the Bolsheviks executed the entire royal family. Germany toppled the Kaiser after he lost the 1914–18 War and, more recently, a number of other monarchs have been unceremoniously deposed and forced into exile—King Umberto of Italy, King Constantine of Greece, King Idris of Libya, the Shah of Iran. They can't even rely on each other. In March 1975 King Feisal of Saudi Arabia was killed by a nephew, Prince Feisal bin Musaid, who turned up at a *majlis*, the traditional meeting place for a desert leader and his people, and pulled a gun from under his robes. In the trigger-happy 1980s no one in the public eye is really safe: you never know where and when some demented (or well-paid) assassin is going to strike next. But there are plenty of rich men and women who would dearly love to join the royal club.

It isn't easy. You can buy a small island in the Caribbean and proclaim yourself king (it has been done), but no one will take you seriously. You can hire an army, take over an obscure country, and get someone to put a crown on your head, but successful coups of that sort are rare in the twentieth century and, in practice, out of the question for a millionaire from Cleveland or Frankfurt, however ambitious he may be. The most effective ploy is one of the oldest and most obvious: marriage. A great deal of time, effort and cash are still devoted to making a royal catch. Some mothers pursue their quarry, on behalf of sons or daughters, with single-minded cunning. The victims are, as a rule, well aware of what is going on and may succumb if the financial stakes are high enough. But suitable royals are in short supply: a Prince Charles comes along once in a lifetime. There are plenty of Arab princes—Saudi Arabia alone is said to have more than three thousand—but socially they have inferior status, at least in the West. Queen Elizabeth is the sixty-third monarch in a line going back one thousand years; the Saudi monarchy was created a mere eighty years ago when Ibn Saud came out of the desert with a handful of followers and took Riyadh. The smell of oil is no substitute for centuries of royal breeding.

The most publicized wedding of recent years—and possibly of the rest of the century—was that of Lady Diana Spencer to the heir to the British throne in the summer of 1981. An estimated 700 million people around the world watched it on television, including countless mothers who, no doubt, wondered what charms Lady Diana had that their little darlings lacked. They saw a twenty-year-old girl, attractive enough but hardly a great beauty, clutching the protective arm of the world's most eligible bachelor. She looked radiantly happy, and who could blame her? The groom was in his early thirties, handsome, wealthy and destined to become the head of what is widely regarded as the most prestigious monarchy of all.

Prince Charles has a large income from the Duchy of Cornwall, created in 1337 by Edward III to support his high-living son, Edward (the "Black Prince"), the third Prince of Wales. The duchy, comprising more than 128,000 acres, mostly in the West Country, makes him one of the biggest landowners in Britain. He also has extensive personal investments, which are managed for him by City professionals. He might have problems if he were seized by an irresistible urge to build grand palaces, but he is sensible enough to realize that those days are over and, in any case, the royals have more than enough of them as it is. The couple's own country home is Highgrove, a modest (by royal standards) eighteenth-century house in the Cotswolds. I dare say that, like most husbands, he gasps when he sees some of his wife's clothing bills, but he doesn't have to lie awake at night wondering how he is going to pay them.

For their wedding, the Prince and Princess were given thousands of presents, ranging from the mundane to the magnificent. They included wooden clothespins, large quantities of glassware, linen, silver and gold platters, a microwave oven, a vacuum cleaner, a first aid kit, coat hangers, salt and pepper shakers, soap, a pincushion and a seven-foot-high thatched birdhouse. The King and Queen of Spain gave the Princess a set of gray leather suitcases embossed with the initial "D," and the Prince a statue of a polo player. The Marquess and Marchioness of Abergavenny sent a dog basket, the Ecology Party a brick paperweight, the Duke and Duchess of Devonshire a visitors' book, the Duke and Duchess of Grafton a porcelain ice bucket, the Sultan of Brunei a silver tea and coffee set, President Reagan a cut glass bowl, the Crown Prince of Saudi Arabia diamond jewelry, and the island of Jersey two cows. The army offered to build them a swimming pool.

They can expect to add to this bounty as they make their way around the world. One of the perks that goes with being a prominent royal is that people insist on being generous hosts. The Queen has, over the years, collected more gifts than even she has house room for. After one Canadian junket, the royal yacht *Britannia* groaned her way home under the weight of four hundred items including a pair of snowshoes, a $10,000 mink coat, a chunk of iron ore, a sixty-pound statue of a bucking bronco, a sackful of spears and polo sticks, a fifteen-foot-long motorboat, a silver maple syrup jug and a painting of a power station. Some of them ended up in one of the Queen's eight residences, but the royals have devised a neat and entirely practical way of dealing with paintings of power stations and other unwanted objects. Any suitable museum can have an appropriate item on permanent loan—the polite fiction being maintained that if, for example, the Queen had a sudden urge to make use of her ceremonial hara-kiri sword from Kyoto, the curators of the British Museum or the Victoria & Albert would instantly remove it from its glass case and send it round by special messenger. The rest is cataloged, stored and kept in running order so that it can be whisked into a prominent position whenever its donor comes to stay.

When he inherits the throne, Charles will get most of the Queen's personal fortune. Very few people know just how large that fortune is; she has always insisted that her private funds are none of the public's business. Some estimates have run as high as £100 million, but that includes the art collection, the stamp collection (reputedly the world's finest), the furniture, the royal jewelry and the country estates, none of which could be sold without a political storm. A parliamentary committee which looked at the monarchy's finances in 1971 was told that the Queen was much concerned "by the astronomical figures bandied about in some quarters suggesting that the value of these funds may now run into fifty to a hundred million pounds or more." She felt, her Lord Chamberlain said, that these ideas could only arise from confusion about the status of the royal collections, which were in no sense at her private disposal, and she wished to assure the committee that these suggestions were "wildly exaggerated." No doubt they were, but "wildly exaggerated" still left room for a substantial bank balance and an impressive portfolio of investments. Like Prince Charles, the Queen has a sizable income from a property company—the Duchy of Lancaster—and she is exempt from both income tax and death duties. No one denies that she is an extremely rich woman. She is also a careful one. Her lifestyle is not extravagant compared with that of some of her predecessors, and she has a good idea of what everything costs. I once discussed money with her at a Buckingham Palace lunch and she complained about inflation: "Everything," she said, "is so expensive these days." The lunch we had was simple—a far cry from the umpteen courses served up by earlier gluttonous monarchs. She is fond of chocolate cake and peaches from the Sandringham estate, but often skips meals altogether because, like all of us, she worries about her figure. Both she and Prince Philip are very moderate drinkers; she enjoys a gin and tonic before dinner and a little wine with her meal, while Prince Philip favors American-style dry martinis or an occasional Scotch.

Their day starts at 8:15 a.m. when servants wake them with a cup of tea. They read the morning papers over breakfast. The Queen, who loves horses, is particularly fond of *The Sporting Life*; Prince Philip prefers to bury his nose in the *Financial Times*. Both are usually at their desks by 9:15 a.m. The Queen has a ground floor office on the side of Buckingham Palace overlooking Constitution Hill. She goes through her letters, looks at government papers, and sees official visitors—sometimes as many as fifteen in one morning. Both like to watch television in the evenings, with their supper on a tray. Her favorite programs include "Kojak," wrestling, and anything with Dudley Moore in it. Weekends free of official functions are usually spent at Windsor Castle. She loves horses and horse racing: "Were it not for the Archbishop of Canterbury," she once told a friend, "I should be off in my plane to Longchamp every Sunday." She heartily dislikes laying foundation stones and having to listen to after-dinner speeches, but patiently copes with both because they are part of her job.

The monarchy itself—once described by King George VI as "the family firm"—is financed by the British taxpayer, though it is said that the Queen has had to subsidize it on occasions. It is the state, not the royal family, that pays for the upkeep of the main residences, including Buckingham Palace and Windsor Castle, and for the splendid yacht *Britannia*. There is also the civil list, which provides millions of pounds in government funds each year to help defray expenses like staff salaries and includes allowances for the Queen and some of her closest relatives, such as Prince Philip, Princess Margaret, Princess Anne and the Duke of Gloucester. The list started in 1761, when George III gave the Crown Lands to Parliament in return for a fixed allowance, and has been the subject of much controversy.

In 1969 the Queen found herself at the center of a major row when she asked for an increase. Inflation had played havoc with the royal finances, as it had done with everyone else's, and it was clear that the monarchy would be "in the red" (as Prince Philip put it at the time) unless Parliament came up with more money. Left-wing M.P.s demanded that the then Labor government should reject the request; if the Queen were hard up she should either economize or meet the extra expense out of her own pocket. The British public was being asked to exercise restraint in pay claims, and the royal family should do the same. Harold Wilson, the Prime Minister, explained that the cash was needed for the Queen's staff, not for herself, but the protests continued and he decided to set up the committee I mentioned earlier. It eventually recommended a substantial rise, making it clear that the payments were reimbursements for operating expenses and not a pay increase for Elizabeth II or anyone else in her family.

The row flared up again four years later when the Queen once more requested extra money to take account of runaway inflation. M.P.s, with help from the press, were particularly critical of Princess Margaret and Princess Anne because, it was said, they were "not pulling their weight." The attacks have continued, on and off, ever since. When the Chancellor announced that the Queen's list would be raised to £3½ million for the financial year 1982–3, the Labor M.P. for Barking said it was "monstrous" that the royal family were not being asked to make some sacrifice. Other Labor M.P.s accused the government of "protecting the rich," and former trade union leader Jack Jones declared that "the government is like a set of scrooges when they treat the old and the disabled, and yet they can dish out money to the royal family in this fashion." Henry VIII would have chopped off his critics' heads, but times have changed: the Queen cannot even speak out in her own defense.

Since 1971 she has had no personal allowance from the civil list: she meets her private expenses from her own purse. Allowances paid to other members of the royal family fall into a much grayer area where the boundary between private pocket money and legitimate expenses for undertaking royal duties is ill defined.

My own feeling is, and always has been, that the value of the monarchy cannot be measured with a slide rule. We either want it or we don't, and if we want it (as most Britons obviously still do) we must be prepared to pay the price. It is right that its finances should come under public scrutiny, and neither the Queen nor Prince Charles would disagree that it should be efficiently run. They have made a number of economies, including cuts in the staff of the Royal Household. Twenty went last year and others are expected to follow. Increasing use is being made of word processors (to save office staff), and instead of employing an army of cleaners the Queen has contracted out cleaning in all but the most private areas of the Palace. Even the liveried footmen have been pressed into multi-purpose service. "They don't just lurk in corners any more; they wait, and act as messengers and porters," says the Queen's press secretary. But a monarchy has to have style, and style isn't cheap. We willingly pay millions for modern military jets and cruise missiles—or at least governments do—none of which, one hopes, will ever be used in a major war. I really cannot bring myself to get all worked up about the comparatively modest cost of the monarchy show.

SCANDAL AT COURT

Europe has six other monarchs—the Queens of Holland and Denmark, and the Kings of Belgium, Norway, Sweden and Spain. In addition there are hereditary rulers of three pocket principalities—Monaco, Luxembourg and Liechtenstein. All perform to some extent what most people would regard as the basic function of a monarchy: they supply a sense of unity, continuity and history. No one can predict with any degree of certainty how many monarchies will survive the next fifty years, or even the next twenty-five, but clearly the institution is far from dead. Spain actually revived it after the long years of Franco's rule.

Europe's kings and queens have managed to adapt themselves to changing circumstances and will continue to do so. The days of imperial (and imperious) Victoria are gone, along with the colonies, and it may well be that new generations will decide that they can dispense with monarchs, too. But presidents are not nearly as glamorous and there are not, today, the same compelling reasons for getting rid of kings and queens as there have been in the past.

I dare say that the existing monarchs have, nevertheless, put something by for the proverbial rainy day. Most of the crowned heads of Europe, Asia and Africa in the twentieth century have placed money in Swiss banks, for basically the same reasons that industrialists and financiers do. If many rich men do not trust their native governments, many rulers hardly trust their own people. The Shah stashed away a huge fortune, not only in Switzerland but all around the world, and King Farouk of Egypt did the same before him. The Shah did not live to enjoy it (he was too busy running from one place to the next), but fat Farouk lived royally to the ripe old age of forty-five, paying his Italian mistresses with Swiss funds to the very end. There is no way of knowing how much money the Swiss are still holding on behalf of other monarchs, and they certainly won't tell, but it seems reasonable to assume that it amounts to many millions. Ex-kings cannot rely on getting a pension from their successors, and it isn't easy to get another well-paid job— there isn't much call for their particular skills in industry. It seems perfectly logical, therefore, that they should keep as much as they can in a country that has always been known for two things: its neutrality, and the ability of its bankers to keep their mouths shut.

The governments of nations which have deposed monarchs, or dictators, almost automatically try to get the money back from the banks, on the grounds that they represent "national" rather than personal wealth. But the first thing they have to prove is that it is actually there, which is extremely difficult under the Swiss laws of banking secrecy. Even the heirs of monarchs sometimes run into problems. King Peter of Yugoslavia was never able to recover any money from Swiss banks, or even to get a Swiss bank to admit that it held any of his father Alexander's assets. The relatives of King Feisal complained of similar trouble after Feisal was murdered in 1958. They were positive that Feisal had money in Switzerland, but like King Peter they couldn't prove it.

Next to Britain's Queen, the richest member of the club is reputed to be Queen Beatrix of The Netherlands. Yet it is the Dutch monarchy which was rocked, a few years ago, by the biggest financial scandal to hit any royal family in the post-war era. Prince Bernhard, consort of Queen Juliana (who abdicated in 1979 in favor of her daughter), was found to have accepted payments from Lockheed, one of America's leading manufacturers of airplanes, for using his influence with the Dutch government to secure defense contracts. The Prince insisted that he thought it was perfectly all right for him to take commissions, and indignantly rejected the charge that he had been bribed. The decision to place orders with Lockheed, he pointed out, had been made by ministers, not by him; he had merely introduced the Lockheed people to them. There was, nevertheless, a huge public outcry. Prince Bernhard had made a considerable number of enemies among his country's politicians and they gleefully seized the opportunity to pull him off his pedestal. The Dutch people were bewildered: they found it hard to understand why he should need the cash. Had the Queen kept him short of pocket money?

She probably had. Juliana was careful with cash (she used to pedal off to the market on her bike and shop alongside her subjects, much to the disgust of the British royals), and he had expensive tastes. But the Prince's surprise at all the fuss was probably quite genuine. The payment of commissions was a worldwide practice (Arab princes *demanded* them) and he hadn't broken any laws. It seemed to him that he had simply become a victim of post-Watergate hysteria.

I went to see him at the Soestdijk Palace near Amsterdam just before the storm broke; he had agreed to be interviewed about his work as the president of the World Wildlife Fund, for which he had raised a great deal of money over the years. If he was worried about the Lockheed affair he didn't show it. He talked, in a study crammed with African wood carvings and other souvenirs, about wildlife conservation and his enthusiasm for riding, scuba diving and flying. He said that a bad back had made it difficult for him to be as active as he used to be—"It makes one very philosophical"—but that there was a great deal left to do. "I'm an optimist; if I weren't, I'd stop trying."

Ironically, in view of what was to follow so soon, he told me during our long conversation about a financial scandal which he had managed to prevent. The World Wildlife Fund had given a large check to the head of an African state (he named him, but I had to promise not to do so in print) to help meet the cost of conservation efforts in his country. The president had said thank you and promptly put the check into his own bank account. "I had personally to threaten him with public exposure," Prince Bernhard said. The money was returned.

The monarchy survived the Lockheed business but you may be sure that the present Queen's consort, Prince Claus, is extra careful. Claus von Amsberg was a professional diplomat when he married the then Princess Beatrix, and he needed all his tact and charm when he first appeared on the public stage. Because he was German the marriage inevitably touched off Dutch sensitivities and gave republican sympathizers a field day. The ceremony was disrupted by protests—even stink bombs—and he had to put up with a great deal of carping for some time afterward. But attitudes softened when the couple's first child was born. It was a boy—the first male born into the family in four generations and now heir to the throne. They have had two more boys since.

Queen Beatrix is an outspoken extrovert, well educated, highly political, determined, impatient. Though she has pointed out herself that she is "no great beauty" (she certainly isn't), she has a lively personality and is, by royal standards, a snappy dresser. Her relationship with the Dutch people has frequently sparked, yet there is no doubt that she has earned their respect.

She was two years old when World War II broke out and she was hastily exiled, traveling (in a gas-proof cot) first to England and then to Canada, where she spent an idyllic five years being brought up in the Ottawa countryside without any of the official fuss which would have attended her in a royal palace. When she returned to Holland the Princess went to an ordinary Dutch school where she was taught in a class with other children and where, aged ten, she moved on to a secondary education with emphasis on such subjects as sociology and politics. She is said to have been a rather awkward pupil, and on one celebrated occasion took exception to being urged to help sweep out the classroom. Punishment, at the insistence of Queen Juliana rather than the teachers, was that she walk home—all six miles.

At the ancient University of Leiden Beatrix studied legal science, parliamentary history, politics and sociology. She became fluent in English, French and German, is a talented musician and sculptress, and a Master of Law. More controversial were the young Princess's efforts to gain direct experience of some of the rougher sides of Dutch life. For a period she worked incognito with the Salvation Army in Amsterdam's red light district and visited the poorest and least salubrious quarters of other cities. No one can claim that Queen Beatrix has led a sheltered life. After she married Claus von Amsberg they traveled extensively on study trips throughout the world, including the Soviet Union, China and the Middle East. Like many of her younger subjects, she and her husband take a deep interest in the problems of the Third World. Many of their friends are writers and artists.

Her personal fortune is a closely guarded secret, but there is no doubt that she is very rich. The family used to live in the charming castle of Drakesteyn, near Utrecht, and was widely expected to take up residence at the Royal Palace in Amsterdam's Dam Square when she became Queen. Instead they have chosen to make their official home in Huis Ten Bosch (the house in the wood) in The Hague. Built in the seventeenth century by Prince Frederik Hendrik, it was often used as a temporary residence by the royal family during the early part of this century, and Queen Wilhelmina spent some of her rather lonely childhood there. When the Germans occupied Holland they decided to demolish Huis Ten Bosch to create an anti-tank area which they thought would make impossible any Allied invasion from the sea. Fortunately, the Dutch managed to persuade them to limit the destruction to two staff dwellings on the estate. After the liberation Huis Ten Bosch was uninhabitable: art treasures had been taken to safety, but the wine cellars and linen cupboards had been plundered, all the windows were broken, and the walls, ceilings and floors had been damaged by bullets and shrapnel. Restoration work was carried out between 1950 and 1956 and Queen Beatrix has added her own touches.

THE "POOR" SCANDINAVIANS

Compared to Queen Beatrix, King Carl Gustav of Sweden is a pauper. His grandfather (and predecessor) left less than $8 million and most of that went to his four children; the young King is said to have collected only about $600,000. The state agreed to continue paying an allowance for the performance of royal duties, but legislation passed in 1974 took away most of his other privileges. He has to pay taxes on his income, like any private citizen, and is also liable to customs duty on anything he brings into the country.

Although an active young man, Carl Gustav has little to do except cut ribbons to open new factories, award prizes at farm fairs, and serve as a symbolic representative of his equality-minded subjects. He may well be the last monarch this ancient kingdom will see; many political observers predict that Sweden will become a republic before he completes his reign.

Denmark's Queen Margrethe has also been forced to adapt herself to the realities of a modern democratic state. The monarchy is popular, but she and her husband, Prince Henrik, are very much aware that they have to tread warily. Prince Henrik was born Henri-Marie-Jean-André, Comte de Laborde de Monpezat; his family home is near Cahors, in the Lot region of France, and although he has changed his nationality he remains unmistakably French. He met Princess Margrethe, as she then was, at a party in London. He was a French diplomat living in Britain; she was a student at the London School of Economics, a breeding ground for socialist politicians. They got to know each other better in Scotland; a lot of their friends seemed to be getting married, so they decided to do the same.

The Danes were hostile at first, but mellowed when Prince Henrik learned their language and involved himself in efforts to restore ancient buildings and protect the environment. He also started to work for the Danish Red Cross, and helped the country's exports by leading trade missions to the Middle East and elsewhere. He is a qualified pilot, but the royal family, although more affluent than the Swedes, has no planes at its disposal—they fly by commercial aircraft. Life at court is unpretentious, and no one could accuse them of being out of touch. One Danish commentator wrote, not long ago, "The Queen and her Prince Consort are a completely ordinary family which simply has a special part to play in society." Prince Henrik laughed when I pointed out, during an interview he gave me in Copenhagen, that ordinary families didn't have three palaces and court chamberlains to greet their guests. "The palaces are not ours," he said. "They belong to the nation. And we *do* try to live like an ordinary family." He conceded, though, that there were many ordinary things royalty couldn't do even in the 1980s. "You have to retain the public's respect, not for your own sake but for the sake of the monarchy. It would never do to have too much to drink, or to tell dubious jokes, or to be seen in a discotheque."

THE GIRL WHO WON THE PRIZE AT MONTE CARLO

Princess Grace of Monaco, formerly film star Grace Kelly, had what many people regarded as the ideal life-style—until it was suddenly and tragically ended, one morning last year, when a car she was driving went out of control on a hairpin bend near the Monaco border and fell some 120 feet into a ravine, turned over several times, and ended up in some trees. Her funeral was attended by dozens of princes, princesses, dukes, Mrs. Nancy Reagan, the Aga Khan, and old Hollywood friends like Cary Grant.

Grace and her husband, Prince Rainier, had their own country in the sun, with a palace and a lovely country retreat. They didn't have to worry about the loyalty of their subjects and they would walk around without fear of assassination. (One morning, some years ago, some tourists stopped an attractive Monégasque who was taking her children to school. Would she mind taking a picture of them posing in front of the Palace entrance? No, said the Monégasque, she didn't mind at all. In fact, she'd be delighted. The tourists handed her the camera and she clicked away, with the children waiting patiently in the background. The visitors thanked her, unaware that the obliging photographer was Princess Grace.)

Monaco is an anachronism—a state within a state, less than half the size of New York's Central Park. There are no barriers at the frontier, and although Prince Rainier rules as an absolute monarch, he and his cabinet are pledged to exercise their authority "in conformity with French interests." De Gaulle forced him to agree that French nationals who are residents of Monaco should pay taxes, and it is always possible that the socialist government of François Mitterrand will one day decide to annex the tiny principality. A treaty signed in 1963, unlike all previous pacts between the two countries, omitted any reference in its preamble to Monaco's sovereign status. But Rainier certainly would not give in easily, and Mitterrand probably feels that he has more important things to do.

During the battle with de Gaulle, Rainier angrily dismissed rumors that he would abdicate if the situation got much worse. "These rumors," he declared, "are absolutely ridiculous. I have no reason to abdicate. I will never do it. Such an idea never came to my mind." Nor did it occur to Princess Grace. To anyone who asked about her feelings she replied, like Marshal MacMahon at Sebastopol in 1855, "J'y suis et j'y reste." (Here I am and here I stay.)

The casino nowadays contributes less than 3 percent of Monaco's budget; the bulk of the principality's revenue comes from tourism, postage stamps, commercial radio and television, and corporation taxes. Rainier himself, like all Monaco citizens, is not allowed to gamble and says he doesn't mind one bit: "I'm just not a gambling man," he told me when I went to see him at his office in one of the towers of the Palace. (The Princess had an office in the twin tower.) The Treasury pays for the upkeep of this grandiose showcase, with its two hundred rooms and staff of one hundred and fifty. The Rainiers did a lot of entertaining, but liked nothing more than to get away to their real homes—a house in Paris and Roc Angel, the retreat 2,400 feet above the sea in the mountains, over the border in France, which he bought way back in 1957.

Roc Angel was originally built in the style of a Provençal *mas* (farmhouse) with sturdy stonework and massive beams. In 1959 the *mas* was enlarged and now looks more like an American ranch; it is, in fact, referred to by the Monégasques as "The Ranch." Set in sixty acres of land it is, as Rainier puts it, "a sort of playground for everyone." The Princess, who loved flowers, had her own garden and also spent a good deal of time in the kitchen, cooking Provençal dishes, curries, and an American version of Polynesian food. Rainier liked to play golf, but his favorite pastime was "to don a pair of blue jeans and retreat into my workshop to do wrought iron work and mend the things I break." It was a relaxed, easy-going way of enjoying what life had to offer and Rainier was heartbroken when he was given news of the accident. He immediately told friends that he was going to abdicate in favor of his son.

Prince Albert, the heir, is a good-looking young man who graduated in 1981 from Amherst College in Massachusetts, with a degree in politics and economics. His father wanted him to continue his studies in Europe, but Albert decided that he needed a bit of fun and went off to exotic places like Tahiti, Martinique and Casablanca. He spent part of the summer after graduation cavorting with a black singer (Princess Grace was not amused); he then joined the French navy and learned to cope with the rigors of pilot training at sea. But it is the couple's elder daughter, Caroline, who has attracted most of the publicity, much to their annoyance. Caroline was sent to a convent school in England at fourteen and later to an exclusive academy outside Paris. She is a bright, attractive girl with a flair for languages, but she was obviously not cut out for the role of demure princess. Her enthusiasm for discos and parties quickly made her the darling of the gossip columns, who linked her name romantically with eligibles like the Prince of Wales, the Grand Duke Henri of Luxembourg and Martin Giscard d'Estaing. At twenty-one she married a Frenchman, Philippe Junot, who was seventeen years older and had a reputation as a hard-living playboy. Her parents were against the match, but could not dissuade her. Two years later the marriage was on the rocks. "If I had not been *Princess* Caroline," she said later, "I could have lived with Philippe before marriage."

No one knows what sort of future awaits the Grimaldi family, but the Monégasques are understandably eager to see history repeat itself. They would be delighted if, like his father, Albert married a beautiful young American heiress. I am sure that there won't be any shortage of suitable candidates.

CHAPTER 5

THE NOBLES

Pride in their port, defiance in their eye
I see the lords of human kind pass by.

OLIVER GOLDSMITH

Monaco has changed a great deal since the days when top-hatted archdukes won and lost fortunes at the casino tables. But so has the aristocracy. The Russian dukes vanished with the Revolution, the hand-kissing Austrian counts are busy running farms and companies, the maharajas have gone into the tourist business, and the English lords are struggling to protect their decaying homes against dry rot and death duties. There *are* still plenty of wealthy aristocrats, as we shall see, but their life-style in the 1980s does not compare with that of the glittering 1880s.

A hundred years ago the Habsburgs were one of the most illustrious families in Europe—the focal point of the chandeliered, waltzing whirl of Vienna. For six centuries they had provided kings and emperors, and the Imperial Palace was the envy of every other royal. Franz Josef I had lost part of his vast realm through two disastrous wars, but he was still the undisputed ruler of Austria and Hungary and his fiftieth birthday, in 1880, was celebrated with loyal demonstrations throughout the monarchy. Clustered around him was a dazzling array of princes, dukes and duchesses, counts and countesses, who devoted most of their time to dancing, gambling, racing and other frivolous pursuits. Lesser folk, including financiers and industrialists, were not admitted at court. The Emperor was prepared to reward a financier who helped to raise a loan, or contributed to some public cause, with the Order of the Iron Crown (which automatically entitled the recipient to place "von" before his name) and, after a further large loan or two, to make him what the dukes and counts derisively described as a *"Finanz-Baron."* But this was an exceptional mark of favor, and the limit to which Franz Josef was prepared to go.

Eight years later the monarchy was rocked by the news that Crown Prince Rudolf and his mistress Mary Vetsera, a commoner, had committed suicide at Mayerling—a romantic tragedy that would have inspired Shakespeare to write an even better play than *Romeo and Juliet* if he had lived in the nineteenth century. Thirty-eight years later, at the end of the devastating 1914–18 War, the proud House of Habsburg collapsed and the monarchy was abolished.

Let us move forward now to November 28, 1980. Uniformed customs officers snap to attention with a friendly salute to a slender man with a pencil moustache crossing the border on the *Autobahn* from Germany to Austria. "Nice to see you, Your Imperial Majesty. Have a good trip." The driver says thank you and moves on. He is Archduke Otto von Habsburg, eldest son of the last emperor and present head of the dynasty. After more than four decades of exile he was granted, in 1967, the right to return to Austria. Once a year he presides over the ancient ceremony of the Imperial Order of the Golden Fleece in the Deutscheordenkirche in Vienna. Otherwise he is a private citizen with no castles of his own; he has renounced his rights to the throne. His home is an unpretentious house in the village of Pocking in Bavaria, where he lives with his wife, Archduchess Regina. They have seven children; the eldest, a girl, is married to a German wine grower.

If the monarchy were still in business, he would be emperor. But Otto von Habsburg is very much a member of the "second society" once derided by Franz Josef's acolytes. He has six university degrees and has written twenty-two books in seven languages on topics of history, world affairs and moral philosophy. In the spring of 1979 he became a democratically elected deputy of the new European Parliament in Strasbourg, representing the Christian Social Union, the conservative party of Bavaria led by Franz Josef Strauss. "Please call me Mr. von Habsburg, or Doctor, if you prefer, because titles of nobility in my present job are really a definite handicap," he insists. The new parliamentarian's election platform was, in his own words: "Equal rights for the middle class. The issue of freedom versus socialism. A greater Europe; that is, the non-recognition of the Yalta line and liberty for all Europeans still ruled by the Soviets."

The Yalta line has, of course, drastically affected the Austrian aristocrats. Although the monarchy ended in 1918, many retained substantial possessions in what had once been the Habsburg Empire; it wasn't until the division of Europe, worked out at the 1945 Yalta Conference, that their big land holdings became part of what is now the Communist bloc. A considerable number of wealthy families were suddenly (though surely not unexpectedly) reduced to relative poverty. Some decided to try their luck abroad rather than remain in a country where they had been the masters; there are more than a hundred Habsburgs scattered around the globe, from Canada to the Philippines, plus numerous members of lesser families.

Fürst Karl zu Schwarzenberg (*Fürst* not only means prince, but also indicates that the title-holder is head of his house) belongs to one of the families who stayed in Austria. It used to provide the Habsburg Empire with cardinals, field marshals and prime ministers; Karl Schwarzenberg provides his country with wood composite building blocks through a company he owns in Vienna, and is in partnership with a carpet firm. The Palais Schwarzenberg, in the center of Vienna, has been turned into a hotel, and is a fashionable place for visiting American millionaires; His Serene Highness devises the menus. Born in Prague, he has degrees in law, political science and forestry from the Universities of Munich, Graz and Vienna, and clearly enjoys his role of successful businessman.

His Illustrious Highness Count Friedrich Karl von Schonborn-Buchheim is another member of the old aristocracy who has turned to commerce. He spent many years in the Eastern Transvaal of South Africa, but decided to come back to Austria, where he is managing director of a company producing electric motors and oil burners. He also looks after more than twenty thousand acres of timberland and agricultural areas surrounding the family seat in the village of Schonborn. It's an eighty-room castle and, he says,

81

too big to live in, so he and his wife, who is the daughter of the Comte de Paris (pretender to the throne of France) have done up one of their other places instead. Schloss Weierberg, near the Czech border, was badly damaged by advancing Soviet troops at the end of World War II, and it took the couple more than four years to make it habitable again.

Several other noble families have gone into the tourist business. Fürst von Khevenhuller-Metsch lived and worked in Spain for thirty years but returned to his native country when he inherited the title and, along with it, Austria's most spectacular fortress—Burg Hohenosterwitz, a turreted bastion which is said to have been the model for Walt Disney's castle in *Snow White*. The Fürst proudly claims to attract an average of five thousand visitors a day. His Imperial Highness Archduke Markus Salvador enjoys showing visitors around his ochre-colored, neo-classical Kaiservilla at Bad Ischl, the princely health spa in the Salzkammergut. The villa was given to Emperor Franz Josef when he married Princess Elisabeth of Bavaria, and he spent more than sixty summers there.

But not everyone has homes to show off or companies to run; a large number of aristocrats have only their fancy titles to remind them—and their fellow citizens—of past glories. The same is true of hundreds of princes, counts and barons in countries such as Italy and France who go on using their titles even though the system which created them vanished long ago. Some are rich, and some extremely rich, but many more have just enough to finance a modest way of life. A title can still help its owner to get a non-executive boardroom seat (though the business world generally is much more concerned with ability these days), and it secures invitations to cocktail and dinner parties organized by social climbers. But it also has drawbacks: waiters expect larger tips from a Count than from a plain Monsieur or Signore, and grocers tend to feel that the nobility can afford to pay higher prices for its baked beans than the rest of us.

Don Francesco Caravita is Il Principe di Sirignano, and he seldom allows anyone to forget it. His title goes back to the days when Naples was a kingdom, and the family still has estates near the city. But Sirignano recognized many years ago that he wasn't cut out to be a businessman, so he did the obvious thing. He handed

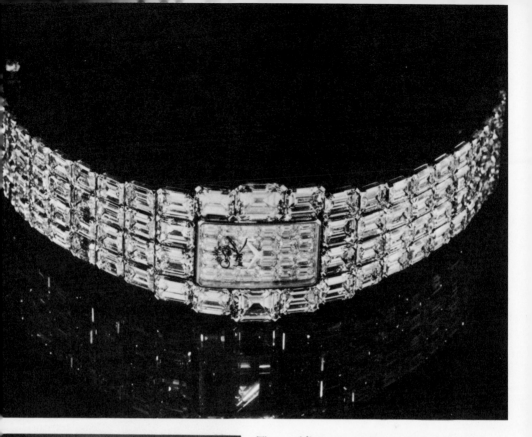

The world's most expensive watch: price, $5 million. It took a team of jewelers 6,000 working hours to make it. (*Vacheron Constantin*)

King of the Road—the Rolls Royce. Some of the super-rich have two or three: one for him, one for her, and one for use when they are at their holiday homes in Florida or the South of France.

One of the stately homes of England,
Blenheim Palace, given to the first Duke
of Marlborough by a "grateful nation"
for his victories against the French.
(*BTA*)

Above Left: Interior of a private jet—
today's equivalent of the golden coach.
(*British Aerospace*)

Left: The Orient Express is back in
business. Adjoining cabins can be
converted into sleeper and sitting rooms
—a method frequently used by monarchs
and maharajahs in the 1920s.

Overleaf: Mansion in Charleston, South
Carolina. Many old plantation houses
have been restored by the *nouveaux
riches*. (*Sylvette Jouclas*)

the estates over to his sons, accepted an allowance, and resolved to devote the rest of his life to the pursuit of pleasure. He argued, logically, that there wasn't much point in doing anything else because whenever he determined to work for a living and embarked on some venture, he invariably lost money. Doing nothing seemed more economical.

Il Principe is a charming man, with a great sense of humor. He speaks several languages, including fluent English (he was brought up by an English nanny, naturally), and charges through life with enviable zest. We first met in Lipari, an island off Sicily, and have since become good friends. He sets great store by friendships, does Il Principe: they are, he insists, far more important than material possessions. At dinner parties he holds fellow guests spellbound with anecdotes about famous people he has known in the past— Noel Coward and the Duke of Windsor among them. His title, impeccable manners and boyish eagerness to entertain an audience— any audience—make him the kind of guest most hostesses are glad to welcome to their homes.

He would, I am sure, feel very much at home in the palace of another colorful and widely traveled noble, His Highness Lt.Col. Fatesinghrao Gaekwad, Maharaja of Baroda. It is an impressive edifice—its frontage is some 500 feet across, and its style an exotic blend of Mogul, Hindu martial, European Gothic and neo-Venetian; its interior is filled with some of India's finest *objets d'art*. Of course it isn't what it used to be. Once it was guarded by twin cannons cast in silver and another pair in gold. There was a carpet woven with pearls and diamonds, and furnishings in ivory and crystal. There were days spent pig-sticking or chasing tigers from the backs of careening elephants. There were sumptuous feasts, a function most days, a spot of polo most weeks. Everywhere there was treasure. There was a diamond bigger than the legendary Koh-i-Noor. Today it is a magnet for tourists and a burden for its owner, who thinks the Indian government should do more to preserve the country's heritage.

The maharajas coped with British rule, but met their match in Mrs. Indira Gandhi. When Queen Victoria became Empress of India in 1858, large parts of that vast subcontinent continued to be governed by rajas, maharajas, nizams, nawabs and others bearing ancient royal titles. Each acknowledged the "paramountcy" of the British Raj, and was hugely influenced by its culture, yet each remained to a considerable extent sovereign in his princely state. Many of these royal houses of India had, after all, seen other empires come and go. They had a pedigree that went back to the eleventh century and the more imaginative rulers claimed direct descent from the oldest Buddhist empires or even from the sun and moon. In many respects, life under British rule could be compared with the chronicle of their history under the Moguls two centuries before; the imperial ruler controlled the coast and rich territories like the Ganges valley or the plains of the far south, while the petty princes ruled the deserts, hills and uplands. Conquered or not, they were left pretty much to themselves. The traditions of their "otherness" survived. It was not until 1948, when the British bowed to the forces of nationalism, that the great Indian princes were at last persuaded to give up their states; but they still managed to cling on as well-cushioned pensioners with their titles and all the social clout that went with them. It was as recently as 1971 that the Indian parliament finally took away the remains of their princely incomes and privilege. Families such as that of the Maharaja of Baroda were left only with their extraordinary history, and palaces doomed to decay.

But the past is not so easily shrugged off. Stripped of all constitutional power the Maharaja may be, yet the fact remains that he is still universally recognized, even revered, in his country. He has unparalleled contacts. He has inherited wealth and a lucrative business. He is India's highest individual taxpaper. He does as he pleases.

When, not long ago, David Taylor interviewed him for *High Life* he was bubbling over with enthusiasm for his business interests. "Rayon," said His Highness, "polyester, nylon: these are what I am doing today." There were four offices for his company, in Bombay, Delhi, Bangalore and Baroda, to each of which he had assigned a managing director from whom he expected the highest efficiency. They understood that, though he did not shout ("What is the point? There is none."), he would not stand any damned nonsense, no nonsense at all. They knew what was required, what was not required, what would not in any circumstances be tolerated. A maharaja had to maintain an authority, a style.

Great-grandfather founded the Bank of Baroda, but that had been nationalized. So had the family zoo. His Highness was busy these days traveling around the world, seeing customers and making deals. He had once taken an interest in politics—was Minister for Health, Family Planning and Sports for the state of Gujarat—but hadn't got the time for that sort of thing now. He did, however, find time for one of his great passions, cricket. He was also involved with the World Wildlife Fund, which was making a determined effort to save the Indian tiger. Had he ever considered a life of exile, tax-free with his treasures? No, certainly not. He would be bored outside India, needed always to be busy, accepting the challenge of tremendous change, trying to give some sort of lead. People expected that in a maharaja.

COMRADE PUJIE

In a private home in Peking an old man, dressed in a plain white shirt and black trousers, feeds his cats. By his own account he is simply Comrade Pujie, a part-time historian living on a government salary of $100 a month. He is surprised that any Western visitor should take an interest in him. But journalists love to speculate on what might have been. Comrade Pujie is the closest living link to the Manchu dynasty—the man who, were it not for two revolutions and a world war, could be ruling China's masses from the seat on the Dragon Throne.

He was only five years old when the last Manchu emperor—his six-year-old brother, Puyi—was deposed by Nationalist revolutionaries and made a virtual captive in the splendid cage of Peking's Imperial Palace. The Manchus and their host of courtiers, concubines and eunuchs finally fled the city in 1924, and for nearly forty years Puyi and Pujie were swept by the winds of war and revolution. They joined hands with Tokyo's militarists during the Sino-Japanese

War, and Puyi became the collaborationist puppet-ruler of Japanese-held Manchuria, with Pujie his heir-apparent. They were postwar prisoners of the Soviets, then inmates in a special Chinese "re-education" camp for former Manchurian officials.

Finally, in 1960 they were made gardeners in Peking's Bei Hai Park, formerly the Emperor's private park reserve. Later that year Prime Minister Chou-En-Lai called Pujie in for a talk. He asked him what he wanted to do with the rest of his life, and granted Pujie's request to do research on Manchu history. Puyi died of cancer in 1967, leaving his younger brother lord of what little remains of the family's once vast estate: a sixteen-room house about a mile from the gates of the former Imperial Palace. Pujie's wife is Japanese (a cousin of Emperor Hirohito) and their only surviving child is a daughter they occasionally visit in Japan. They have two state-paid servants, a far cry from the three-thousand-strong palace staff, which specialized in such tasks as trimming the young Prince's toenails or picking dangerous bones from his delicately cooked fish. But the man who would have been lord of the Celestial Kingdom says he has no complaints. "In the past I was a drop of dirty water," he says. "Now I am immersed in a sea of a billion people."

ALL THE QUEEN'S MEN

Unlike their brethren on the continent of Europe and in the ex-colonies, Britain's hereditary peers retain the right to play an official role in the shaping of the nation's laws without going through the tiresome business of getting elected. They are entitled to sit in the upper house of what is proudly known as the "Mother of Parliaments" and to pass judgment on legislation introduced by the hoi polloi in the Commons next door. The only stipulation is that a member of the Lords must be over twenty-one, must not be bankrupt, and must not be a lunatic. By no means all of them take advantage of this right, which the majority enjoy through accident of birth rather than merit, and the power of the Lords is not what it was. The upper house no longer *makes* laws; it merely delays or corrects those it doesn't like. And most of the speeches delivered by their lordships during a parliamentary sitting are ignored both by the government and by the national press. There is a strong possibility that the system will not survive into the twenty-first century; it may not even last out the 1980s. But for the moment their lordships can still comfort themselves with the thought that their opinions matter.

They are a motley crew—some bright, some stupid; some pompous, some dotty; some deeply interested in politics, some totally indifferent to the world around them; some poor, some among the richest people in the country. Earl Nelson of Trafalgar, descendant of the hero admiral, earns his living as a police sergeant and prefers to be known as Pete Nelson. Lord Mitford is a member of the Communist Party, the only Communist to sit in either Houses of Parliament. The Earl of Derby, the "uncrowned king of Lancashire," sports the largest herd of elephants to roam freely outside Africa at his grand house, Knowsley, in a Liverpool suburban park. Lord Cowdray presides over a business empire which ranges from merchant banking to a group of regional newspapers plus the *Financial Times*, and is reputed to be worth several hundred million pounds. And so on. The only generalization one can really make with confidence is that none of them is allowed to vote in parliamentary elections or sit in the Commons, and that all are exempt from jury duty, a privilege they share with convicted felons, M.P.s, barristers, lunatics and persons with undischarged bankruptcies.

At the top of the tree are the dukes. The title of Duke is the rarest honor the Crown may bestow on a person not of royal blood, and those who hold it are addressed officially by the monarch as "right trusty and entirely beloved cousin," and by everyone else as "Your Grace." (Not everyone, though, manages to grasp the distinction. A little boy was introduced to the Duke of Sutherland, whom he called "Sir" to the consternation of his proud father who dug him in the ribs and loudly whispered: "No, boy! Your Grace." The boy looked the Duke in the eye and said: "For what we are about to receive may the Lord make us truly thankful.") In George I's day there were forty dukes; today there are twenty-five, plus three who are members of the royal family, including the Duke of Edinburgh. There have been none (except royal) created since 1900, and there are not likely to be any more.

Some of the present company had ancestors who, like Marlborough and Wellington, won great battles for their country. Others owe their exalted status to men who performed outstanding service in political and public life. Several can thank a king's fondness for the fair sex; Charles II made dukes out of six of his bastards, born to four different mothers.

Until the reforms of the nineteenth century the dukes enjoyed extraordinary prerogatives. They were above the law; they could commit crimes without fear of arrest and prosecution in the courts; they could run up debts to infinity without punishment; they had control of Parliament. All this is over. Even royal dukes nowadays have to watch their step; recently, the Duke of Gloucester was fined $70 and had his license endorsed for driving at nearly 50 m.p.h. in a 30 m.p.h. zone. Governments manage to get along without them; the last duke to be prime minister was Wellington in 1828. But most of them still have considerable wealth, at least on paper.

The basis of ducal fortunes has always been land. Original grants were augmented by well-planned marriages to owners of other estates or heiresses who could afford to add to the ancestral acres. The institution of primogeniture allowed the heads of families to pass on their lands intact to their eldest sons, who were taught from childhood that it was their duty to preserve and if possible to increase the family holdings. Death duties have played havoc with the system in the twentieth century, but several dukes still own more land than the Queen. Cash in hand is another story; some of the present-day dukes appear to be perpetually strapped for ready money. ("Land gives one position," says Oscar Wilde's Lady Bracknell in *The Importance of Being Earnest,* "and prevents one from keeping it up.")

The largest fortune is generally reckoned to be that of the young Duke of Westminster: it has been put at $1 billion and could well be considerably more; even he is not sure of the figure. The dukedom was created by Queen Victoria in 1874, ostensibly to reward the Marquis of Westminster for services to the Liberals, but in reality because she felt obliged to acknowledge the fact that he was richer than she was—or so it's said. The family's prize possession is nothing less than the whole of Mayfair and Belgravia, which one of the Duke's ancestors acquired through marriage in 1678. (It was marsh and meadow at the time.) The Grosvenor family also owns land in eighteen British counties, an "industrial island" off Vancouver, a sheep station in Australia, a beach hotel in Hawaii, and other properties in Ireland, South Africa and the United States. The administration of this far-flung private dominion is in the hands of trustees; the Duke himself lives in Cheshire and keeps a low profile. He is a slim, boyish-faced six-footer who travels many thousands of miles each year to attend board meetings and supervise his estates. To his employees and tenant farmers he is known as "Himself." They say he is pleasant, unassuming and likable. He married former *Vogue* secretary Natalia Phillips in 1978 and they have two daughters. His sister Jane is married to another wealthy young nobleman, the Duke of Roxburghe, who was left several million in his father's will and has as his seat the delightful Floors Castle, set in eighty thousand acres in the Borders.

Next to Westminster, the largest ducal landowner is the Duke of Buccleuch, a descendant of King Charles's son by his first mistress, Lucy Walters. Lucy once claimed to be Charles's wife and he often addressed her as such. If it were true, the Duke would have a better right to sit on the throne than Elizabeth II, but no one has ever been able to prove that a marriage actually took place. There is a story that when the fifth Duke of Buccleuch was looking through old papers in the time of Queen Victoria he came across a black box containing the marriage certificate. He summoned his son and heir to his presence and said: "I am now going to do something which should have been done a long time ago. The publication of this document in my right hand might have severe repercussions. It is something no loyal subject should possess." He then threw it on the fire. It no longer matters whether the story is accurate or a piece of romantic fiction; none of his successors has pressed their case and it seems highly improbable that any future duke, lacking convincing evidence, will attempt to do so.

The current holder of the title sat for many years in the House of Commons, as the Conservative member for Edinburgh North. He had to leave when the eighth Duke died in 1973, and he assumed responsibility for more than a quarter of a million acres of England

and Scotland, estimated to be worth more than $150 million, together with a number of magnificent homes and one of the finest collections of furniture and paintings in the world. He rarely goes to debates in the House of Lords; he says he prefers to lobby behind the scenes.

The Duke of Devonshire, who owns large tracts of land in Derbyshire and Yorkshire, as well as much of the seaside resort of Eastbourne, has also withdrawn from active politics. In the 1960s he was Minister of State at the Commonwealth Office, but when the Tories lost office he decided to concentrate his energies on his estates and stable of racehorses. He later switched his allegiance to the SDP. The dukedom is one of the oldest—it was created in 1694—and the main family residence, Chatsworth, is among the half dozen best-known stately homes in the country. He is probably worth at least $100 million, but says he has to be careful: present-day taxes have "made life very difficult for the big landowners." Chatsworth has been open to the public for two centuries and attracts large numbers of tourists, but keeping it going costs a staggering sum each year. There is a sizable staff and constant repairs are needed.

One of the most celebrated aspects of Chatsworth is a cascade (a garden waterfall), and when that required a major overhaul it took two years and cost $40,000. The Duke decided that drastic action was called for. He put one of his heirlooms, a famous painting by Poussin, on the market and announced that with the proceeds he would turn Chatsworth into a charitable trust. It meant that part of the house, the eighty-acre garden, and the $30 million art collection would be leased to the trust for another hundred years. If he had to sell off another picture to fix the heating or mend a staircase he would not be subject to capital gains tax. He said the move had been forced on him by inflation. "Once I had eight or ten racehorses. Now I can afford only two. But I shall never call on the taxpayer for money. I think anyone who owns even one leg of a racehorse should not ask for public money. I am one of the most fortunate people in the country."

His Grace does not mind in the least that admiring visitors from many countries troop through his home—they are, after all, paying customers—but he eschews the showbiz gimmicks that have turned another ducal home, Woburn Abbey, into the most popular stately residence in England. Woburn is the family seat of the Dukes of Bedford and the thirteenth Duke has long been a maverick, a showman who has exploited his title with obvious relish. He is the only one of the breed to have joined Equity, the Actors' Union, so that he could appear in films and television shows. I have met him three times, always in television studios where he was plugging Woburn Abbey with all the skill and determination of a thorough professional.

The Bedfords used to own elegant mansions and lucrative parcels of land in the better part of central London (the family connection is still commemorated in over seventy street names), but unlike the Westminsters they have not managed to keep them. Death duties are one of the principal reasons: the deaths within fifteen years of the eleventh and twelfth Dukes, neither of whom had taken adequate steps to protect the estates, are reckoned to have cost more than $15 million. Even Woburn no longer belongs to the Duke; as a result of arrangements made by his father and grandfather, who did their best to prevent him from setting foot in the place, the owners are the Bedford Estates whose trustees have absolute discretion over what should be done with it and who should live there. In his youth the Duke worked as a reporter, and for a while lived in South Africa where ᵾe learned farming. He returned to Britain when he inherited the title in 1953, and persuaded the trustees to give him a limited tenancy while he rescued Woburn from neglect. He decided that the only way to make it pay was to attract as many tourists as possible, and tackled the job with vigor and imagination. He was, among other things, the first duke to take in paying guests— mostly Americans who happily paid large sums for the privilege of dining with the Duke and Duchess. His ideas were copied by others, despite the reservations of people like the Duke of Devonshire, and today tourists have a wide choice of diversions, including game parks and motor museums. In 1974 the Duke handed Woburn over to his son, Lord Tavistock, so that he could get to know the stately-home business, and went to live in a modest apartment in Paris with his French wife Nicole who (not surprisingly) used to be a television producer. They have since spent a great deal of time traveling around the world. Lord Tavistock, who is a stockbroker by profession, has kept the turnstiles clicking. His Lordship, who occupies only two of Woburn's hundred-odd rooms, belongs to a peers' cooperative formed in 1975 to publicize Britain's stately homes abroad. Calling themselves the Magnificent Seven, they include the Duke of Argyll and the Duke of Marlborough, whose palace, Blenheim, was given to his illustrious ancestor by a "grateful nation" for his victories against the French.

I daresay that the ghosts of past dukes are appalled by the whole business, but as another member of the cooperative, the Marquess of Bath, said to a reporter recently: "We have no alternative. No one lives like a proper lord these days—it's a question of getting the poor to feed the rich."

CHAPTER 6

BLACK GOLD

The hand you cannot bite, kiss it.

BEDOUIN SAYING

It is easy to make fun of oil-rich sheiks in their flowing robes and odd headdresses; it hardly ever seems to occur to those who do that Europe's nobles must have looked equally comic to the Arabs when they first ventured forth into the desert in their tight-fitting suits and solar topees. Over the past decade, ever since OPEC reminded the West how dependent it is on oil, millions of patronizing words have been written about the strange little men and their amusing habits: their penchant for blondes and solid gold bath-taps; their love of gambling (so sharply at variance with the austere approach to life in their own countries); and their tendency to hang laundry from the windowsills of their expensive London homes. There are stories galore about their vulgar attitude toward money, their fondness for kitsch and extravagant follies like buying $20,000 mink coats to use as bathrobes, and ordering Cadillacs by the dozen. Some of the stories are undoubtedly true (though they could just as easily be told about some of the nouveaux riches in the West), but some are apocryphal and others are based on remarks that were intended to be humorous but were taken seriously because it was assumed, wrongly, that Arabs have no sense of humor. The Sultan of Oman, who went to a boarding school in England and then spent two years at Sandhurst, delights in playing to the gallery. Ordering $40,000

97

worth of perfumes at Harrods, he was warned by an assistant that it would evaporate. "Don't worry, it's for the bath," he replied. And when his private D.C.10 was delayed on the runway for three hours during a strike at London's Heathrow, he relayed a message to the control tower asking how much it would cost to buy the airport. It was his idea of a joke, but the press thought he meant it.

We tend to be envious of Arab wealth, and because we are envious many of us are resentful. We tell ourselves that they have done nothing to deserve all those riches; the oil was discovered by Western geologists. But we are not so resentful that we resist the opportunity to channel some of that cash in our own direction. When Saudi Arabia's Crown Prince let it be known that he was planning to make his first official visit to Britain, and expected the Prime Minister to be at the airport to greet him, we did not tell him to get lost. Harold Wilson, then the occupant of 10 Downing Street, duly drove to Heathrow and kissed the royal hand. The Queen invited him to lunch. Not so very long ago such courtesies would have been unthinkable. The Arabian peninsula was a patchwork of sheikdoms until Ibn Saud came out of the desert with fifty Bedouin tribesmen, conquered the mud-walled settlement of Riyadh, and created his own kingdom. It would have remained of little interest to anyone if it had not emerged, many years later, that it held the world's greatest reserves of black gold. Europe's nobility would have continued to view the Arab king and his galaxy of princes—more than four thousand at the last count—as upstarts who could safely be ignored. But we can no longer afford such lofty attitudes. Britain may have oil of her own, but her industries need the Arab world's business. So does every other Western country, including the United States.

American resentment of Arab riches is just as great, if not greater, than Europe's. When the oil embargo was imposed in 1973 there was much angry talk of invasion: America, it was argued, was entitled to keep what her geologists—and oil companies—had created. But even the most gung-ho American politician has come to accept that times have changed. *If* the Soviet Union were to invade first, or *if* the present rulers were threatened by the kind of revolution which has already taken place in Iran, the White House would feel justified in taking military action. Until then, however, America has little choice but to be nice to the Arab billionaires.

The amounts of cash at stake are truly staggering. In 1980 Saudi Arabia alone—a country with less than a tenth of the population of Britain—had an income of $110 billion and spent more than $35 billion on imports. Defense accounts for the largest slice, much to the delight of Western arms manufacturers and middlemen like Adnan Kashoggi. Billions more went on industrial development—notably petrochemical plants—and on grandiose projects like Jeddah's third airport, the world's largest. Riyadh, the capital, has been turned into a vast urban sprawl with giant three-lane highways, huge five-star hotels, and a computerized mega-hospital. And still the money pours in. No wonder that Western politicians, faced with rising unemployment in their own countries, flatter the sheiks and princes. No wonder that industrialists and bankers hide their resentment, and put up with irritating delays and other inconveniences.

Unlike some of the other oil-producing countries, Saudi Arabia has ample reserves. It owns forty-seven oil fields, but so far has used only fifteen. The others wait, capped off, against the future. Rock dome formations suggest that oil is present in other, still unexplored parts of the country. Some estimates have put its probable reserves at 350 million barrels, which gives it enough oil to last until the year 2070.

The only threat to its prosperity, apart from the risk of military conflict or internal rebellion, is that of falling world demand. The worldwide economic recession induced by high prices has already led to a sharp decline, and Western countries have not only learned to conserve energy but have also pushed ahead with the development of alternative sources—coal, solar power, thermal energy, alcohol and nuclear energy. Sheik Ahmed Zaki Yamani, the world's best-known sheik, recognized the danger in a celebrated lecture not long ago:

If we force Western countries to invest heavily in finding alternative sources of energy, they will. This will take no longer than ten years and would result in reducing dependence on oil to a point which would jeopardize Saudi Arabia's interests. . . . Saudi Arabia's interests lie in extending the lifespan of oil to the longest period possible to enable us to build a diversified economy supported by our industry, agriculture and other endeavors. Unless we do that, there will come a time when this developing country will receive a violent shock.

But the House of Saud, which runs the country like a family firm, can console itself with two impressive facts. Its oil is cheap to produce; it costs only about 60 cents a barrel to tap the stuff. And its earnings during the past decade have allowed the government to pile up vast financial hoards all over the world. The size of these hoards is in constant dispute; the official Saudi estimate of $110 billion in 1980 is almost certainly conservative. Last year, the best guess was that the Saudis had around $180 billion overseas. No one is quite sure where these and other Arab funds are invested; the Gulf States tend to be secretive about their foreign assets. But there is no doubt that many billions could easily be brought back if the need arose.

Huge additional sums are held abroad by Saudis privately. As there are no exchange controls in the kingdom, even the Central Bank has little track of them. Part of the money is almost certainly stashed away in various numbered accounts in Switzerland, in the Bahamas, and other tax havens. Billions more are invested in land, property and business enterprises.

When the sheiks and princes first embarked on massive foreign investments, early in the 1970s, many people in the West felt uneasy. *The Economist* calculated that the OPEC countries were raking in enough cash to buy all the companies on the world's major stock exchanges in fifteen years and eight months. (The London Stock Exchange would take less than ten months. New York needed longer: nine years and three months.) Were a handful of autocratic Arabs going to take over what it had taken the rest of us so many years to build?

In Britain there was a public outcry when it was revealed that Arab interests had acquired the Dorchester Hotel. London's dining rooms were buzzing with all kinds of rumors. The Arabs, it was said, were on the point of buying Fortnum & Mason's. They were even after *The Times*, so that they could get favorable publicity for their cause. "Arabs may buy Knightsbridge," threatened the *Guardian*. Questions were asked in Parliament, and the government was urged to pass preventive legislation. It was perfectly in order to allow British insurance companies and pension funds to invest their money abroad and to let a Canadian own *The Times*. It was *not* in order, it seemed, to permit Arabs to do the same.

But by no means everyone was displeased. Bankers, stockbrokers and real estate agents made discreet trips to the Gulf to persuade the new masters that they had just the right deal for them. Hard-pressed businessmen relished the prospect of selling their ailing companies to people who, they hoped, had more money than sense. Even middle-class families joined in the hunt. One friend of mine, lumbered for years with an expensive property which no one seemed willing to buy, had a full color brochure printed in Arabic and bought small ads in Arab newspapers. (It worked.) Others gleefully swapped tales about the outrageous prices paid for London flats and mock-Tudor homes in the better suburbs. South Kensington became known as Saudi Kensington.

The press soon reported other notable acquisitions. Fort Belvedere, where King Edward VIII had signed his abdication, passed into Arab hands. So did Coppins, the former estate of the Duke of Kent, and Mereworth, near Tunbridge Wells. Property tycoon Nigel Broackes sold his country house, Wargrave Manor, to the Sultan of Oman. Adnan Kashoggi bought an apartment in Eaton Square, and Sheik Yamani became the owner of an apartment in Cadogan Place and a house near Ascot. Sheik Zaid of Abu Dhabi acquired Buxted Park, and a group of investors from Abu Dhabi and Dubai bought London's Park Tower Hotel. But the Arabs appeared strangely reluctant to take over British industry. *The Economist*, it seemed, had got it wrong. Even *The Times* stayed out of their clutches; it was bought by another foreigner, this time an Australian.

What really happened, of course, is that the Arabs decided to operate more discreetly. The Dorchester episode had demonstrated the perils of letting people know that Arab interests were involved. It clearly made more sense to buy through companies that were run by British businessmen but which were, in reality, owned by Arab investors. This has been the strategy ever since, both in Britain and in other Western countries, including the United States. Elaborate care is often taken to get around disclosure rules; a British firm may be the subsidiary of an American company, which in turn is controlled by a company in the Bahamas, which in turn is owned—through a trust—by Arabs. In many cases the British or American directors don't really know who ultimately has the power to pull the strings.

I would not wish to give the impression that, through such sinister-sounding machinations, the sheiks and princes have quietly managed to become lords of all they survey. That would be absurd. (It would also be foolish; who would want to risk having it all seized by Tony Benn?) What I am saying is that Arab money, today, is a much more powerful force than is generally realized.

For millions of people, Sheik Yamani is the symbol of that power—it is his face, after all, which appears most often in our newspapers. But he is servant rather than master, a non-royal who holds his position because he understands the West, is a shrewd strategist, and possesses formidable negotiating skills. The title of sheik doesn't really mean very much. It is used for courtesy and means, literally, "old man"; it does not denote aristocratic lineage. "I'm just a simple Bedouin," he once told an interviewer. He is not, but such modesty goes down well with the people who pay his salary. There is no doubt that he is a millionaire, but there are plenty of Saudis who are much wealthier. Adnan Kashoggi, that darling of the gossip columnists, is one of them. Suleiman Olayan, a Saudi entrepreneur who started out when the going was tough in 1947 and now owns Saudi Arabia's biggest joint-venture holding company, is another. Olayan, who has managed to keep a low profile, is said to have made substantial land deals in Florida and to be the man behind several important U.S. enterprises. He is known to be the principal private shareholder after David Rockefeller in the Chase Manhattan Bank.

Adnan Kashoggi—A.K. to his associates—is a flamboyant character, a wheeler-dealer who was the model for the principal character in the best-selling Harold Robbins novel, *The Pirate*. His father was personal physician to King Ibn Saud; it established a royal connection which has been useful ever since. Adnan was sent to a British-style boarding school in Alexandria, where he scored his first entrepreneurial success: he introduced the father of one classmate who wanted to import towels to the father of another who owned a textile factory, and received a present of $400. He later took a course in business studies at California's Stanford University and, when he returned to Saudi Arabia, became an agent. He soon had the Saudi agencies for Marconi, Fiat, Chrysler and Rolls Royce aero-engines. His royal links got him involved in lucrative arms deals. He was paid a commission of $45 million from the sale of French tanks to the Saudi army and, in the years that followed, earned more than $100 million from Lockheed and another $54 million from its rivals, Northrop. The Lockheed and Northrop deals first brought him to the attention of the American public: it was alleged that the fees paid to him had been bribes. Kashoggi denied it; he insisted that the proper term was "commissions." He issued a press statement which argued that:

> This is what the free world economy is all about. The more you produce, the more you are rewarded. This is how companies sell their products and it was on this basis that the American economy was founded and still thrives today. We have offices in six cities and five countries and seventy or eighty persons who work on the business we are trying to develop for our clients. If we don't produce for them we get no return for our work. Is 50 million dollars for all that work by all those people in the company working for five years wrong? I don't believe that anyone who believes in the free enterprise system would think it's wrong, or anyone who wants to see more prosperity and more jobs in the U.S. thinks that a sale which produces 4 billion dollars is wrong.

John D. Rockefeller and his fellow "Robber Barons" would have accepted his case; his American critics, still shaken by Watergate, didn't. Nor, it seems, did the Saudi government. The Ministry of Defense no longer buys weapons through Kashoggi or any other Saudi middlemen. But Kashoggi does not have to rely on agents' fees, these days, to finance his extravagant life-style. He has built up a formidable business empire outside Saudi Arabia. His Triad group, based in Liechtenstein, is a conglomerate with operations in thirty-eight countries: banking, property development, hotels, ship chartering, meat packing, insurance, fashion, hospital management and so on. It owns property in Florida, Texas and Arizona; steak houses in San Francisco; an industrial trade zone in Salt Lake City; and two California banks. (There was strong resistance when he tried to buy a third, the First National Bank of San Jose.) Kashoggi, a small, portly man blessed with great energy, flits from one country to the next in his private jet. He has eight homes waiting for him, in London, Rome, Paris, Cannes, New York, Beirut, Riyadh and Jeddah. He also has a luxurious yacht which is reckoned to have cost him $25 million, and a fleet of expensive cars. He likes to give lavish parties and is invariably surrounded by beautiful women. Islamic puritans may disapprove, but he is unrepentant: he says he enjoys living pleasantly and can afford it.

CHAPTER 7

GODS AND MAMMON

*Men make their choice; one
man honors one God, and one another.*

EURIPIDES

"We like to get him the very best," the British branch of the Divine
Light Mission said when it bought a magnificent gold-colored Rolls
Royce for its guru, Maharaj Ji, who was just fourteen at the time.
"It's the same as Jesus riding into Jerusalem on a donkey."

Well, not quite. But the boy "god" was by no means the first
leader of a religious cult to acquire the world's best-known symbol
of wealth, and I am sure he won't be the last. The gurus like to
live well. Maharaj Ji, who had made only a few visits to Britain,
was also provided with a "Divine Residence" in Highgate, a cook
who was required to be on call twenty-four hours a day in case he
felt hungry, and other incentives to bless his British followers with
his presence. When he expressed an interest in flying, the Mission
paid for lessons and told him that it would buy a private plane.
But the British had to accept that they were not the only adoring
disciples. The teenage guru claimed more than a million adherents
around the world, including some fifty thousand in America who
were prepared to be even more generous. During the next few years
the American branch provided him with a *fleet* of cars (including
the obligatory Rolls), an expensive retreat in Malibu, California,
and another in the Rocky Mountains near Denver. He also acquired
an American wife—a former airline stewardess who dutifully pre-

sented him with a daughter—and a less welcome symbol of success, an ulcer.

The guru phenomenon is one of the most curious features of an allegedly sophisticated age. There are, to be sure, others who have made fortunes out of religion. The Aga Khan, spiritual leader of twenty million Ismaili Moslems, is one of the richest men in the world. His grandfather used to be weighed against gold, diamonds and platinum at an annual conclave of the faithful, and although most of the proceeds were later used for charities, the old man, who spent much of his life in playgrounds like Monte Carlo, had amassed great wealth by the time he died in 1957. The present Aga Khan, who is in his forties, owns an immense estate outside Paris, a collection of racehorses, and a lavish resort in Sardinia. But the Rolls Royce gurus operate for the most part in countries where organized religion has seen a dramatic decline in the last few years. Many of the clergymen serving the Christian Church are literally struggling to keep the roof over their heads. It is remarkable, in the circumstances, that so many people are willing to give up their earnings and live on bare necessities in order to please self-appointed masters who obviously feel that none of the rules imposed on their followers apply to them.

When Maharaj Ji first arrived in Britain he came equipped with a simple slogan: "Give me your love, and I will give you peace." It seemed an impudent message—how could a child make such a bombastic promise?—but it quickly attracted several hundred followers. They severed contacts with their past lives and gave up sex, meat, money, drinking, smoking, TV, movies, marriage and worldly activities to live in "ashrams"—monastery-like communes dedicated to the guru. He talked to them from time to time, but for most of the disciples the mere existence of this precocious, fat-faced little boy appears to have been enough. He nominated *mahatmas* who taught courses in meditation which they called "the knowledge." People with "the knowledge" were supposed to see a "divine light" which gave them peace and contentment and convinced them of the guru's wisdom and divinity. It clearly worked for some; they brushed aside all questions about how much they were giving the guru by saying that this gift to them of divine light was of immeasurably greater importance. Others stayed for a while, clearly enjoying the novelty of it all, and then grew disillusioned and returned to their former way of life.

Since then, other gurus have made equally impressive hauls on both sides of the Atlantic. Bhagwan ("Lord God") Shree Rajneesh, ousted from his controversial Poona *ashram* amid loud complaints from the locals, set up a New Jersey-based "Rajneesh Meditation Center," and became a multimillionaire through the sale of tapes, books and video cassettes. He took out ads in *Time* and other mass circulation journals, emphasizing the sexual aspect of his path to enlightenment. "Search all the nooks and crannies of your sexuality," urged one. "Never repress it. Sex is just the beginning, not the end. But if you miss the beginning, you miss the end also." Recently he used $6 million collected from devoted followers to buy a vast tract of land in Oregon on which he is building his world head-quarters. Rajneesville, he declared at the time of the purchase, would be "an experiment in spiritual communism . . . a community to provoke God . . . a space where through meditation we can create human beings free from obsession with the ego." The guru, who clearly has a considerable ego himself, allows his press aides to describe him as "the self-proclaimed living God, totally beyond time in a state of continuous endless bliss." Who wouldn't be, with so many devotees eager to fulfill his every wish?

Another movement that has attracted a lot of attention, and formidable sums of money, is the so-called World Government created by the Maharishi Mahesh Yogi. The Maharishi made his British debut in the early 1960s and a few years later claimed some ten thousand converts to his doctrine of Spiritual Regeneration. His biggest coup was the recruitment of the greatest idols of the dec-ade—the Beatles. George Harrison's wife, Patti, had joined the movement in 1967 after hearing a talk by one of his lieutenants, and she persuaded the four Beatles to accompany her to a lecture given by the guru himself at his hotel, the Park Lane Hilton. They listened with apparent rapture as the little Asian gentleman, wearing robes and an unruly beard, described in his high-pitched voice, interspersed with giggles, an existence which seemed a lot more interesting to the jaded pop millionaires than mere hippydom. The "inner peace" that the Maharishi promised could, apparently, be obtained with comparatively little effort; to be spiritually regen-

107

erated, they were told, they need meditate with him for only half an hour each day. The next morning they joined the guru on a course of indoctrination at University College, Bangor, North Wales, and a small army of incredulous press and T.V. reporters saw them off at Paddington Station. They had a second audience with the holy being, who occupied his own first-class compartment, squatting on a sheet spread over British Rail's green upholstery. He held up a flower and explained that its petals were an illusion, like the physical world. Spiritual Regeneration, he said, was like a bank from which its practitioner could always draw dividends of repose.

As newly enrolled members of the movement, the Beatles were liable to pay a week's earnings per month to support it. They also undertook to visit their guru's academy in North India to further their studies and ultimately to qualify as teachers of meditation. They went off some months later, with Ringo taking along a consignment of baked beans because he couldn't bear the thought of eating nothing but curry for several weeks. The *ashram* to which their pocket-sized guru welcomed them was comfortable enough, with stone bungalows, English hotel furniture, telephones and running water. The Maharishi himself occupied an elegant residence, equipped with a launching pad for the private helicopter in which he would periodically view his domain. There were frequent excursions and parties, but Ringo had had enough after only ten days. Paul and his girlfriend stayed for nine weeks, and John for eleven. When the Maharishi demanded to know why he was leaving, John said: "You're the cosmic one. You ought to know."

Paul told journalists afterward that they had made a mistake. "We thought there was more to him than there was. He's human. We thought he wasn't." The press gleefully reported this verdict, and it is not difficult to imagine the Maharishi's feelings when he heard about it. But the defection of his most prominent disciples proved to be only a temporary setback. His "World Government" continued to recruit followers, and during the next few years it grew so rich that it was able to buy two hotels near Lake Lucerne, where it established its international headquarters, and several expensive properties in America and Britain, including Mentmore Towers, the Victorian mansion in Buckinghamshire which was formerly the home of the Rothschild family.

When the Maharishi visited London early in 1982 the press was summoned, as usual, to hear his latest theories. Sitting cross-legged on a sofa surrounded by flowers in the Royal Suite of the Royal Garden Hotel, Kensington (cost: $800 a day without breakfast), he said that London had been chosen as the testing ground for his view that it needs only a figure of one square root of 1 percent of a country's population (in Britain's case, eight hundred people) to levitate together, for all the ills of that country to be neutralized and eradicated. The guru likened the effect that his eight hundred "fliers" would have on British life to the impact of a washing machine in India. All our individual and collective anxieties and aggression would, he claimed, be sucked in and washed away by the super biological action of cosmic consciousness. Alas, his track record so far is not impressive. The 250-strong group who have been levitating together for more than a year at Skelmersdale, near Liverpool, do not seem to have radiated much order and calm to their near neighbors in Toxteth. Nor is Hackney, where an experiment was launched in 1978 to teach 1 percent of the inhabitants to meditate, noted among London boroughs for its low crime figures.

It's easy to mock people like Rajneesh and the Maharishi, and to dismiss their disciples as gullible fools. But it is only fair to acknowledge that their movements have also been responsible for a good deal of social work. The same is true of the Aga Khan, who takes an active interest in the various charitable and self-help institutions set up by his grandfather. The Aga Khan Foundation puts considerable effort into rural health, education and housing, in collaboration with national bodies and international agencies like the World Health Organization and UNICEF. There is also a group of some sixty companies, with mobilized assets of about $200 million, which is deeply involved in Third World development problems. The Aga Khan resents the notion that he is simply a millionaire playboy. There is, nevertheless, a marked contrast between the lifestyles of the gurus and most of their flock, and this certainly applies to the oldest institution of all—the Vatican.

Christ was a man who came from a poor family and who chose all the apostles from among poor people. He not only chased the merchants and the moneylenders from the Temple but issued a terrible warning that it is "easier for a camel to go through a needle's eye than for a rich man to enter into the Kingdom of God." "Go sell whatsoever thou hast, and give to the poor," he repeatedly told his listeners. He didn't believe in making provisions for future necessities; divine providence would somehow take care of everything. "Consider the ravens: for they neither sow nor reap; which neither have storehouse nor barn; and God feedeth them: how much are ye better than the fowls? Consider the lilies how they grow: they toil not, they spin not; and yet I say unto you, that Solomon in all his glory was not arrayed like one of these." One wonders what he made of the behavior of his Church in the centuries that followed. A long line of popes, cardinals and archbishops not only welcomed the rich back to the Temple but also did their best to assure them that the needle's eye could be conveniently widened if the right price was paid. Christ's vicar lived in regal splendor while the poor lined up outside the gates for a glimpse of His Holiness, who was often far too busy tucking into a sumptuous meal to find time for his flock. In the early years of the sixteenth century Pope Leo X had 683 courtiers and servants, including a court composer, several jesters, and a keeper of the elephants. He kept his own permanent orchestra and theater company, and when he went on one of his frequent hunting expeditions he was accompanied by two hundred riders, among whom were cardinals, musicians and comedians. To pay for it all, he pushed the sale of benefices and indulgences to such extremes that it provoked Luther's revolt and the Reformation. He appointed numbers of cardinals, from whom he extorted a great deal of money, and created and sold no fewer than 1,200 new offices. These officials often had curious names, like Knights of St. Peter, portionarii, and squires, but no duties to perform.

The present Pope, who knows from personal experience what poverty is like, is a much more modest man. In any case, the days of hunting expeditions are over. But the Vatican still makes all the guru residences look like hovels, and the Pope's Summer Palace (complete with swimming pool) is the envy of many a millionaire.

The Holy See has its own team of financial advisers who keep a watchful eye on its investment portfolio. By pressing a button they can get the latest quotations on the stock markets of Wall Street, the City of London, Zurich or Milan. At one time the Pope's business empire was largely in the hands of Italian princes, counts and other protégés, but they proved to be more adept at spending money than at making it, and were gradually replaced by clerical and lay financial experts, each a specialist in his own particular field. The Vatican also accepted an offer of help from a Sicilian financier, Michele Sindona, who in 1969 became its chief financial consultant. Sindona established private banks in Switzerland, transferred funds to various tax havens such as Liechtenstein and the Bahamas, and indulged in a series of speculative deals which, in 1974, led to the collapse of his empire, the closure of his banks, and a twenty-five-year jail sentence in the United States for the supposed whizz-kid of high finance. Deeply embarrassed officials admitted that the Vatican had lost a great deal of money through its association with Sindona's affairs.

But other scandals followed, including the Vatican's involvement in the ill-fated Banco Ambrosiano. In June 1982 the bank's president, Roberto Calvi, was found hanging ("like a salami," as one Italian newspaper put it) from scaffolding under London's Blackfriars Bridge. Calvi, who had taken over Sindona's role, was known to the popular press as "God's banker." The British police said he appeared to have committed suicide—a verdict that was greeted with astonishment throughout Italy. Calvi had good reason for leaving this world without saying goodbye; his bank was in an appalling mess, but why should he stage such a bizarre exit? It would have been simpler to take an overdose or jump from the top floor of the nearest building, as his secretary had done the day before. Some of the newspapers felt sure he had been dispatched by the Mafia.

"God's banker," it emerged, had been at the center of a complex financial web involving companies in Panama, the Bahamas, and Liechtenstein. Some of his deals had gone badly wrong, leaving the Banco Ambrosiano with debts of at least $1.4 billion. The Vatican, through its Institute of Religious Works, was not only an important shareholder in the bank but had provided Calvi with "letters of comfort," which its creditors assumed to be guarantees. Archbishop Paul Marcinkus, the head of the Institute, was a director of its offshore subsidiary in the Bahamas.

Marcinkus, son of a Lithuanian-born Chicago window cleaner,

111

seemed a curious choice for the job. Known to his staff as "the gorilla," because he is built like a rugby forward, he frequently acts as the Pope's bodyguard on overseas trips. But he clearly has poor financial judgment. Years before he had been taken in by the persuasive charms of Sindona and, it seemed, history had repeated itself. The Bank of Italy declared that it was holding the Vatican responsible for the entire debt. The Pope, thoroughly alarmed, appointed three independent financial experts to look into the affair. Marcinkus said nothing.

The Vatican has always been reluctant to talk about its investments, but it is known to have substantial share stakes in a great many business enterprises, including General Motors and I.B.M. Most of its capital used to be invested in Italian industry, but over the last decade or so a lot of it has been switched abroad—notably to the United States, Canada and Australia—partly because of the shaky state of the Italian economy, but also because of the risk that, at some date, Italy might elect a Communist government determined to take both companies and real estate into public ownership. The Vatican also has dozens of numbered accounts in Swiss banks.

Presiding over all this is an office called the Prefecture of Economic Affairs of the Holy See, headed by a cardinal. It draws up an annual budget for the Pope's approval, provides balance sheets for all Curia departments, and supervises the Vatican's economic operations. In essence, the Prefecture serves as the Vatican's equivalent of a finance ministry.

Officially, the Pope has the last word on everything. He can be judged by no man, and there is no appeal from his decisions. The greatest worry of Vatican officials is that any new man will (like Christ) take an "irresponsible" view of money. There have been some notable examples of papal generosity: officials still recall with horror Pope Benedict's custom, in the earlier part of this century, of keeping huge sums of money in his desk drawer and handing them freely to any priest who came to him with a tale of woe. His successor, Pius XI, was another prodigal spender and, more recently, Pope John XXIII had a reputation of being an easy touch. One day, walking in the Vatican gardens, he met a group of gardeners. He asked them about their families, and the conversation soon got around to their wages. "What?" he exclaimed when he heard what they were paid. "No family with children can live on that. What has become of justice? Just wait . . . that's going to change." On his order, a general review of all Vatican wages and salaries was made and he ordered an across-the-board increase.

In 1979 Pope John Paul decided that the time had come to publish an annual balance sheet. There was strong resistance from conservative cardinals who argued that donations would dry up if the Church was seen to be rich, but the Pope was adamant. He discovered, soon after his election, that the annual budget was actually in the red. The Vatican had huge running costs: it not only had to meet a payroll of several thousand employees but was also involved in missionary work, relief agencies and other worthy causes. Losses were mounting rapidly. The Church could sell some of its assets but that would merely postpone the day of reckoning. It needed more income.

The main source of income, apart from bequests and dividends from investments, is "Peter's Pence"—money collected among the world's 750 million Roman Catholics. A custom that developed in Britain over a thousand years ago, when a yearly tax was imposed on householders in favor of the Pope, Peter's Pence is now strictly voluntary. Every year on a certain day in all the Catholic churches of the world a collection is held for the Pope. Contributions from each diocese vary enormously according to its size, the wealth and the religious zeal of its inhabitants, and the efficiency of its clergy. But it is also heavily influenced by the charisma of the reigning Pope and the view people take of his needs. A hundred years ago, when the Holy See came close to bankruptcy, parish priests in many European countries distributed to the faithful picture cards depicting the Pope lying on a bed of straw in a dark dungeon to corroborate the legend that he was a prisoner of the wicked Italians and reduced to extreme poverty. Money poured in. If they tried such a ploy today, the Vatican would be besieged by T.V. cameramen and reporters, half of them trying to persuade the Pope to make the picture postcards come true and the other half exposing the whole thing as a diabolical fake. It makes much more sense, in a media-dominated age, to reveal the facts and hope for the best.

Pope John Paul gets no salary and certainly cannot be called rich. He does not drive around in a Rolls Royce and he doesn't have a private plane. But it is reasonable to ask whether the Vatican really requires such a large staff, and whether it needs all that pomp. Many young Christians, including radical young clergy of all denominations, would like to see the Church return to basic principles. They are dismayed that the Holy See can spend $20 million on an Ecumenical Council while, at the same time, paying lip service to the virtues of poverty.

Vatican officials tend to dismiss this kind of argument as "moral simplicity," but one of the present Pope's predecessors, Pope Paul, acknowledged the contradiction between the ideal of poverty preached by Christ and the wealth, or the supposed wealth and its appearances, of the Holy See. In a memorable speech on June 24, 1970, he told an audience in St. Peter's: "The Church must be poor and appear to be poor." He went on:

> One could easily demonstrate that the fabulous wealth, which now and then certain public opinion attributes to her, is of a quite different nature, often insufficient to the modest and legitimate needs of ordinary life, to the needs of so many ecclesiastics and of religious, beneficent and pastoral institutions. But we don't want to make this apology now. Let us instead accept the desire which today's men, especially those who look at the Church from the outside, feel for the Church to manifest herself as she should be: certainly not as an economic power, not appearing to have great wealth, not engaged in financial speculations, not indifferent to the needs of indigent persons, institutions and nations. We notice with vigilant attention that, in a period like ours which is completely taken up by the acquisition, the possession and the enjoyment of material goods, one feels that public opinion, both inside and outside the Church, desires to see the poverty of the Gospel and that it wants to recognize this even more where the Gospel is preached and represented: in the official Church, in our own Apostolic See. We are aware of this exigency, internal and external, of our ministry. And just as, by the grace of God, many things have already been accomplished to renounce temporal power and to reform the style of the Church, so we shall proceed, with the respect due to legitimate *de facto* situations, but with the confidence of being understood by

the faithful, in our effort to overcome situations which do not con-
form with the spirit and the good of the true Church.

His officials were appalled, and the cardinal in charge of the
Prefecture of Economic Affairs took the first opportunity to explain
in an interview: "When the Pope said that we need more money
and are a poor Church he meant exactly that!" He went on to list
the Vatican's investment priorities and boasted that "We are more
peformance-minded now." It never seems to have occurred to him
that all the talk of boardroom control, current assets, price-earnings
ratios and real estate holdings totally missed the point—or if it
did, he clearly felt that the Pope's sudden lapse into "moral simplicity" was a serious mistake.

The present Pope has been more careful. He has encouraged the
Vatican to publicize the fact that it has a budget deficit—that,
indeed, it has been in the red for years. The result has been gratifying: the 1981 deficit was entirely covered by an increase in Peter's
Pence. A commission of cardinals set up to look into the Vatican's
finances announced in March 1982 that operations were continuing
to run at a loss: the deficit for 1982 would be around $30 million;
but it refused to publish budget details, so it is still impossible to
say how much money the Church really has. The figure of $30
million does not take into account the operations of the highly
secretive Vatican Bank run by Archbishop Paul Marcinkus, and
tells us nothing about the Church's worldwide assets. All that is
known is that they remain very substantial: possibly as much as $8
billion.

Let me end this chapter with a few words about the Church of
England. It, too, is "performance-minded," but its wealth is less
obvious than the Vatican's and therefore attracts less attention. A
body called the Church Commissioners administers more than $2
billion of assets (excluding churches and parsonages) under the
chairmanship of the Archbishop of Canterbury. The assets include
office and residential property, some of which has been left to the
Church in the wills of rich businessmen, and substantial stock
market investments. The Commissioners will not buy shares in
companies operating wholly or mainly in armaments, gambling,

breweries or distilleries, tobacco, newspapers, publishing and broadcasting, theater and films, and southern Africa. This policy limits the scope for making money, but they do their best. Millions more are donated each year by what they call "the man in the pew," but the Commissioners say that the amount of money at their disposal is inadequate. Churches have to be repaired, and even clergymen have to eat. Most of them earn less than the average skilled worker; in today's materialistic terms they are indeed poor and seen to be poor.

The question we really have to ask ourselves, as individuals, is whether we want organized religion and, if we do, what form it should take. A guru's commune? A showplace like St. Peter's, filled with priceless treasures? A simple parish church? Christ did his work without any of these things, and if we truly accept his teachings we should be able to do the same. But organized religion gives comfort to millions of people, and on that score alone seems far more worthwhile than most of the frivolous pursuits of the twentieth century.

CHAPTER 8

RED AND RICH

Capitalism means exploitation of man by his fellow man.
In socialism, it is precisely the other way round.

MOSCOW JOKE

Officially, individual wealth does not exist in the Communist world; in practice it most certainly does, even in the Soviet Union. The rich keep quiet about their financial affairs for obvious reasons, but from time to time "show" trials produce some astonishing revelations. Some years ago the KGB arrested a Moscow black marketeer, Yan Rokotov, and accused him of making a personal profit of $16 million. He had, they said, escaped earlier detection despite the impressive scale of his operations, by systematically bribing top officials. A month after his arrest the KGB picked up three of them, including Moscow's Deputy Police Commissioner. Rokotov was shot; the officials got lengthy prison sentences but were released after three years. In another famous case, Boris Roifman and his cousin Peter Order confessed that they had been in business underground for more than ten years. One turned over more than 200 million roubles' worth of valuables to the KGB, and the other about three-quarters of that amount. More recently, one Mikhail Leniev was formally accused of speculation and illegal sales of gold, allowing him to accumulate assets valued at $3.5 million. He was sentenced to death—not, his wife claimed, because he had money but because he was a Jew.

The KGB has a special section dealing with "economic crime"

and punishment is severe. One cannot help wondering why people like Rokotov and Leniev should have wanted to amass such large fortunes—it isn't easy to spend millions in a drab country like the Soviet Union. But greed is a powerful driving force and I daresay that, like most millionaires, they got as much satisfaction from the pursuit of riches as they did from the actual cash. The fact that they managed to avoid detection for so long suggests that the KGB is not nearly as efficient as it likes to pretend, and there is every reason to believe that the Soviet Union still has plenty of clandestine operators who are doing very nicely. The trick, clearly, is not to get *too* big. Large-scale operations carry correspondingly large risks; more people have to be bribed and there is the ever-present danger that someone will blow the whistle.

Sometimes the KGB hesitates because the people involved have close connections with the Soviet hierarchy. In Khrushchev's day, one of the most notorious underground millionaires in Georgia, Otar Lazeishvili, did absolutely nothing to conceal his wealth: he prided himself on the luxury of his two villas, one outside Tbilisi and the other on the Black Sea shore; he gave fabulous evening balls, had four limousines and half a dozen mistresses. The KGB knew all about him, but did not dare to act because he was a close friend of Vasily Mzhavanadze—the Party leader of Georgia, candidate member of the Politburo, and personal chum of Khrushchev. Lazeishvili gave lavish gifts, including diamonds, to the Party leader's fun-loving wife. It was not until Khrushchev's downfall, and the subsequent removal of Mzhavanadze from all his government posts, that the KGB made its move. Lazeishvili was sent before a firing squad and his associates were dispatched to labor camps.

Lazeishvili had been the silent owner of three large factories and twenty-eight cooperatives. Officially they made goods called for by the state plan, which appeared on the books and were distributed through the usual channels; unofficially, they also produced substantial quantities of goods not registered in any documents—easily salable merchandise like fashionable raincoats and sweaters, ladies' underwear and leather jackets. Unaccounted for, they were known (in underground jargon) as "left-hand goods." They were made on the same machines as the official merchandise, operated and supervised by the same personnel, but the supplies needed for their manufacture, as well as the labor costs, were paid for by Lazeishvili. In other words, private enterprise co-existed under the same roof, and the same name, with a state factory.

Lazeishvili was not the first to use this path to riches nor, despite his fate, has he been the last. Dissidents who have left Russia during the last few years say that similar enterprises flourish in most, if not all, the nation's major cities. According to them, alongside the state system exists an organized "second economy"—an underground system of companies and family clans that own dozens of factories and have access to a nearly national sales network. Factory workers are paid extra money, higher than the official rates and not subject to tax, and therefore have good reason to cooperate. Shop employees, too, get a substantial cut, often as much as a third of the retail price.

If the KGB is really determined to get an underground businessman it can always find people who are willing to give evidence, but even KGB officials can be persuaded to accept discreet bribes: many are just as eager to grab their share of the good life as the rest, providing they think they can get away with it. If they were incorruptible, the factories could not last for more than a few weeks. They may not actively participate in private enterprise, but for the right kind of payoff (generally untraceable cash, handed over at a secret rendezvous), many will gladly look the other way. If the entrepreneurs are exposed by, say, an idealistic journalist from Moscow, which has been known to happen, they simply claim that they had no idea such things were going on.

But the "second economy" isn't all underground. Its most important legal produce is the crops and livestock that Soviet citizens raise on private plots, then sell at public markets. The plots are small, and represent only 3 percent of all Soviet farmland, but they are used so efficiently that they account for a quarter of all Soviet farm products. During the long winter months these growers are often the only people who sell fresh fruit and vegetables. The law also allows some people who provide services to make money of their own. Doctors, for example, may treat patients at home; the fees, though, are fixed by the state and taxed heavily. The obvious answer is to moonlight and that is, in fact, what happens. Moonlighting is far more popular than the authorities acknowledge. It is often the only way to get things done; if one wants to get a car repaired the quickest course is to go to one of the many unlicensed car mechanics and pay under the table.

The black market, too, continues to flourish. Yan Rokotov, the man who was shot for making $16 million, got his start when foreign tourists first began to arrive in large numbers during the late 1950s. He offered to buy their clothes, watches, cigarettes and other personal belongings at high prices, knowing that these precious items would fetch far more when he subsequently sold them to his fellow Muscovites. (Many of the tourists were dismayed to find, after the transactions had been concluded, that there was little they could buy for their roubles.) His next move was into the lucrative "hard currency" business. He soon had a small army of touts who accosted foreigners and offered to exchange their dollars, marks, francs or pounds at double the official rate; the line outside the Lenin Museum was a favorite mark. Rokotov also traded in gold, after making the acquaintance of some Egyptian Arabs who were students at a nearby Soviet military academy. They were able to fly in and out of the country through special military airports, where their luggage was not examined, and they agreed to use his dollars to buy gold in Cairo. It was a highly lucrative ploy for all concerned, but it turned out to be his undoing. A Russian plane carrying the Egyptians crashed outside Kiev and every passenger was killed. Investigators sifting through the wreckage found hundreds of gold coins, and reported their discovery to the KGB who soon established the link with Rokotov.

His much-publicized trial, ironically, had an effect which the KGB should have foreseen but didn't—all Moscow was made aware of the profits that could be made from foreign tourists. During the years that followed, the number of small-time operators grew considerably. On each of my three visits to the Soviet Union over a period of ten years, I was approached at least once a day, usually in the street, by a young man who said, in good English, that he could give me a far better rate than the official agency. I always declined, not because I had any moral objections to doing business with a Russian tout but because I had been warned that the KGB made a habit of using its own people to trap tourists in this way, and I didn't fancy the idea of ending up in the Lubianka. (I learned of another trick on my last trip. Con-men would pose as KGB officials, "arrest" both the tout and the tourist, confiscate their cash, and then vanish.)

There were good reasons why so many Russians were willing to take risks in order to get hard currency. Moscow and other cities had special stores where they would buy goods not available to the proletariat—Scotch whiskey, French perfumes, American cigarettes, Japanese stereo sets. These stores existed for the benefit of tourists and the Russian elite; prices were given in dollars.

The Kremlin propaganda machine makes strenuous efforts to perpetuate the myth that the Soviet Union is a classless society, but the reality is different. A large number of officials enjoy all kinds of privileges; they don't have to risk their necks to get them— the perks go with the job. The top men may not be millionaires but they certainly live like millionaires. They have large apartments, servants, special clinics, country dachas, and chauffeur-driven limousines that speed down the special center lane of main avenues, the lane reserved for VIP cars. Still further benefits are gained by using influence or pressure; high officials, for example, get their offspring into universities and institutes and place them in good jobs afterward.

Muscovites know all about these perks but there is nothing they can do, except make jokes about them. There is a story about Brezhnev which has been making the rounds for some years. The former Soviet leader, so the story goes, brought his mother from the Ukraine to show her how well he had done in the capital. He took her around his ample town apartment, ordered a chauffeur-driven car to take them to the airport, and flew her to his dacha in his personal helicopter. He escorted her through the large dining room, into the gun room, and finally when he settled the troubled and ill-at-ease old lady in the ample living room, he asked: "Tell me, Mama, what do you think?"

The old lady hesitated. "It's good, Leonid. But what if the Reds come back?"

Ordinary citizens can only dream of luxurious dachas, but the law does not prevent them from buying their own house or car if they have the necessary cash. The enterprising young man or woman has, therefore, considerable incentive to earn income by moonlighting or through some other clandestine activity. The growth in tourism has not only made it easier to get hold of hard currency, but has also opened up a market for other items, such as antiques. Foreigners are known to be particularly enthusiastic about icons, so many people scour the countryside for them. The government does its best to prevent the illegal exporting of antiques but it is rare, these days, for tourists to be clapped in jail if they are found in possession of such goods, and sellers generally take care to ensure that they cannot be traced back to them. Many antiques are smuggled out in diplomatic pouches.

Not long ago, *Literaturnaya Gazeta* published a revealing article about what it called the nouveaux riches. It told of big spenders from the freewheeling Caucasian republics who squander their money in holiday resorts like Sochi, on the Black Sea, and behave like the old aristocracy on visits to Moscow. Whenever they arrive in the city, the paper said, people scurry around to compete for their custom, offering chic and expensive furniture, imported toilets — still the acme of fashion and the yardstick of success for the parvenu — as well as matching pastel baths and basins. Two cars carry their purchases back to their treasure-store outside the city. A huge, well-packed container is sent to the station with furniture supplied on the strength of a special stamp in their Moscow residence permits. No matter that the law forbids its export from the city; wads of banknotes circumvent that small difficulty.

The paper went on to tell the story of two minor officials. Mr. Firidum Kadyov was director of the social security office for industrial enterprises in Azerbaijan. For a consideration he would divert cars intended for invalids to the garages of perfectly healthy people. This profitable sideline enabled him to buy two flats in Baku, a country dacha with a swimming pool, and his own orange grove. He had, of course, the requisite imported toilet, and was particularly fond of black swans. He decorated his town house with antique pictures and kept objets d'art in his glass display cabinet. At his arrest the total amount of gold in his possession weighed 75 lbs.

In the central Asian oasis town of Urgench, Mr. Kadam Rahmanov found an equally rewarding occupation — at least materially — as director of correspondence courses in the teachers' training college. After his arrest for selling diplomas he was found to have 3 cars, 23 dinner services for 380 people, 74 suits, and 149 pairs of shoes.

Similar reports appear from time to time in other journals. Some tell of a growing traffic in marijuana and other drugs. Some say that fortunes have been and are being made out of gambling. Russians are, traditionally, inveterate gamblers, and the government acknowledges the fact by operating state lotteries. Buying a lottery ticket from a street kiosk and scanning the papers for the winning numbers is a national pastime which, in the absence of football pools and off-track betting on horses, occupies a central position in many people's lives. The main lottery is held every six weeks and is called rather prosaically Money and Things Lottery: prizes include cars, carpets, motorcycles, refrigerators, cameras, vacuum cleaners and so on. But this is not enough for big-time gamblers, who play for much higher stakes in private homes.

Large-scale corruption is occasionally shown to extend to the very top of the hierarchy. In the early 1960s, the KGB opened the safe of an official who had died in a car accident. They found packages of precious stones and huge bundles of money. They were all clearly labeled, and it turned out that some of them belonged to Frol Kozlov, a member of the Politburo and, in effect, the second man in the regime. Discreet inquiries revealed that he had been accepting large bribes through the official, in exchange for performing various services such as appointing people to responsible and prestigious posts, general protection, and using his influence to halt criminal proceedings against underground businessmen wealthy enough to pay for such influence with bribes amounting to hundreds of thousands of roubles. But Kozlov did not lose his membership in the Politburo. He retained all his posts and privileges and, under the pretext of illness, was merely removed from active service. When he died, he was even buried with full state honors in the Kremlin Wall on Red Square.

Satellite countries like Romania, Hungary and East Germany offer even greater scope. They do considerable business with the West, and it is generally easier for an entrepreneur to make money on the side here than it is in the Soviet Union. Visiting businessmen are treated with considerable courtesy, and although the authorities frown on private currency deals they are reluctant to make a fuss. Bribes are commonplace. When I crossed from Romania into Bulgaria not long ago my companion, who lived in Bucharest and knew the score, placed several packets of American cigarettes on top of our luggage in the trunk of his car. The customs officer opened the trunk, saw the cigarettes and picked them up.

"What's this?" he asked.

"American cigarettes," my companion said. "Would you like some?"

The officer silently took the packets and waved us on. We could have a ton of gold with us for all he cared. I later learned that the Romanian border police were operating a thriving black market operation of their own: they smuggled across the border coffee and other goods which at that time were hard to get in Bulgaria, and sold them at fancy prices.

Yugoslavia is perhaps the easiest place in which to run a private enterprise. Tourists frequently express surprise that this is a Communist country, since there is so little sign of it. One can eat in privately owned restaurants and pay with an American Express credit card, buy all kinds of goods, and make all kinds of deals. The coastline is studded with the plush villas of the well-to-do, and the hotels are among the best in Europe.

In Hungary, too, free enterprise has made a comeback. Under new regulations announced recently, private businessmen are being given much more freedom to do their own thing. They can employ more people; tax concessions make it easier to raise money for partnerships; and they are being encouraged to lease small businesses which were previously state-run. The authorities say that, by doing all this, they hope to "unleash the creative possibilities of the Hungarian people."

In Poland, a few years ago, a friend showed me around one of the suburbs of Warsaw, Zoliborz, where he said the rich had their homes. The houses I saw were impressive, with swimming pools in the gardens and Western cars parked outside the door. All the homes, my friend assured me, were privately owned. Some time later, just before the declaration of martial law, Solidarity analyzed the perks available to what it called the "power elite." They included an "envelope enclosure" system by which large sums of money were handed over on national holidays, and special name-day presents were given to officials and their wives. Some of the elite, Solidarity said, also had the power to decree which Western companies could acquire a monopoly of services to Poland and this brought with it many bonuses, apart from the illegal possibility of commissions and bribes. Many members of the hierarchy were tax-exempt, and they were able not only to borrow state treasures indefinitely to furnish their homes, but could also use state labor to build private houses and maintain estates.

The Military Council, keenly aware of the effect these disclosures had on public opinion, promised to take appropriate action. One of its first moves was to order the trial of Majec Szcepanski, the chairman of Polish Television under former Party leader Edward Gierek. Szcepanski (who was said to have a yacht, seven cars and three mistresses) was charged with taking bribes and misappropriating millions of zloties' worth of state property. In court, on the opening day, he defiantly stated that he was "not ashamed of having earned money or having served my Party." Yes, he had a yacht; yes, it was bought with state funds. But it was hired out to foreigners in some months and earned the country hard currency; in other months it was lent out to naval cadets. Poland's problems, he insisted, were not the result of yachts and cars but of economic mismanagement.

China, too, occasionally feels compelled to stage show trials, though the West seldom gets to hear about them. Mao's Cultural Revolution was intended to "purify the system," but his successors take a more lenient view: they only tackle the more blatant cases of corruption. The profit motive has made a comeback, and the Peking leadership has openly declared that "egalitarianism is a petty-bourgeois socialist utopian idea."

Some of the wealthier citizens of Communist countries have numbered accounts in Switzerland, just in case they should feel compelled to leave at some point in the future. The Swiss are not particularly enthusiastic about this class of trade, but it isn't really difficult to find an obliging banker if the amounts are large enough: the Swiss may not have any love for Communism, but they love the smell of money. Some also admit, privately, that they maintain such accounts for Communists living in Western countries such as

France and Italy—though, of course, nothing would persuade them to disclose their names to journalists or, for that matter, to tax inspectors. Western Communists, including mayors, are understandably reluctant to advertise their wealth, but they are certainly not averse to making the most of whatever moneymaking opportunities come along. Socialist millionaires in the West don't even bother to disguise their riches. They argue that one doesn't have to give away one's fortune in order to prove that one believes in socialism; they see nothing wrong in leading a life of ease and plenty while lecturing the rest of us on the merits of enforced equality.

One of the best-known of Britain's socialist millionaires is Lord Lever, who has held various posts in the Labor governments of Sir Harold Wilson and Jim Callaghan. Much of his wealth comes from share transactions. In 1962 he married Mrs. Diane Zilkha, a Lebanese heiress who brought with her a fortune variously estimated at between $4 million and $8 million. They live in a sumptuous apartment in London's fashionable Eaton Square which he calls "My Taj Mahal": it has a marble hall, a Louis XIV staircase, ten bedrooms and seven bathrooms. They give lavish dinner parties and are among the most charming and attentive hosts in the country; I have spent many pleasant hours there debating the merits of nationalization, high taxes and other causes dear to every socialist's heart.

Another well-off politician is Tony Benn, though he is hardly in the millionaire class. Born Anthony Neil Wedgwood Benn, he decided some years ago that Tony would be more appropriate to an aspiring champion of the militant left. In 1960 he inherited his father's title of Lord Stansgate; he fought a long and ultimately successful campaign for a law which allowed people like him to renounce their peerage, and few people now remember that he was once a viscount. He has even made strenuous efforts to shed his upper-class accent. He did not, however, renounce the family's possessions. His mother, Lady Stansgate, owns an estate that will be divided between Mr. Benn and his younger brother David on her death. His wife, Caroline, comes from a wealthy American family; when her mother died she left $350,000 in trust for the Benns' four children.

There are numerous other examples, in Britain and elsewhere, of affluent socialists who claim to speak for the poor but clearly have no wish to join them. George Orwell summed it all up in his splendid satirical novel *Animal Farm*. The farm, you will recall, is taken over by the pigs, who make sure that they have more food—and do less work—than the rest. Challenged, they explain that "all animals are equal, but some are more equal than others." Quite so.

CHAPTER 9

CRIME AND WEALTH

Crime is a logical extension of the sort of behavior that is often considered perfectly respectable in legitimate business.

ROBERT RICE

I mentioned, in an earlier chapter, some of the problems involved in trying to compile lists of the richest men and women. Let me now add another: it is difficult, if not impossible, to include those who have made their fortune through crime. The laws of libel are one reason. I could tell you about successful criminals of the past but it could cost my publishers a huge sum if I were to make a serious effort to give you the names of all the rich crooks who are alive today. Confining the list to those who have been caught and convicted would, inevitably, give you only a small part of the story. *Forbes* magazine estimated, not long ago, that organized crime is America's second biggest industry after oil, grossing more than $150 billion a year. Because of the freedom from taxes it is enormously profitable: it has probably made more millionaires than the Harvard Business School. In Europe, too, crime is a growth industry. But no one really knows the *full* extent of the link between crime and wealth, because criminals are experts at covering their tracks. A great deal of Mafia money, for example, is invested in respectable "fronts"—hotels and hotel chains, office buildings, pleasure resorts and even in banks. It is comparatively easy, in the 1980s, to "launder" the proceeds of activities such as robbery, smuggling, embezzlement and peddling in drugs. Only the most ignorant gangster still buries his loot in the backyard or hides it under floorboards.

The popular image of the big-time criminal has been greatly influenced by Hollywood directors and authors like Mario Puzo, who wrote *The Godfather*. The movie machine has cranked out countless portrayals of vicious Little Caesars who gunned down anyone who got in the way during their relentless climb to the top. Mention big-time crime to most people and they will automatically think of thugs like Al Capone, or of the actors who played men like him—Edward G. Robinson (in real life a charming fellow whose hobby was collecting fine paintings), Humphrey Bogart, Marlon Brando. There is no doubt that such characters still exist, but few would qualify for a place in a list of the wealthiest villains. Things have changed a lot since the 1920s and 1930s. Today's emperors of crime regard Al Capone as a foolish young man who made two quite unforgivable mistakes: he loved publicity and he went to jail for, of all things, income tax evasion. The Godfather is considered an even more ludicrously old-fashioned figure. The new-style Mafioso is usually a fat little man with a briefcase who knows that he can enjoy a luxurious and relatively peaceful life if he avoids the limelight, puts his ill-gotten gains into a legitimate business, collects dividends, and pays taxes on them like everyone else—after, of course, taking his accountant's advice on what is legally deductible.

I have a house in Sicily and I once went to interview fifteen alleged Mafia leaders who had been banished to the small island of Filicudi. There was Rosario Terasi, who looked like Anthony Quinn; Calogero Sinatra (yes!), a sly, intelligent-looking man who struck me as capable of anything; Giacomo Coppola, a thickset, aggressive type who proudly displayed an immensely hairy chest; Antonio Bucellati, a short, powerfully built Sicilian who shouted every word and underlined his arguments with swift karate chops that made the heavy table tremble; and a quiet, white-haired man who wouldn't give his name, but told me in excellent English that he admired the late Winston Churchill "because he knew what he wanted and got it." A movie producer would have hired them on the spot, but they looked like small-fry who had been sacrificed to demonstrate that the police were doing their job and to divert attention from their masters. "The real Mafiosi," Sinatra insisted, "are in Rome, sitting behind beautiful desks, with servants to wait on them." The others nodded agreement. Most of them had been in the construction business, a notoriously corrupt industry in which the biggest profits are made by faceless men with political influence who are experts at steering government funds into their own pockets. Who needs to kill when one can make millions by altering the books?

Trading in drugs—a far nastier game than Al Capone's defiance of prohibition—is the best-known criminal activity in the 1980s, but even bigger money is being made out of what an American sociologist has labeled white-collar crime. It takes in everything from embezzlement and fraud to bribery, stock market manipulation and industrial espionage. The white-collar criminal rarely makes use of violence: he depends chiefly on stealth, deceit or conspiracy. He is generally wealthy, and in many cases a pillar of the local business community. He can afford to employ expensive professional advisers, and if caught tends to get a much lighter sentence than the common criminal, even though far bigger sums may be involved. His lawyers invariably make the most of the complexities of the case, its nonviolent nature, and his client's "respectability." In many cases, he is let off with a fine.

In short, this is crime in the grand manner with relatively mild penalties and immense rewards. The growing complexities of the economic system, and an increasing reliance on technology in business and government, constantly create new opportunities. It is a growth industry and, in the long run, much more dangerous to society because it undermines public morale and spreads social disintegration. Yet most of us—and that includes the press—take much less notice of it than we do of more familiar types of mugging. We condemn the burglar and the mugger, but we often show a sneaking admiration for the rich individual who is clever enough to get away with fancy schemes. We raise hell only if his crafty manipulations score a direct hit on our pockets. The hauls from most bank robberies are petty cash compared with the fortunes made from financial swindles. Tino de Angeles made a great deal more by raising money on the strength of nonexisting stocks of salad oil. So, in an earlier era, did Ivar Krueger, who issued $500 million worth of fictitious bonds.

Crime and Wealth

The principal ally of the financial swindler is greed. It makes people—including many who claim to be experts—extraordinarily gullible. They will believe almost anything provided it is stated with enough conviction and holds out the promise of easy profits. Dr. Emil Savundra caught thousands of motorists in his net by offering insurance on their cars at premiums well below the going rate. He shoveled as much of the proceeds as possible into his own bank accounts, most of which were overseas. The game went on for quite a while: his company kept going by meeting accident claims out of new premiums. It was only when the flow dried up, and claims began to exceed the amount in the company's coffers, that the enterprise collapsed. Savundra might have got away with it if, like train robber Ronald Biggs, he had left for Brazil in good time. But he stayed around, was arrested, and was sent to prison. The trick is to know when to call it quits.

In the mid-1970s a French-Canadian named Jean Doucet proved another point: it is foolish to rob a bank when you can start one of your own and rob your depositors in comfort. Doucet exploited the attractions of tax havens; he went to the Cayman Islands in the Caribbean, and launched two companies—Interbank and Sterling Bank. He pulled in a lot of cash, which he invested in his own projects. When depositors began to develop doubts about those projects and asked for their money back, Doucet left for Costa Rica in a Lear jet loaded with gold bullion. The banks closed their doors the next day. He later returned voluntarily to face prosecution and served eight months in the island's tiny jail—a far lighter sentence than he would have got if he had held up the banks at gunpoint.

Governments are constantly passing new laws designed to prevent financial juggling (Savundra would find it hard to repeat his game today), and enforcement agencies keep a close watch on the business scene. But there is ample scope for the smart crook.

One of the most fascinating developments of the past decade is the growth of computer crime. The FBI reckons that in America, where this lucrative racket began, the annual haul now adds up to $300 million, with the *average* take per incident in excess of $500,000.

Once a computer fraud has been discovered it generally doesn't take long to find the culprit; most of the money is stolen by employees with inside knowledge. But experts believe that only a small proportion of these crimes are detected, chiefly because there is very little intervention once the program has been written—it is just left to the computer to do its own thing, whether or not it has been tampered with. People have become so confident of the accuracy of the beast that its output is never properly checked, yet it is comparatively easy to rig a computer if you know what to do. Anyone in possession of the proper codes can get away with breathtaking manipulations. He can put millions into his own pocket, order merchandise without payment, steal valuable trade secrets, or simply add the name of a fictitious employee to the payroll. To date, no adequate protection against such frauds has been devised and most that have come to light have done so through accident or a tip-off.

A few years ago, a California computer scientist named Stanley Mark Rifkin robbed a bank of more than $10 million. He had worked at its headquarters as a freelance consultant and was a familiar face to its employees, so no one said anything when he told them, one day, that he had work to do on computers in the wire-transfer room where the bank moved funds by cable. Once inside the room he learned the day's "key"—the secret code which had to be included in any transfer. The same afternoon he telephoned the transfer room, identified himself as an officer of the bank's international division, and quoted three codes. With that information he gave orders for the transfer of $10.2 million from one of its branch accounts to his own account in New York—from which he promptly moved the money to Switzerland.

He should have been content with that, but his next move was to fly to Geneva and use $8 million of the haul to buy diamonds from Russalmaz, the Soviet trade organization dealing in diamond exports. Five days after his original coup he was back in Los Angeles, having smuggled a large quantity of diamonds through customs. He set up a syndicate to sell them, but at this point the whole enterprise fell apart: someone tipped off the FBI, Rifkin was arrested, and the story of his ambitious venture came out during interrogation. He was eventually sentenced to eight years in jail for "transporting stolen property across state lines." For once the victim came off best. The bank not only got back the balance of the money left in Switzerland (the Swiss, not surprisingly, don't approve of people who rob banks), but also became the legal owner of the diamonds which, by then, were worth over a million dollars more in the United States, even after paying customs duty, than they had been when Rifkin bought them in Geneva.

In another case not long ago, an American mutual fund discovered during its monthly audit that more than $1½ million was missing. Investigations revealed that it had been transferred twenty-eight days earlier to the account of a Brazilian national at the Virginia National Bank. The Brazilian had previously invested $2,500 in the fund with directions that the interest should be paid into his account. A young female employee of the fund, also Brazilian and a close friend of his, had apparently used her access to computer codes to transfer the $1½ million in a single transaction. He withdrew $50,000 a few days later and switched the rest to Zurich; both he and the young woman had vanished.

Financial institutions are generally reluctant to talk about their experiences, partly because it could undermine public confidence, but also because more of their employees might be tempted to make a quick fortune if they knew how easy it is to beat the computer. In Britain, the banks were dismayed when it emerged that even telex data could be misused. A team of five men, led by a company director, were jailed for changing telex messages from banks in Nigeria so that large amounts of money were switched into accounts which they operated in London. They made a million dollars before they were caught; none of the money was recovered. Shortly before, the banks had been alerted to a flaw in a new code system they were about to adopt. The alert was sounded by a computer expert, Mr. Leslie Goldberg, in a bizarre manner. He entered a magazine competition on "How to Think like a Thief" and won $200 with an entry that showed how one could use a $400 kit (sold openly in New York) to tap telex lines which carry messages transferring funds between banks, and insert a fictitious transaction. The banks hastily plugged the loophole.

American experts say that "electronic burglars" are the criminals of the future, and that many are learning their trade at public expense. Computer programming and data processing is the most popular training program in U.S. prisons; it used to be lockmaking.

Another lucrative racket, which is reckoned to have yielded several hundred million dollars in the last few years, is a modern form of piracy that involves the scuttling of ships by their owners. The technique is simple: you buy a ship, get her insured for more than her market value, sail her to somewhere deep, sink her, and write to those nice people at Lloyd's. The director of the International Maritime Bureau said in 1981 that of forty-eight ships to go down in Far Eastern waters, twenty-eight of the sinkings had proved to be fraudulent.

Some of these capers include cargo theft. If you sink your ship, it is wasteful to sink the cargo too. So you unload it, for cash, in some port where they know how to keep their mouths shut, and ask Lloyd's to compensate you for the loss of the cargo as well as the carrier.

In the biggest maritime scam to date, a gang promised a South African oil-purchasing agency a cargo of oil. The agency paid down $12 million, which the gang used to buy a supertanker. They named it *Salem*, and loaded it with oil in the Gulf. They sent it to Durban, temporarily changed its name to *Lema*, secretly unloaded the 196,000 tons of oil, arranged to have $43 million paid into their Swiss bank accounts on the same day, and proceeded to the coast of Senegal, where the tanker, now once again the *Salem*, mysteriously foundered. The gang then tried to collect $34 million insurance on the cargo and the tanker. Unfortunately for them, a British ship had arrived on the scene in time for her officers to take movie-camera films of the *Salem*'s crew casually abandoning their charge, suitcases in hands. A subsequent investigation brought out the whole story.

Other gambits include bogus bills of lading. A bill of lading is the standard document in international trade which shows that goods have been put aboard a ship, ready for export. You will have a letter of credit from the importer's bank; show that bank the bill of lading and you can draw money against the letter of credit. With a little ingenuity, or a home printing outfit, you need not trouble to produce any cargo, or even a ship.

Then there is the charter party fraud. For this you need an exporter, an importer and some sea between them. You agree to transport the goods on a ship you will charter for the purpose. Hirers of ships, like hirers of anything else, put down a deposit and then pay the rent at certain intervals. You, however, are ahead of the game, because the exporter has paid you in full. So, having paid the shipowner his deposit and perhaps one installment of rent, you see no need to stay around.

Insurance firms are hitting back by screening problem companies, monitoring questionable voyages, and sending undercover agents on suspect ships to flush out frauds. But with such huge sums of money involved the perpetrators can afford to take elaborate steps to cover their tracks, and it is often difficult to collect enough hard evidence to bring them to court.

The same is true of yet another type of white-collar crime, known as the advance fee fraud. It works like this: a businessman is offered a contract from an Arab "sheik," with 10 percent commission from the "agent." The businessman is then introduced to an "Arab," or even flown to an Arab country to meet the "sheik." He signs the contract, which may be for as much as $20 million. The agent collects his 10 percent, or $2 million, commission and vanishes, along with the sheik.

The FBI, the City of London Fraud Squad, and the police forces of other countries are doing their best to keep up with all the new ploys, but it has proved to be an uphill job. The bulk of police work is still devoted to the more conventional type of crime. The white-collar criminal has a great deal of expertise on his side, and mass air travel has made it relatively easy for international fraudsmen to slip in and out of countries like Britain, America, France and Germany. It takes a lot of time, skill and patience to bring a complex case to a successful conclusion. Tracking down and recovering the proceeds of a crime is even harder because of the proliferation of tax havens.

The head of Britain's Fraud Squad would like to see much closer cooperation between different countries. It would certainly help, but what is also needed is a greater recognition, on the part of both governments and the public, of the growing menace of white-collar crime.

THE MONEY LAUNDRY

I said at the beginning of this chapter that it was comparatively easy to launder the proceeds of illegal activities like robbery, smuggling, embezzlement and peddling in drugs. Let me now tell you how it is done. I am not trying to provide a manual for amateur crooks who want to join the ranks of the rich; my purpose is to draw attention to a game that seems to me every bit as obnoxious as the crimes themselves.

"Laundering" is a term used by the financial community as a label for various maneuvers designed to obscure the real origin of money. When practiced on an international scale it involves three basic operations: smuggling "dirty" money to a secret Swiss or Caribbean bank account; altering its nature; and repatriating the "newly clean" money and using it for investment, pleasure, or in some cases bribery.

A tax haven is the ideal money laundry. A few years ago the BBC's "Money Program" asked me to go to the Cayman Islands— scene of Mr. Doucet's exploits—and make a film about its activities. I interviewed dozens of people, including the colony's Financial Secretary, who told me that, yes, their secrecy laws could be abused by criminals but it was the price one had to pay for the substantial benefits which tax haven status brought to the islands. "You have to have evil with the good," he said. It is a curious attitude for a government official, but he was quite serious about it. The islands had been poor before they discovered this splendid wheeze; now they had a major source of income besides tourism, and their inhabitants could afford to buy some of the things which the rest of us have long taken for granted. A local bank manager assured me that I would have no need to worry about income tax inspectors or the British police, even though the Caymans were a British colony. "We would show them the door."

On a more recent visit to another tax haven, the Bahamas, I asked a banker in Nassau if he would take a suitcase full of cash. (Many big-time criminals employ couriers because they are still the best insurance against a paper trail of cables, transfer slips and canceled checks that might connect them to a foreign bank account.

The suitcase is a favorite method of transporting dirty money, though many couriers, mindful of how often airlines manage to lose baggage, prefer to carry large-denomination banknotes in hand luggage or strapped around the waist.) The banker gave me an appraising look. Where was the suitcase? I said that I didn't actually have one, but that I was interested in finding out what would happen to those who did.

"Well," he said, "we don't usually open accounts for people we don't know. But there are banks down the road who would be happy to accommodate you."

I said that I rather liked the idea of doing business with *his* bank. What would it take?

"We would need a reference from a bank you've done business with in the past."

"And *then* you would accept my suitcase?"

"Yes, certainly."

"But wouldn't you want to know where I'd got the money, and why I had chosen to transport it in this unorthodox and cumbersome fashion?"

"We would ask you, but if you decided not to tell us we wouldn't insist that you did."

I don't know how often this kind of conversation takes place in the dozen or more tax havens around the world, but I am sure that it is quite common. The banks know perfectly well that people who lug around suitcases stuffed with cash are up to no good. They may be dodging taxes or exchange controls, or they may be trying to hide the proceeds of crime. But the banks also know that tax havens wouldn't stay in business for long if they asked too many awkward questions. *Pecunia non olet*, as the Romans used to say. Money has no smell.

Tax dodgers have it easy. So do people who try to hide the money from creditors, or from a wife or husband prior to divorce proceedings. Criminals have to be a bit more careful, at least in Switzerland. The Swiss have become increasingly touchy about suggestions that they make life easy for the underworld and seem quite ready, nowadays, to give the game away if it can be proved that the depositor has taken part in a robbery or criminal fraud. But one can always hire expert laundrymen, and in places like the Cayman

Islands and the Bahamas the banks will keep quiet unless they are ordered to tell all by a *local* court—which in practice rarely happens.

Only a small percentage of the money is invested on the spot. Like Switzerland, Caribbean tax havens act as a way station—cash deposited in a Nassau or Cayman bank account can be transferred immediately to a Swiss bank or used to buy property and shares in the United States and other countries. A regular ploy is to set up a paper corporation that handles all such transactions. It insulates the owner still further from his dirty money: the actual deals are made by local people and his own identity is shielded by the secrecy laws, which apply just as firmly to this kind of company as to individual bank accounts. (The Caribbean tax havens have gained a lot of business by taking a tougher line than the Swiss: bank employees who talk about a client's affairs, or even admit the existence of a secret account, risk going to jail for two years. Some *have* been known to accept bribes from American and British agents— former employers are reckoned to be particularly susceptible to bribery—but the threat of imprisonment is, on the whole, an effective deterrent.) Some of the companies have rather bizarre names but the majority sound dignified enough and there is no reason why a Wall Street broker, or a California real estate salesman, should not do business with them. The laundry has done its work; the money is clean.

Wealthy criminals may own dozens of companies in a variety of tax havens: it reduces the risks. If a shady operator in one of the havens should embezzle their money it would be difficult for them to bring a court action, so it makes sense to diversify. It also gives them greater flexibility: different companies can be used at different times.

Bringing "clean money" back home may, of course, lead to other problems. A drug peddler who normally masquerades as, say, a news dealer may find it difficult to explain his new-found wealth to the authorities. If he leads an extravagant life-style on what appears to be a modest income he can certainly expect to be asked some awkward questions. He can make a trip to Las Vegas, and tell the authorities that he has won a fortune at the gambling tables, but that is not a ploy which can be used too often. The shrewd criminal knows that it is dangerous to draw attention to oneself by a sudden transformation from a relatively humble way of life to the ostentatious display of riches; it is a lot safer to make a gradual transition. He also knows that it is best to let the paper companies own the properties or business enterprises which he may acquire.

Some of America's millionaire criminals use "loan back" schemes to disguise large amounts of once dirty money. They enter into an agreement to buy a legitimate business for, say, $2 million and make a down payment of $200,000 in clean money, which has been declared to the government and taxed. They then take out a $500,000 mortgage from a local bank and "borrow" the remaining $1.3 million from one or more tax haven banks. This $1.3 million is, in fact, money from their own accounts disguised as a legitimate loan. They pay interest in the normal way, and in due course repay the loan, but since both flow back into their accounts they lose nothing by the transaction. The money thus repaid can be "borrowed" again for the next acquisition.

The U.S. government knows all about these schemes—and many more. Like other governments, it makes strenuous efforts to catch the people who use them. But unless and until all the tax havens decide that they ought to give their full cooperation, the clever criminal holds a lot of aces.

CHAPTER 10

PLEASURES AND EGO TRIPS

It's what God would have built if he had the money.

GEORGE KAUFMAN ON THE ROCKEFELLER ESTATE

One of the greatest pleasures of the rich has always been the possession of impressive homes. There is something quite basic about the urge to live in a grandiose residence; it is a personal advertisement, a status symbol which tells the world that the owner is an important member of his tribe. The pharaohs had the greatest palaces and tombs; the Roman nobles had the biggest mansions and seaside villas; medieval barons had the biggest castles; Indian chiefs had the biggest tents. Comfort often had little to do with it — many of these places were, and are, distinctly uncomfortable. The principal aim was to show that the occupant was someone special.

For centuries, the grandest homes in Europe belonged to the aristocracy: the monarch set the pace and the rest followed. Few dared to build a home that was bigger than the monarch's; he was liable to find some excuse to requisition it, as Henry VIII did when he saw Cardinal Wolsey's Hampton Court. But it was unthinkable that a duke or marquis should live in a modest house or, God forbid, an elegant apartment. If he lacked the means to build an

140

edifice commensurate with his status, the government sometimes lent a helping hand. John Churchill, First Duke of Marlborough, was given the magnificent Blenheim Palace after his victory in 1704 over the French. Glory wasn't enough; a grateful nation felt compelled to build him an imperial edifice.

When commoners started to make fortunes during the Industrial Revolution one of their first acts was to buy or create mansions which would proclaim that they, too, stood above the herd. The industrialist or financier was not content with piling up the cash; he wanted the whole world to see that he had arrived. In Britain, many tried to outdo the aristocracy. In America, which did not have a traditional ruling class, the new millionaires copied the homes of the European nobility. Many of these nouveaux riches were immigrants of poor stock who, in their youth, had looked longingly at the magnificent mansions of the rich and titled. They could not hope to acquire a title, but they could certainly acquire some of the other trappings of the privileged classes, so they not only built opulent homes but also ransacked the art treasures of the countries they had left behind. Medieval castles were stripped of their carvings and tapestries, whole staircases and ceilings were ripped from their place of repose through the centuries, and shiploads of crystal chandeliers, old Tudor chests and bedsteads, Louis XIV furniture, old armor, statuettes, porcelain and paintings by European masters made their way across the Atlantic.

New York's Fifth Avenue became the premier showplace in the latter part of the nineteenth century. So many mansions and châteaux of French, Gothic and Italian style lined both sides of the two-mile stretch of boulevard that the newspapers dubbed it "Millionaires' Row." One of the grandest belonged to the Vanderbilts, whose fortune had been founded by "Commodore" Vanderbilt, a ruthless, self-made man who made millions in the shipping business despite his lack of any formal education. Built in neo-Grecian style, the Vanderbilt house was the setting for lavish society balls and dinner parties. Guests entered through two massive doors which were superb copies of the famous Ghiberti Gates of Paradise at the Baptistry of Florence Cathedral. Inside there was a grand staircase of Caen stone, a huge ballroom, a library, dining halls, salons, a gymnasium, a Japanese parlor worthy of an emperor's palace, and a picture gallery that occupied the entire rear of the house and was filled with hundreds of paintings and sculptures. (When the owner was asked which of his paintings he liked best, he replied, with stunning simplicity: "I like them all.") The drawing salon had a ceiling painted by Gallaud of Paris. The massive frames of its doors were encrusted with gold, while the woodwork was a mass of sculpture, gilded and glazed with warm tints. The walls were hung with pale red velvet, embroidered with foliage, flowers and butterflies encircled with cut crystal and precious stones. Vases, upheld by female figures in solid silver, stood on pedestals of onyx with bronze trimmings.

Just about everything, including the beds, had been brought in from overseas. The result was a glorious hash of styles—French tapestries, Florentine doors, African marbles, English china, Dutch old masters, Japanese knick-knacks. W. H. Vanderbilt was delighted when *Harper's Weekly* called his palace "The Taj Mahal of New York"; other commentators were less flattering.

A contemporary account of one of the Vanderbilt balls, in 1883, will give you the flavor of life inside this pleasure dome. More than twelve hundred guests arrived at 10:30 p.m. or later. Footmen in powdered wigs and knee breeches relieved gentlemen of their coats and directed ladies upstairs to a state bedroom where maids in French peasant dress attended to their needs. The host was dressed as a French *duc*; the hostess as a Venetian princess. Another Vanderbilt appeared as Louis XVI, in fawn-colored brocade trimmed with *point d'Espagne* lace and a waistcoat of olive hue with pointings of silver; with this he wore a diamond-hilted sword. One of the guests was Queen Elizabeth I, another Mary Stuart. The company sat down to an eight-course meal with eight different vintage wines, and danced until 6 a.m. King Louis XVI himself, one of the newspapers said the next day, would have felt at home amid such splendor.

The splendor did not last. The Vanderbilt palace was closed forever in 1945 and most of the other mansions have disappeared. New York has always shown a restless urge to banish the past, and today Fifth Avenue is lined with elegant stores, office blocks and apartment buildings. But there are plenty of reminders of the period throughout America.

The Vanderbilts created many other residences, including an ornate French Renaissance château near Asheville, North Carolina. It had 250 rooms and was set in 146,000 acres, with a three-mile drive from the gate to the main house. George Washington Vanderbilt II, grandson of the Commodore, built it in 1895 at an estimated cost of $7 million. To replace such a showplace today might cost as much as $60 million, one reason why few people would dream of attempting it—any more than they would of dream of building another Blenheim Palace. The rich still like to have luxurious homes, but they tend to build on a much smaller scale than their aristocratic and plutocratic forebears. Apart from the cost, they are uneasily aware of present-day problems like the possibility of unwelcome attention from burglars, kidnappers and the tax collector.

Britain's peers, struggling to maintain their inherited homes, generally use only a few of the rooms available to them. They may give the occasional party, but they are happier if they can rent the ballroom to IBM for a generous fee. Many of the great town houses of London, Paris and New York have been turned into clubs, museums and apartments. Castles occasionally change hands (one can always find a parvenu who wants to show off), but most of them are cold and empty relics. In France, splendid but neglected châteaux can be bought for relatively modest sums because their owners are reluctant to do battle with a socialist government which seems determined to reduce everyone, and everything, to the lowest common denominator. In Italy, no one in his right mind would want to acquire the *palazzi* of earlier generations because the joys of ownership would be outweighed by the penalties imposed by a society ruled by envy. In America, privacy is widely considered more important than the ostentatious display of wealth. Millionaires would rather own a sumptuous apartment on Fifth Avenue or Park Avenue, plus a smart place somewhere less conspicuous, than a Vanderbilt mansion. They want to impress each other, but they are no longer so eager to impress the public. It doesn't pay.

One interesting result of this concern with privacy has been the growth of the compound, or multiple estate, containing many large residences for different members of an extended family. The Kennedy compound at Hyannisport, Massachusetts, is the most pub-

143

licized example. The Rockefeller estate at Pocantico Hills, New York (the one "God would have built if he had the money"), is another. Completely surrounded by a high stone wall, it has scores of buildings, including a playhouse that holds bowling alleys, tennis court, swimming pool and squash court.

Islands also hold great attractions for the rich. They are comparatively easy to protect, and they allow their occupants to feel like sovereigns of their own little world. A number of prominent American families have island colonies and they rarely change hands; others own hideaways in the Pacific and the Caribbean. In Europe, Greek shipping millionaires have long shown great fondness for island retreats. When Aristotle Onassis bought Skorpios, he invested $3 million to turn it into a flower-decked gem with six miles of roads and riding paths through the olive groves, a harbor for his yacht, a villa, a dozen luxurious guest chalets, stables and a telephone exchange. It now belongs to his daughter Christina. His great rival, Stavros Niarchos, bought the island of Spetsopoula, fifty-three miles from Athens, and transformed it from a barren tract into a personal Arcadia. His lovely villa is surrounded by guest bungalows and there is a hangar to house two helicopters on the landing field where he and his visitors arrive and depart. Niarchos even has his own church.

Modern methods of transportation have played an important role in changing the habits of the rich and famous. Air travel has made it a relatively simple matter to commute between two or three different homes. The rich have always had their summer residences, but today they tend to be in far more exotic places. It is quite common for American multimillionaires to have a penthouse in New York, a weekend home in the country, and another house in Florida, Mexico, Hawaii or the Caribbean. Some also maintain lavish, fully-staffed residences in London or Paris. The British have their own apartments in New York (it saves having to pack, you see), and like to have summer homes in the South of France— ideally in Monte Carlo, the area behind Cannes, or Cap Ferrat. The Germans like Spain, especially the Costa del Sol. The Italians love Switzerland, not because of its climate but because it offers political stability and low taxation. The Arabs used to like London, but nowadays go just about anywhere. So many have bought property in America that some states, alarmed by this foreign "invasion," have passed legislation which makes it more difficult for them to do so.

A traditional way of keeping out unwanted neighbors is to form a club, and nowadays there are numerous private clubs where the rich can live without having to come into contact with the lower orders—except, of course, servants. The British are generally thought to be the greatest clubmen, but Americans outdo them. They have more country clubs than anyone else, and the best select their members with considerable care. Wealth alone does not guarantee admittance, but without it one cannot even get a hearing. Once in, one shares all the privileges and obligations associated with such institutions, but there is usually a strict social order. A new member is expected to take a back seat, even if he has more millions than any of the others. (As in Britain, elitist clubs in the U.S. take a dim view of people who talk about how much money they have. It is taken for granted that everyone is rich; the actual amounts do not matter.)

Every nation has its favorite playgrounds, but some have achieved international status. Fashions change, but here is a brief list of some of the places where the world's money elite likes to congregate.

Gstaad and St Moritz, Switzerland
The Côte d'Azur, France
Aspen and Vail, Colorado
Beverly Hills and Los Angeles, California
Lyford Cay, Bahamas
Marbella, Spain
Acapulco, Mexico
Geneva, Switzerland
Palm Beach and nearby resorts, Florida (mainly American, but increasingly popular with foreigners)
Mayfair, London
Manhattan, New York
Montego Bay, Jamaica (neglected for some years, because of the political situation, but making a comeback)
Bermuda, Barbados, Antigua

Here are some of the things to do when you get there:

Order a bottle of Crystal champagne at the Palace Hotel in Gstaad and pretend not to notice any of the celebrities.

Arrange to be greeted by the owner of the Moulin des Mougins or L'Oasis on the Côte d'Azur.

Secure invitations to the more stylish parties in Aspen.

Be seen, at least once, at the Bistro in Beverly Hills.

Arrange to play golf with Arthur Hailey and his friends at Lyford Cay.

Have dinner with Prince Alfonso in Marbella and tell him—loudly, so that everyone can hear—that you really prefer the Aga Khan's place in Sardinia.

Tell the Acapulco set that you are tired of all the noisy conventioneers and have decided to move on to Las Hadas in Manzanillo.

Open an account with one of Geneva's private banks and ask its chairman to give advice to some of your friends.

Join the Polo set in Florida.

Take afternoon tea, and cucumber sandwiches, at the Ritz in London and try to join Annabel's.

Get the best table at the Four Seasons restaurant in Manhattan and at the 21 Club.

Stay at the Half-Moon Hotel in Montego Bay, Jamaica, or rent one of the private houses from your neighborhood millionaire.

Take a suite at the Sandy Lane Hotel in Barbados, and tell everyone that you despise Bermuda and Antigua because they are so full of tourists.

YOU SIMPLY MUST SEE MY PICASSO

Grand homes require grand décor, but the approach to interiors has also changed since the days of Vanderbilt ostentation: the rich have become more discriminating. Some, it is true, still fill their houses with suits of armor, mighty fireplaces, elaborate chandeliers, and life-size statues of Roman emperors, but many more prefer a modern setting to the cluttered, swaggering pomp of the past. There is greater concern with quality than with quantity, and much more emphasis on practical amenities. Americans who visit Versailles for the first time, invariably express amazement that the king who could build such a magnificent edifice managed to do without a single bathroom. For today's wealthy families three or four stunning bathrooms are an absolute must. If you want to win the approval of the younger set you should also have a sauna, a jacuzzi, a large swimming pool (outdoors in warm countries, indoors elsewhere), a squash court and several tennis courts. You will also be much admired if you have a private zoo.

Self-made millionaires do not, as a rule, devote much time to furnishing their homes. They claim to be too busy, but the truth in many cases is that they don't know how to go about it. They are much more familiar with balance sheets than with wallpaper, sofas and porcelain. They want a home that reflects their status and which provides them with reasonable comfort, but they are quite content to leave the details to their wives. It is the wives who spend long hours in stores and auction rooms, and who make the key decisions. The husband's job is to sign the checks.

Occasionally, though, they may be called upon to express an opinion. It tends to be confined to comments like "Yes, that's nice," or "I don't care for it, but if it makes you happy go ahead." Big, gilded mirrors generally meet with instant approval. Oriental carpets are something else; a man who is hooked on new products finds it hard to understand why some women should want to spend thousands on that "threadbare thing." He gets even more confused when he is asked for his views on paintings. He has never bothered to study art, but has always claimed that he knows what he likes. It usually means large paintings in rich color that "tell a story"— battle scenes, pastoral glimpses, and animals of all sorts. When confronted with a work by an artist like Picasso he will either reject it out of hand (if he dares), or confess that "I don't understand what the fellow is getting at." Wives can generally win the argument by pointing out that Picasso paintings are an excellent investment and that neighbors and colleagues will be *green* with envy. (Picasso himself was well aware of this kind of attitude. He despised it, but was also shrewd enough to make the most of it. A group of wealthy

The Rich: A Study of the Species

Americans once spotted him at his favorite restaurant on the Côte d'Azur and asked him to "draw something." Picasso smiled, and with a few swift strokes covered the sheet of paper which served as a tablecloth. The Americans couldn't decide what, if anything, the drawing was supposed to mean but they gladly paid him enough to finance his meals for the rest of the year. No wonder he became the richest artist in history.)

Newspapers and business magazines, taking their cues from the wives, nowadays give a great deal of coverage to the investment aspect of works of art. Auctions are widely reported and there are tales galore about the stupendous increases in prices of everything from Victorian landscapes to old musical instruments. Banks, pension funds and other financial institutions have also managed to get into the act. They have been buying art by the carload, not because they think it will give their executives and shareholders any particular pleasure, but because they are hoping for capital appreciation. I don't know what the Medicis would have made of this crass approach to culture, but I can see why a businessman's eyes should light up when he is told that a painting or sculpture will be worth twice as much a year after purchase.

Many, alas, take the same view of books. I was astonished, during my years as the editor of *Punch*, when a bookseller told me that some of his wealthy clients bought dozens of old *Punch* volumes solely because they looked good. They were quite frank about it. No, they had never read *Punch*, but the binding looked nice— although it would have been better if it had been green because then it wouldn't have clashed with the wallpaper. They had bought this big house, you see, and it had a library, and you couldn't have a library without books, could you? It clearly did not occur to them that, if they felt that way about books, it would have been better to turn the library into a gameroom or whatever.

The blame must sometimes be put on professional decorators rather than on the rich themselves. Many haughtily ignore the personal preferences of their clients, and design the rooms *they* would like to live in. The poor rich often don't have the courage to argue with their decorator's verdicts. They feel that if they pay a top man or woman a small fortune to do up their home, they are obliged to accept that person's decisions. So the designer blithely goes ahead and orders whatever takes his or her fancy. The outcome may be a home which the clients hate, but which will at least give them the satisfaction of being featured in society magazines like *Town and Country* and *Harper's and Queen*. It is the ultimate in pointless snobbery.

But it would be unfair to give the impression that all rich men are philistines. Some are not only extremely knowledgeable about art, but are also skillful collectors whose judgment is widely respected. They, and the corporations they control, have done much to keep the arts alive. They take pride in their possessions, but they are also surprisingly willing to share them. Both Britain and America would be culturally much poorer if it were not for the help these men give during their lifetime, and the treasures they leave to museums and galleries after their death. Some may be motivated by a desire for reflected glory (the rich are rarely great artists themselves), but many have been, and still are, inspired by a very real sense of personal fulfillment. New York's Museum of Modern Art was started by a Rockefeller, and museums like the Guggenheim would not exist if it were not for the enthusiasm and generosity of the families whose names they bear. Some second- and third-generation heirs have devoted their whole lives to patronage of the arts. Paul Mellon, whose father founded the National Gallery in Washington (it houses his art collection), is a prominent example. He has not only given many millions more to the gallery, but has also been responsible for creating the Yale Center for British Art, which has the largest collection of British paintings, drawings, watercolors, prints and rare books anywhere outside Britain. He once told an interviewer that he had taken as his life's work the goal of "spending my fortune sensibly."

Perhaps it is unreasonable to expect a man who has struggled to make his millions to adopt the same relaxed attitude as one who has come by them without any sort of effort. It would clearly be foolish if he were to pretend that he is interested in art when all that really matters to him is the state of his bank balance. But one cannot help wishing that, like Paul Mellon, other people would spend more time thinking about ways of spending their fortunes sensibly and less about doubling them.

I am no authority on art myself, and I am certainly not an expert interior decorator. I, too, tend to leave such matters largely in the hands of my wife, whose taste is, on the whole, better than mine. But I have seen enough of the homes of the rich—and talked to enough critics—to be able to offer a brief list of items that are "in" and those that are definitely "out."

OUT

A television set in the main room
Plaster cherubs
Suits of armor
Artificial flowers under glass
Tiger skin rugs
Onyx pedestals
Portraits of the owner painted by his wife—and vice versa
Three-piece suites
Paintings of angels and Napoleonic battles
Trophy room
Royal wedding souvenirs

IN

French and English antique furniture
Japanese screens—in fact, almost anything Japanese
Antique mosaics
Rare Persian carpets, however old
Sculptures by Renoir and Henry Moore (if you can get them through the front door)
Paintings by Picasso, Turner, Chagall, Miró and most of the Impressionists
A pool pavilion
Baccarat crystal

One of the most daring things I have ever seen was on a visit to the stylish château of a wealthy French count. He had, believe it or not, the original of a well-known Toulouse-Lautrec painting in the *smallest* room. I was so surprised that I nearly wet the floor. It takes a great deal of aristocratic nerve to indulge in that kind of showmanship; I doubt if, say, a property developer could get away with it.

PARTY TIME

Having acquired and stocked a luxurious home, a rich man (or, rather, his wife) will naturally want to do some entertaining. How else are people going to get a chance to admire his possessions?

Like everything else, parties are not what they were. Few people could nowadays invite twelve hundred people to a ball at home, even if they wanted to. The rich haven't lost their taste for affairs of this kind but most of them are quite content to use some other premises, usually the nearest five-star hotel. Charity balls have become increasingly fashionable—perhaps people don't want the world to think that they are dancing the night away purely for their own amusement. But by far the most popular forms of entertainment are the cocktail party, the dinner party, the dance, and the weekend house party.

Some of the super-rich rarely go to any of them. They prefer their own company to that of others, though few cut themselves off as completely as Howard Hughes did in his later years. They have never bothered to make friends, and they often can't stand their relatives. Their idea of a whoop-up is a Scotch or two before dinner and, perhaps, a recording of Beethoven's Ninth Symphony. In the early days neighbors invited them to parties but were rebuffed. The invitations soon dried up.

But most of the rich and super-rich *love* parties of one kind or another, not only because they provide an opportunity to flaunt their wealth but also because it allows them to mix with their own kind and, in the case of a nouveau riche, to gain social advancement. In Britain, social divisions are not nearly as strong as they used to be, but they certainly have not vanished altogether. A rich man with "old money" might invite his doctor to a party, but he wouldn't dream of asking his plumber. Someone with "new money" might do so, if only because the plumber went to school with him, but

151

other guests will generally take a dim view of such thoughtless behavior and stay away on the next occasion. An equally unforgivable faux pas is to ask vulgar businessmen who can't hold their liquor and insist on telling dirty jokes. That sort of thing might go down well at the local bar, but it simply won't do in polite society. Employees, too, are generally excluded unless they happen to belong to the upper echelons of management, and even then only on condition that they don't talk about their work.

To make any sort of impact, one should invite at least one guest with a title—preferably one with a hereditary peerage, not one of the socialist life peers. A Russian prince will do, but an English earl is better. Ambassadors also rate a fairly high place on the social scale. In Britain the greatest ambition of every host and hostess is to capture a member of the royal family. The ultimate dream is summed up by this recent extract from that hilariously snooty chronicle of society life, Jennifer's Diary in *Harper's and Queen* magazine.

> Back home to change and on to Syon House, Brentford, the beautiful home of the Duke and Duchess of Northumberland, who had so kindly lent it to Mr. and Mrs. Douglas Fairbanks, Jr., who were giving a small party of around a hundred and fifty friends, to meet the new American Ambassador and Mrs. John Louis, and Miss Kimberley and Miss Tracy Louis.
>
> The Duke and Duchess of Northumberland, who are such wonderfully warm and kind hosts themselves, were at the party. Earlier in the day the Duchess had helped Mary Lee Fairbanks arrange the beautiful flowers for the party, which were all home-grown from the Syon garden center. It was a graciously informal, and beautifully arranged 6:30–10 p.m. reception, with a light two-course cold buffet, the second course being very English summer pudding. The Queen honored the Duke and Duchess of Northumberland, Mr. and Mrs. Fairbanks, and the American Ambassador and Mrs. Louis, by coming to the party quite informally.

Americans, too, would gave a great deal for *that* kind of publicity. (Mrs. Stuyvesant Fish, that mischievous hostess of an earlier generation, once dared to make fun of the American love of European titles. She invited the *crème de la crème* of Newport society to a dinner in honor of Prince de Drago, who had just arrived in the country from far-off Corsica. The "Prince" turned out to be a bewildered monkey attired in full evening dress. The other guests were *not* amused.) Presidents, of course, enjoy equal status providing they are still in office. Former occupants of the White House have a certain curiosity value—Richard Nixon gets a lot of invitations—but they are not nearly as desirable as a sitting tenant, even though his visit may be brief and will, inevitably, involve tiresome security measures. (Many a perfect lawn has been wrecked by clumsy members of the White House security detail.) Senators are on a par with ambassadors, but politicians on the make tend to be shunned on both sides of the Atlantic, especially if they hold left-wing opinions.

In Britain, the prime minister is considered a catch but an M.P. is not—there are, after all, so many of them. The head of a civil service department can count on getting numerous invitations, not merely because of his position but also because he will generally have impeccable manners. A mere civil servant, though, is treated as just that—a servant. Bishops, like generals, are nowadays well down on the list. So are actors and actresses, though the nouveaux riches tend to be rather fond of them. Television personalities are held in equally low regard. The presenter of a prestigious program like "Panorama" may occasionally be invited to an upper-crust party, but a comedian is expected to stick to his own kind. Musicians don't rate unless they are in the Menuhin class. Journalists are asked for one purpose and one only: to report the proceedings in flattering terms. Authors are reckoned to be bores. If they are invited at all they are generally treated with the same sort of condescending amusement that a former Prince of Wales dished out to the author of *The Decline and Fall of the Roman Empire*. ("Always scribble, scribble, scribble, eh Mr. Gibbon?")

The Queen herself tries to be a little more democratic. She, too, prefers to be with her own kind (i.e., members of old aristocratic families), but her annual garden parties at Buckingham Palace are attended by people from all walks of life—actors, T.V. personalities, textile manufacturers, engineers, shopkeepers, politicians and even authors. She manages to deal with as many as seven thousand people each afternoon, which detracts somewhat from the prestige of the occasion, but invitations are nevertheless eagerly sought and proudly displayed on mantelpieces all over the country. The prime minister gives dinners and cocktail parties for prominent visitors (generally politicians) from other countries, but to be invited to those one generally has to have some commercial or political link with the countries concerned. (A former prime minister, Harold Wilson, tried to break the mold. He made a point of asking trade union leaders and showbiz stars to parties at 10 Downing Street. The right-wing press was outraged; so were the nation's snobs. Margaret Thatcher has been more circumspect.)

There are, of course, all sorts of other parties outside the platinum ring of society—parties given by wealthy people who couldn't care less about the "standards" imposed by the so-called establishment. A millionaire entertainer isn't going to lose any sleep over the lack of invitations to dances and dinners organized by social climbers in Ascot and Mayfair. A businessman who is proud of his humble origins, and reluctant to lose old friends, will be equally casual about the whole business—and rightly so. But an awful lot of people are keen to win the approval of those whom they regard as their social superiors, and this seems as good a place as any to lay down some broad guidelines. If nothing else, it will help to provide further clues to the attitudes of the rich.

COCKTAIL PARTIES

The usual format is to have an "At Home." Elegant invitations are sent out some time in advance, and it is ill-mannered not to send a prompt reply. It is also ill-mannered to arrive on the dot, bring friends, get drunk, or stay until the last moment. In easy-going California, or in Australia, a cocktail party may end up with everyone jumping into a pool or rustling up an informal barbecue, but it won't do in Ascot or Boston. The British, the French and the Italians like to have champagne on tap; in most of America, the word "cocktail" tends to mean just that. If possible, the "At Home" should be given in honor of some prominent visitor. Business can be discussed, providing it is done discreetly.

DINNER PARTIES

These are much more serious affairs and are usually planned with meticulous care. The guest list must include at least one of the people I mentioned earlier. Three or four are better but one should not overdo it: prominent men and women hate having to compete for attention. If you can get royalty, you don't need *anyone* else. Some hostesses prefer to circulate their guest list in advance, but this is regarded as an obvious ploy to persuade others to come. Top people prefer to have it taken for granted that eminent members of the establishment will be there. Men should be asked to wear dinner jackets and black tie; women should wear evening dress, but it won't do to turn up looking like a Christmas tree—tiaras should be left at home. It will naturally be assumed that, if you are rich, the servants will be your own rather than freelancers hired for the evening. You should, therefore, be on familiar (but not too familiar) terms with the butler. It is enough to know his surname: "That will be all, Bates," has a nice, reassuring ring about it. If he makes a mistake, don't berate him in front of your guests. A raised eyebrow should appear to be enough, even in these rebellious days. Some hostesses like to have a silver bell on the table that can be used to summon the help, but it is much better to be able to press a little button *under* the table. In the best homes, needless to say, neither are considered necessary: servants are so well trained that their timing is always perfect.

In Vanderbilt days, it was the custom to place favors under the napkins of one's guests. These were usually attractive little trinkets, though in at least one reported case the hostess (a nouveau riche, naturally) felt compelled to provide solid gold watches and bracelets. It is no longer necessary to go to such lengths; the rich *love* presents, but they are liable to be acutely embarrassed by obvious bribes. It is, however, essential not to be mean with the food and wine. Champagne should be available before and after dinner, and the wines should be of impeccable vintage.

In Britain, the ladies still tend to excuse themselves after dinner and leave the gentlemen to their cigars, brandy and boring chat about politics and business. Women's lib is forgotten, though one is likely to encounter the occasional hostess who feels compelled to strike a blow for equality. In America, the *ladies* may ask the gents to leave while they concentrate on their cigars, brandy and boring chat about politics and business. (It is unlikely, I must admit, but I wouldn't like you to say that you haven't been warned.) A handwritten thank you note should be written the day after the party. Flowers are more risky; if sent by a woman, the gesture may be taken as a sign that she disapproved of the ones she saw in the house, and if it's a man the host may get suspicious.

DANCES

The main objective of a dance is to enable the offspring of the rich to meet "suitable" young men and women. It is the parental alternative to dangerous places like discos, where they are liable to team up with undesirables like plumbers and secretaries from working-class areas. Old-money people recognize that they have to move with the times (which are hard), and they no longer mind inviting young men who are engaged in trade, but they feel the need to draw the line somewhere. Bankers, real estate agents, lawyers and stockbrokers are acceptable; plumbers, carpenters and clerks are not. The nouveaux riches also tend to have strong views about this. Having worked his way up from nothing, Daddy does not want his daughter to fall in love with some handsome working-class lout.

WEEKEND HOUSE PARTIES

The weekend house party has a long history and still seems to be as popular as ever. In London it generally means going off to "the country," which can be anywhere from fifty to a hundred miles away. Some of the old-fashioned rich still frown on the use of the word "weekend"; the phrase used to be "Saturday to Monday."

There will generally be around a dozen guests (sometimes more), and a good host is careful not to invite people who are known to hate each other's guts. Engaged or newly married couples should also be avoided because they have an irritating tendency to keep the other guests awake at night. Each guest should be provided with a spacious room containing a canopied bed, plenty of flowers (all the year round), a bottle of Malvern water, a book about art or horses, and a push-button telephone on which one can reach the servants in every part of the house—the kitchen, the butler's room, the pool area, and so on. Other facilities should naturally include a sauna and a tennis court. Some houses also have a cinema and, as mentioned earlier, a private zoo is much appreciated by some guests providing the animals are kept under control. (It is bad manners to allow tigers to roam freely around the premises.) The atmosphere should be informal, but everyone should be obliged to dress for dinner.

A proper British weekend should also include a shoot on Saturday. It is advisable to inquire about this beforehand, because you will not only be expected to bring your own Purdey guns but also plenty of cash so you can tip the loaders and keepers. Some hosts prefer to go riding, or to play golf, and it is bad form not to be properly equipped for either pursuit. It is also essential to be reasonably proficient at bridge—or, in the case of younger hosts, backgammon—and to know one's way around a billiard table.

HOMES ABROAD

These are also eminently suitable for parties, especially if they are in the sun or in the snow. Impressive as weekends in the country can be, there are times when one's friends want to get away from it all. Ideally one should have a villa in the South of France, a chalet in Gstaad or St. Moritz, and a home somewhere in the Caribbean. (Majorca and Benidorm can safely be left to the poor.) Comparatively few people achieve this state of perfection, but those who do are never short of companionship. Renting is more popular than the rich care to admit, and although it is very much second-best there really is no shame in it; the rent on a decent house in any of these places can, after all, come to several thousand dollars a *week*.

For the English, the French Riviera has been the "in" place for more than a century. They were the first to turn it into a holiday playground for the rich: they built the Promenade des Anglais in Nice, planted the palm trees, and made Cannes fashionable. Cannes was "discovered" by Lord Brougham, then Chancellor of England. When he first saw it, in 1834, it was a small fishing village. He

157

liked it so much that he built himself a villa; other aristocrats followed. (There is a statue of him near the Croisette, donated by the grateful citizens.) Today hundreds of wealthy English couples have splendid homes all along the Côte d'Azur. They used to go there mainly in the winter, but now prefer the summer months, and the harbors are full of yachts flying the English flag. House guests on the Côte d'Azur tend to spend most of their time around the pool—millionaires wouldn't be seen dead on the crowded beaches of Nice and Cannes—and in the spacious gardens. There is no shooting, but tennis is popular. One flies down there for long weekends; some people stay a week, but it isn't done to outstay one's welcome—the rich tend to get bored with each other after a week. The cook and the maids will be French, but the butler will usually be English—not necessarily because he is better, but because *someone* has to be able to talk to the guests in their own language. There are occasional forays to the casinos, especially those of Monte Carlo.

CHAPTER 11

THE TOYS OF THE RICH

The rich, like other men, are perhaps more simply human than otherwise. But their toys are bigger; they have more of them; they have more of them all at once.

C. WRIGHT MILLS

Getting around in style is as important to the rich as having the right place to live. For centuries, the answer was the carriage — from kings in their golden coaches to country squires in their gigs, men of wealth displayed their standing by the splendor of their équipage. They had a very bumpy ride until good springs were first used in the middle of the eighteenth century, but they were an imposing sight as they splashed through the mud with their teams of fine horses.

In the latter part of the nineteenth century private railroad cars became an equally important symbol of wealth, especially in America. Many of them looked like miniature stately homes, with gilded ceilings, expensive French furniture, and even pianos. When the motor car appeared some of the rich were skeptical, and some downright hostile, but the more daring gave the new toy an enthusiastic welcome. By the 1920s, a Rolls Royce had become almost *de rigueur*. The super-rich, anxious to outdo each other, ordered models which incorporated some of the features of the private railroad car: Rolls Royce still points with pride to some of its creations, like the sumptuous drawing room on wheels it built for a French buyer in 1927: the upholstery was woven by Aubusson and the ceiling was painted with rococo cupids.

159

The Rich: A Study of the Species

Cupids are out of fashion, but the Rolls is not—it is one of the first things people acquire when they have made a little money. Some of the super-rich have two or three: one for him, one for her, and the other one for use when they are in their homes in Florida or in the South of France. Their offspring may also have a Ferrari or a Maserati. In car-mad California there are people with so many of these expensive toys that they find it difficult to make up their minds which one to wheel out for the day. A gleaming new Rolls no longer attracts any comment; if you want to get attention you have to get hold of one of the older models, like the pre-1939 Silver Ghosts.

You should also have a private plane. This is the real equivalent of the golden coach or the private railroad car, though some people will tell you that a yacht (of which more in a moment) is even better. America has by far the largest number of private planes, which isn't surprising when you consider the size and affluence of the country, but they are used just about everywhere. Oil-rich Arabs love them. Helicopters are also popular; they are *so* convenient when one's wife wants to do some shopping.

A word of warning, though. Small planes are not nearly as practical as their owners like to pretend. A single-engined aircraft is fine for island-hopping but not much good if you need to cover any great distance. A modern jet will do the job, but one can often get there faster and in greater comfort by scheduled aircraft. If you want to go across the Atlantic it is certainly far more convenient to use the Concorde.

An American friend of mine who used to have a Learjet says he sold it because it turned out to be more trouble than it was worth. He didn't mind the cost (as in so many cases, the bill was picked up by his company), but he did mind the refueling stops, the time spent on maintenance, the bumpy rides, and the constant worry about whether the pilots would arrive at the appointed hour. A jet, he says, is a lovely ego trip but on balance one is better off flying first-class with a commercial airline. I am inclined to agree, but I can quite understand why so many multimillionaires are deeply attached to their playthings.

Yachts are not primarily used to get anywhere in particular: they are made for pleasure. Like jets, they tend to be hideously expensive but such considerations do not bother the super-rich. (J.P. Morgan, the famous American financier, once told a guest who wanted to know how much a yacht like his cost, "If you have to ask, you can't afford it.") One can get a modest yacht for a million dollars, and make do with a crew of two or three, but if you really want to compete with the super-rich you have to be prepared to pay several million and to spend another small fortune each year on keeping it afloat. The late Aristotle Onassis, whose *Christina* was more like a small private ocean liner than a yacht, spent more on his dreamboat each week than most business executives earn in a year.

The younger set tends to prefer sleek and powerful yachts built by Italian firms like Benetti and Riva. A sixty-six foot Riva boat will cost around $2 million, but nubile young ladies swoon at the sight of one. It's all a matter of priorities.

I well remember my own first time as guest on a substantial yacht. My hosts were members of two of the wealthiest Greek shipping families, and we were sailing toward Athens. We drank gallons of Dom Pérignon and tucked into caviar served by attentive flunkeys. This, I thought, is the life. Between mouthfuls we discussed business. My hosts seemed deeply depressed. Shipping, they confided, was in a frightful mess. Prospects were grim. Guiltily, I spent a whole three seconds considering whether to say no thank you, I won't have another portion of caviar. Then I remembered what one of their fraternity, Basil Mavroleon, had told me years before: "Shipowners are always complaining. And when they die they leave a fortune." The rest of the voyage was every bit as pleasant as the beginning. The second time I was on one of those sleek power yachts, owned by a well-known British property tycoon and moored in the harbor of Antibes. I boarded it on a bright, sunny day and gratefully accepted a glass of champagne. The host proudly showed me around his domain and, like most nouveaux riches, dwelled at length on the price he had paid and the smart tax deal he had managed to work out. We then set off on an aimless spin along the Côte d'Azur during which his charming and attractive wife was seasick. Our main satisfaction lay in waving a casual "hello" to another British millionaire who was chugging along in his dignified but old-fashioned yacht. I decided there and then that *I* would never buy a yacht even if I were one day to make as much money as my host; it seemed much more sensible, if ever I felt the urge to test the waves, to be an admiring guest.

Another business acquaintance of mine keeps his yacht in the old harbor of Cannes. He doesn't particularly like the sea, and he can't speak French. Indeed, he can't do anything very much when he is on holiday except drink whiskey, which he does for most of the day. He desperately misses the office, but he feels that a man in his position *must* have a boat. It seldom moves out of the harbor, but people are always ready to accept invitations to join him on board for a drink. I feel sorry for him, but I suppose I shouldn't: he is doing his own thing.

THE SPORT OF KINGS—AND TYCOONS

The same is true of all the multimillionaires who indulge in that other expensive pastime, the ownership of capricious horses. Earlier generations used them for transport; today's owners are much more interested in winning races, which most of these splendid creatures stubbornly refuse to do. I have yet to meet a rich man who does not complain, at great length, about the expense and the disappointments involved in the "sport of kings," but when one inquires why they persist they seem amazed that anyone should ask such a foolish question. One owns a horse because it is the thing to do and, besides, it may one day be first past the post and make a lot of money.

English racing was originally the preserve of the aristocracy and of country gentlemen. They made matches with each other's horses and frequently rode in the races themselves. Though racing gradually increased in scope and became more highly organized, it was still dominated by the aristocracy throughout the nineteenth century. The situation is entirely different today. Most owners are business tycoons and people who are coyly described in some magazines as "foreign gentlemen"—the Aga Khan, Nelson Bunker Hunt, Prince Khalid of Saudi Arabia, and others. The Jockey Club nowadays allows syndicates with up to twelve members to register ownership, so there are quite a number of people who race their horses in partnership.

The normal way of acquiring a racehorse is to buy a yearling at a Newmarket auction. In Britain and Ireland well over 30 percent of thoroughbreds foaled each year are sold as yearlings. Prices vary: at the December 1981 sales they averaged $30,000. But, of course, that is only the start: you also have to pay for feeding, stabling, training and, in due course, for entering your horse in a race and transporting it to and from the course. In the happy event of a successful foray, 10 percent of the winning prize money goes to the jockey and further percentages are taken by the stable.

Some people have tried to make a business out of it. In the early 1970s David Robinson, who used to be in television rentals, set up a stable of 120 horses with the specific aim of making a profit from prizes. His venture succeeded in that he regularly won over a hundred races a year, but the prize money involved was never enough and he virtually gave up. Millionaire Robert Sangster is another tycoon who has done his best to prove that the turf can be lucrative. His method is different: he is almost entirely concerned with breeding stallions.

In every year's racing new stallions emerge. If a colt wins one of the world's greatest races—the British Derby, the Kentucky Derby, the Prix de l'Arc de Triomphe—he automatically becomes extremely valuable. If he is reckoned to be a truly great horse (perhaps two or three emerge in each decade) he can be worth an enormous sum. A stallion covers at least forty mares a year, and a famous racehorse can command a stud fee of anything up to $100,000. If he lives to twenty-five, the equine equivalent of threescore years and ten (assuming that he stays fit and his early progeny win good races), he will earn at least $80 million. Sangster combs the major thoroughbred sales of the world for likely-looking foals, paying an average of perhaps $100,000 for each, and also breeds his own horses with the same objective of finding a stallion. He has had considerable success: a horse he bought in California for $120,000, for example, twice won the Prix de l'Arc de Triomphe and has since earned substantial fees. If he turned up such a horse just every three years it would keep the operation profitable, even if the others turned out to be worthless—which they are not.

Sangster takes his job seriously, but for most rich people it is a dilettante activity. They like gambling, and they like the idea of proudly showing off a winner bearing their very own colors at one of the famous racetracks. In Britain, the grand events are the Derby, the Grand National (the most grueling jumping race in the world), Goodwood, and of course Ascot. Everyone would like to win the Derby, but Ascot is the main social occasion. During Ascot week, recessions and the perils of socialism are forgotten. Each day's racing opens with a royal procession down the middle of the course in front of all the enclosures. The Queen is always in the front carriage—open, unless it is raining—with Prince Philip and their two most important guests, who may be members of European royalty or the Aga Khan. Then four or five other carriages follow holding the Queen Mother, the Prince and Princess of Wales, and the remaining guests from luncheon at nearby Windsor Castle. Splendid grays pull the carriages, with postilions on each coach, and drivers resplendent in the royal colors of gold and purple with white breeches and black caps with gold tassels; men doff their top hats while all the women curtsey—however distant they are.

The ideal way to enjoy the racing is to have one's own box. One need never move (except, of course, to greet the sovereign), and silent flunkeys obligingly place bets. There is an excellent restaurant in the Royal Enclosure and a plethora of splendid bars around the course serving champagne or Pimms. To get into the Enclosure one has to secure permission, well in advance of the meeting, from Her Majesty's representative. Up until the early 1960s people who had been through the divorce courts were banned; so were journalists and members of other unsuitable trades and professions. But the rules have been relaxed, and nowadays nearly ten thousand people make successful applications for admittance every year. Men are expected to wear morning dress and a gray topper; women have an opportunity to display the latest creations of the leading fashion houses. (Some go to extraordinary lengths to grab the limelight; hats, in particular, tend to be quite remarkable concoctions.) Weather allowing, picnics take place—with butlers serving from the backs of Rolls Royces—in the adjoining parking lots.

Yachts in Cannes Harbor. Financier J.P. Morgan once told a guest who wanted to know how much a yacht like his cost, "if you have to ask, you can't afford it." (*Sylvette Jouclas*)

Aldo Gucci, expert in the art of pleasing the rich. (*Gucci*)

Above: Tax havens like the Cayman Islands not only have lovely beaches but also strict banking secrecy laws—a great attraction for people who want to hide their fortunes. (*Sylvette Jouclas*)

Left: Henry Ford called gold the "most useless thing in the world," but the rich still choose to use vaults like these to store their wealth.

Above, far left: Curling in Gstaad, one of the favorite winter playgrounds of the wealthy; and (*below*) the equally expensive St. Moritz. (*Swiss Tourist Office*)

Overleaf: Las Vegas—plastic, neon, garish and greedy. (*Las Vegas News Bureau*)

The Toys of the Rich

Ascot is an anachronism of privilege that is passionately condemned by the left, but even its critics concede that it is a magnificent show. The rich love it, and so do the tourists. I have no doubt that it will survive, even if there is another socialist government.

In the U.S. the Kentucky Derby is a must (the crowning social event is the Lexington Ball), and the rich also like to be seen at such racetracks as Saratoga and Belmont Park in New York, Hialeah Park in Florida, and Santa Anita in Los Angeles. The oldest private club of racing is Belmont's Turf and Field Club, founded in 1895, whose 560 members strive to uphold the value of a more gracious era. Its Board of Governors includes Jockey Club members like Paul Mellon, Alfred G. Vanderbilt, and C. V. Whitney.

America's blue-chip auctions of yearling thoroughbreds are held each summer at Keeneland, Kentucky, and Saratoga in upstate New York. They are big business: at Keeneland alone, sales of these young, untried horses can easily reach the $100 million mark in just four days. Buyers come from all over the world, including the oil-rich Arab states.

To raise a thoroughbred champion is the determined dream of thousands of breeders who foal around 39,000 spanking new colts and fillies annually. Every time a fuzzy, wide-eyed and gawky potential Triple Crown contender hits the ground, each breeder has the hope that this will be a king of racing. But only 37 percent make it to the racetrack; a handful reach the winner's circle, and only *one* wears the coveted wreath of roses on Kentucky Derby Day.

All kinds of methods are used to narrow the field, including computer technology. Computers can analyze stallion and broodmare performance, and figure out which crosses might work and which won't work. Richard Broadbent's data bank in Lexington can instantly establish the five-cross pedigree, race record, and other relevant details of an American thoroughbred foaled since 1920, and of most major international-stakes horses. The complete race results of over 800,000 horses, accurate to within three days, are available with lightning speed.

But even the most brilliant technocrat cannot project the idiosyncrasies of biology or tabulate the courage in a racehorse's heart.

Luck still plays an enormously important part—which is why so many millionaires continue to back their instinctive judgments with small fortunes.

A "GIFT" FROM YVES

Although they dress up for occasions like Ascot, men are generally less interested in clothes than women. Earlier generations were far more daring. Wealthy Englishmen still go to their tailors, but a surprisingly large number of people who could well afford to buy the best, make do with clothes bought off the rack. The same is true of other countries, including America. Look around you at a business meeting and you will, as a rule, find nothing but drab conformity. There are exceptions (notably in places like Florida and California), but I don't think anyone would dispute that, when it comes to clothes, most men have lost their sense of adventure. They may take a chance on weekends or on holidays, but rarely in everyday life. Even dinner jackets are dull.

Many tycoons claim that they are too busy to find time for something as frivolous as fashion, and I daresay there is some truth in that. But I suspect that the real reasons are different. The business world tends to equate conservative dress with financial responsibility, and no one wants to be thought irresponsible. Big corporations don't much care for individualism, and the man at the top feels compelled to set an example.

Wives are seen in a different light. A well-dressed woman is regarded as a walking advertisement for her husband's affluence: she simply cannot be expected to shop at Marks & Spencer or Sears. The women's lib movement fiercely resents the notion that females are merely elegant playthings, and I can quite understand why libbers feel the way they do. The fact remains, however, that most wives (who are usually much more powerful than women's lib tends to acknowledge) happily accept their role. They *like* to dress well, and they are more than willing to let their husbands pay for it.

The Toys of the Rich

Mink coats have long been a status symbol, but so many middle-class women wear them nowadays that rich wives feel they must have at least two or three furs—plus, of course, a cape. (Enterprising designers have come up with other versions: mink blazers, mink sweaters, mink shawls. In America, one designer has even gone as far as designing a $10,000 mink jogging suit.) If you can get Yves St. Laurent to create something for you, so much the better. Labels are terribly important to women. A coat, suit or dress made by a perfectly good but unknown designer does not carry nearly as much prestige as one which bears the label of a famous couturier.

The fashion industry has cashed in on this particular type of snobbishness: there are numerous ready-to-wear boutiques around the world where one can buy clothes with magic signatures like St. Laurent, Cardin and Dior, and the practice has been extended to cover other items like perfumes, sunglasses, luggage and shoes. But for the super-rich all this is much too vulgar; their mecca is the haute couture collection.

The fabled five thousand—as they used to call the rich and privileged international set who could afford to indulge their tastes for custom-made clothing in exclusive fabrics—is said to have dwindled to a lean two thousand. But that is a story put out by the Paris fashion houses who have a vested interest in persuading customers that they are even more special than they used to be. Italian designers have taken a great deal of business away from the French; many women insist that they have more flair. Whatever the number, Paris still goes to a lot of trouble and expense to please them. The twice-yearly haute couture shows invariably lose money, even though a dress or suit may cost $10,000 or more, but they are the indispensable flagships of a vast marketing exercise. To market a name you must have a name, and there is no better way of getting publicity than to have the rich and famous sitting on gilded chairs in one's salon and, next to them, gushing fashion writers to record their reactions.

Yves St. Laurent once said that "each couture dress I sell is a gift to my clients," but it is a gift which brings in rich rewards. If it weren't for the celebrity-studded spectaculars that confirm his talent, and reaffirm the excitement which his name can generate, the clothes in the Rive Gauche ready-to-wear boutiques from Abu Dhabi to Hong Kong would be less hotly sought after, and the sales of the perfumes and some sixty other products from sunglasses to soap that bear the YSL imprimatur would start to fall.

St. Laurent, who has never made any secret of his preference for men rather than women, first achieved fame as the protégé of the late Christian Dior. After Dior's death, he was fired for wasting money on what his critics claimed "looked more like crocodile motorcycle jackets than clothes." He started his own fashion house and has done well ever since. He is shy and introspective, but knows what women want to hear. "I am a crazy, mixed-up man," he told an interviewer a few months ago. "It takes me six agonizing weeks to design a collection and the clothes come to me like visions. I literally see them in the air and then sketch what I see. The creative side is hell and I hate it. I keep telling myself not to get so anguished but I can't help it." How can *any* woman resist such tortured genius?

A DIAMOND'S BEST FRIEND

Even a St. Laurent dress requires accessories, and there are plenty of people who are eager to provide them. Basics like crocodile handbags and Piaget gold watches are taken very much for granted; what makes one rich woman really different from another (or so they tend to think) is the quantity and quality of their jewels. Secretaries and suburban housewives with diamonds the size of a pinhead are held in amused contempt—anything less than a one-carat stone does not begin to rate. The ideal is a flawless gem which is big enough to draw envious glances. Richard Burton had the right idea when he presented Elizabeth Taylor with a 69 carat pear-shaped diamond that cost him more than a million dollars. (The lucky lady later sold it for twice that sum.) If a mere actor can do it, thousands of women must have told themselves when they read the news, a property developer or shipowner should be able to do the same. (Oil-rich Arabs certainly can. King Ibn Saud bought a beautiful heart-shaped diamond of 62.50 carats from the renowned New York dealer Harry Winston. He subsequently returned it in part payment for $2 million worth of other jewelry, explaining that he really needed four big diamonds exactly alike, one for each of his wives.)

An engagement ring is generally reckoned to be the first rung of the ladder, but many attractive women start a good deal earlier than that. A rich man is expected to hand out baubles from the moment he makes an advance. A pair of diamond earrings can do a lot for his cause. A mistress will try to persuade him to add other gifts as the affair progresses; a wife will insist on it. Expensive jewelry can compensate for a great many things, including neglect ("You are always working") and sexual inadequacy ("You are always tired"). Quarrels, birthdays and Christmas provide suitable excuses for the formal handing over of diamond bracelets, emerald necklaces and other trinkets. Designers are constantly encouraged to explore fresh and exotic avenues, but true snobs hanker after jewelry with an interesting history: a necklace that belonged to Marie-Antoinette makes a much better conversation piece than one which has just emerged from the workshop.

The industry has made strenuous efforts, over the years, to convince men that they should also buy diamond rings, tieclips and cuff links for themselves, but it has had only a limited success. Some American jewelers say the drawback is the image created by flamboyant characters like Diamond Jim Brady, a salesman-cum-swindler who was a familiar figure around racetracks in the Gay Nineties. Because of him, they claim, many people associate diamonds with gangsterism. Others say that showbiz people like Liberace (who gets a lot of headlines by walking around looking like a human chandelier) have made them a sign of vulgarity. But I think there is a much simpler answer: diamonds, like flashy clothes, are widely seen as proof that a man who wears them cannot be taken seriously. Women have come to accept—without, it seems any great reluctance—that their husbands do not dare to overstep the mark, so they tend to restrict their gifts to silver cigar-cutters and pillboxes, and jeweled swizzlesticks. But the stores have not given up. Harrods not long ago offered a set of emerald worry beads, a snip at $20,000. And the annual Christmas catalog of Neiman Marcus, the famous Texas bazaar of the rich, always includes a variety of items designed to tickle the fancy of the Man Who Has

Everything. One year there were midget submarines, islands, gliders fitted with turbo-jets and life-size portable replicas of customers or their loved ones "programed to laugh as long as you like at your jokes or say yes in any language you choose at the touch of a remote control button." This was followed by gold omelette pans, supplied with four dozen double-yolked eggs; a pair of buffalo calves, male and female, for the man with a bit of prairie in need of restocking; guitar lessons from José Feliciano and dancing lessons from Mitzi Gaynor; and, when the energy crisis started to make headlines, his-and-her windmills. For children, there was a complete miniature duplicate of their own home. For Christmas 1981 the number one bargain was a domestic robot who could open doors, serve guests, water the plants and walk the dog.

Another Texas store, eager to do even better, has advertised private performances by "the world's largest tented circus" for only $47,500; for another $150,000, it promised to get Andy Warhol to write, produce and direct a home movie of the event. It has also offered customers a chance to build their own amusement park. Disneyland designer Roland Crump, the store declared, would put it together for a laughable $2 million per acre, including maintenance facilities, running water and a parking lot for guests. Bizarre? Convincing proof that the rich have more money than sense? Well, yes. But in a free society the rich, like everyone else, have the right to make fools of themselves, and I see no reason to abolish freedom just because some of them do.

CHAPTER 12

THE GREATEST APHRODISIAC?

0, what a world of vile, ill-favored faults,
looks handsome in three hundred pounds a year!

ANNE, THE MERRY WIVES OF WINDSOR
WILLIAM SHAKESPEARE.

Countless paperback novels have encouraged the view that the rich lead more interesting sex lives than the rest of us. Some undoubtedly do. One does not *have* to be wealthy to indulge in sexual games-manship, but it helps. A rich man can afford to set up mistresses in cozy apartments; a rich woman has the means to buy the attention of handsome and ardent lovers. Money is a great aphrodisiac. So, of course, is power. Put the two together and you have a combination which many people find irresistible.

Much has been said and written about the alleged sexual antics of Hollywood film moguls like the late Darryl F. Zanuck: if half the stories are true, one wonders how he and his rivals ever found the time and energy to get their work done. Looks had nothing to do with their sex appeal—some of them were downright ugly. Money and power was (and is) everything. The same is true of others who are able to promote the careers of ambitious people. Hugh Hefner (that aging playboy) has kept in shape, and no doubt some women would find him attractive even if he could not guarantee the centerfold of his popular magazine. But how many glamorous young women would line up outside his bedroom door if he were a struggling insurance salesman?

Captains of industry may have less obvious appeal, but they also have many useful advantages. They can, and do, invest money in films and stage plays on condition that their mistresses are given leading roles. They can, and do, help career girls to make the right contacts and win business. They can, and do, offer women the opportunity to lead lives of idle luxury. They can, and do, divorce wives (who have been with them through the tough years) in order to marry younger, more attractive companions.

The divorce rate among the rich is comparatively high because they tend to be more restless, more easily bored, more tempted to change for the sake of change. They find it easy to persuade themselves that a new partner will provide greater happiness. It doesn't always work out like that, of course, but they can afford to experiment.

Money, by itself, is of little importance. Its value lies in what it will buy. For most of us that means a house, a car, a vacation in some exotic playground. For a rich man it may mean a younger and more beautiful wife. For a rich woman it may mean a charming husband who is prepared to give up all thoughts of a career and become an attentive and obedient poodle. Divorce no longer carries the social stigma it once did; too many people have gone through the process.

Self-made tycoons are notoriously vulnerable. They tend to marry early, often choosing dull but supportive wives who cook their meals, make good martinis, bring up their children, listen to their plans, and applaud their ambition. Sex soon becomes a once-a-week chore because they are too tired, or too preoccupied with other matters, to indulge in more frequent performances. Their wives seldom complain, either because they don't dare to or because the act no longer gives them pleasure anyway. Some take lovers, but it is a dangerous thing to do because the would-be tycoon, though unwilling to play the part of ardent stud, fiercely resents the idea that his wife might find other men attractive. It undermines his self-confidence.

He reserves the right to flirt with younger women and may occasionally embark on a brief affair, but he carefully avoids getting entangled in serious relationships. His work comes first, and he is not going to jeopardize his chances of business success by rocking the marital boat.

The moment of danger arrives when he has climbed to the top

of whatever hill he has chosen. He can afford to relax, to turn his attention to the other good things in life. Loyalty is no longer the main consideration when he looks at women. His wife, worn out by years of caring for him and his brood, suddenly seems intolerably dreary. She knows all his faults (which is irritating), and she is a poor advertisement for a successful man. Yes, she knows how to dress and how to entertain his friends, but she doesn't make other men envious of him.

It is at this point that he is liable to fall heavily for a glamorous young woman. She openly admires his success (which is gratifying), refrains from criticism (which is comforting) and revives his interest in sex. Friends comment on her beauty and he basks in the prestige of his new conquest. Because he is vain and knows next to nothing about the wiles of women, he finds it easy to believe that she is interested in his finer human qualities and his prowess in bed, rather than in his money.

In the early stages of this exciting venture she seems quite content to play the role of mistress. She gladly settles for whatever he is willing to offer. She is delighted when he takes her out to dinner, or asks her along on a business trip. She nods, reassuringly, when he explains why he still has to spend his nights, and the weekends, with his family. She never complains, and she always looks her best.

Gradually, the pressure builds up. It begins harmlessly enough, with the occasional "wouldn't it be nice if...?" Then there are hints that other men are interested in this adorable creature. She is, of course, happy to be with him but a girl has to consider her future. What future does she have with someone else's husband?

He wavers. He asks himself if he can possibly live without her. She is such *fun*. With her by his side, he could really enjoy his wealth. But he is not yet ready to commit himself. All kinds of awkward questions demand an answer. What would his children say if he divorced their mother? How much alimony would he have to pay to a furious wife? Would he have to give up part of the business he has worked so hard to create? He makes vague promises, hoping that they will enable him to postpone the day of decision. Eventually, though, the day arrives when he has to make up his mind.

The behavior of the wife/mother during this trying period is of crucial importance. If she learns of the affair and keeps her mouth shut, there is a good chance that he will in time grow bored with her rival. If she makes a fuss and insists that he must never see her again, he may well take the plunge. It isn't easy to stay silent, but if she wants to preserve her marriage (which may not necessarily be the case) she would be wise to keep quiet.

The scenario I have described is, of course, a familiar one at *all* levels of society. And I would not wish to suggest that it only happens because some grasping female is after a bundle of money; her love may be genuine. What I am saying is that self-made tycoons are a comparatively easy target for attractive women who seek the easy way to riches. There are male fortune hunters who prey on wealthy females (more of that in a moment), but self-made female tycoons are not in abundant supply—and, in any case, they tend to be much less gullible. It is the male who most frequently finds himself caught up in a situation which he did not anticipate when he so eagerly embarked on that agreeable romp.

Let us take a brief look at some of the other species—male and female—whose wealth enables them to play a variety of sexual games.

THE SHOW-OFF

He, or she, is not interested in lasting relationships. The show-off may not even be greatly interested in sex. The main reason for acquiring a glamorous companion, or a string of companions, is to impress the rest of us. We are expected to gasp in admiration when the fat rich man arrives at a party with a stunningly beautiful blonde, or when the elderly rich woman arrives in the company of a handsome and adoring acolyte. We are not only meant to be envious but also to be deeply impressed by his, or her, ability to attract such desirable objects. They are not people but possessions, like the Rolls Royce or Cadillac, the yacht, the private plane.

The male wants us to know that he is a winner in bed as well as in business. He may be potbellied and bald, but gorgeous women can't keep their hands off him. That, at least, is the impression he tries to convey. He *may* enjoy a wild sex life—some women regard success as a bigger turn-on than physical charms—but it is much more likely that he is simply using his companion as an advertisement. There is no shortage of good-time girls who are more than willing to allow themselves to be used in this way. He might be surprised if he could hear what they say about him when he is not around, but as long as they perform their assigned duties with style and discretion he doesn't really care about their views. If they step out of line they can always be traded in for another model.

The female show-off wants the world to believe that, although she is long past her prime, young men still find her devastatingly attractive. They don't necessarily have to perform in bed—indeed, she may find that part distasteful—but they do have to perform everywhere else. There must never be the slightest hint that he is not the besotted, boyishly eager lover he is supposed to be. Like the male show-off, she is prepared to pay for such services; it is a cynical transaction which leaves each free to go their own way when they can no longer stand each other or when someone who is richer, or more handsome, comes along.

THE PLAYBOY

The playboy has made—or, more probably, inherited—a substantial sum of money and is determined to spend the rest of his life in the pursuit of pleasure. Work has absolutely no appeal for him. His chief interests are clothes, cars, sports, gambling and sex, though not necessarily in that order. He prefers the night to the day, and seldom gets up before noon. Women like him because he is amusing and because, unlike the self-made tycoon, he doesn't spend all his time talking about deals. But there is no guarantee that *he* likes women—he may well prefer his own sex.

Many playboys are the spoiled scions of wealthy families and display the effortless arrogance one expects from their kind. They do not have any particular talents but nevertheless consider themselves to be superior. They take good care of their bodies, but their minds are often blank. They know (or claim to know) all the best restaurants in cities like London or Paris, but they couldn't give you the name of the current secretary of state. They find politics almost as boring as business.

179

The playboy does his best to dodge marriage because it would impose annoying limitations. If he does marry, he invariably chooses someone who is richer than he is. He wouldn't dream of tying his future to a woman who is poor, however beautiful she may be. An heiress is much more acceptable.

THE LONER

The loner is a man or woman who has always been afraid to let anyone come too close. There is a thick wall around his or her personal emotions.

Many loners have had unhappy childhoods, or have been badly hurt at some stage in their lives. They fear that if they let down their guard, the same thing may happen again. Deeply insecure, they are afraid of being ridiculed or having their weaknesses exposed. Business is easy: they are in control. Love is difficult.

The loner hates parties and other social functions. They make him feel awkward and, anyhow, he doesn't really like people. He has few, if any, friends. His subordinates at the office provide all the reassuring flattery he needs, and there is usually a devoted secretary and/or housekeeper who can be relied upon to take care of tedious domestic details. He is often an enthusiastic collector of paintings, which can be enjoyed in the privacy of his home. Paintings don't talk, and therefore do not cause problems.

The loner tends to have a low sex drive, but if he feels the urge he has the telephone number of a sophisticated call girl who will take care of the matter without demanding anything more than a generous check. The female loner may pick up a suitable male for an uncomplicated one-night stand.

THE SEPTUAGENARIAN SYBARITE

The septuagenarian sybarite is desperately trying to make up for lost time. His greatest remaining ambition is to sleep with as many women as possible before the curtain falls. For many years he was too busy for sex. He also worried that business colleagues might think him irresponsible if he started to play around. He now bitterly regrets his foolishness and tries to seduce every attractive female he meets. He gets a lot of indignant refusals, but he also has a fair number of successes. Nubile young things like his distinguished appearance, his elegant manner, his silver hair, and his obvious eagerness to please.

One of his favorite ploys is to invite two or three women to spend a weekend on his yacht. It sounds safe enough, so they accept. He plies them with champagne and soft music, and hopes that at least one of them will be sufficiently stirred to leap into bed with him. Ideally, of course, he would like all three to accompany him to his luxurious, softly-lit cabin. He has a collection of Chinese or Japanese erotic paintings, and the dainty gold boxes on his bedside table contain powdered rhinoceros horn, pot, and other revivers.

The septuagenarian sybarite is a generous man. He reckons that it makes a lot more sense to buy diamond bracelets for likely prospects than to leave his fortune to the government or to some college. But he is also a crafty man. One septuagenarian sybarite I know—an immensely wealthy property developer—has developed a neat little ruse that seldom fails. On the very first date, he gives the lady of his choice the keys to a gleaming new Rolls Royce. She is so dazzled that she readily accepts his invitation to stay the night. The next morning he allows her to drive home in the splendid toy and then sends an aide to collect it. Challenged, he explains that he had merely wanted her to try out his latest acquisition: he can't imagine how she could have thought that it was a gift. There are no witnesses, so she angrily accepts that she has been tricked. She naturally refuses to see him again, but he clearly doesn't care: the ruse has worked and there is always someone else who will fall for it.

THE MERRY WIDOW

You can see her on Caribbean cruises—she is the one with the blue rinse, Yves St Laurent dress, and Cartier diamond necklace. Her wealthy husband died from a heart attack in his late fifties or early sixties, and left her everything. She mourned him briefly, and then decided to enjoy herself. During his lifetime she played the role of a dutiful wife; now she eagerly tries to be the *femme fatale* she always wanted to be. She gives lavish parties and flirts with any reasonably good-looking male who catches her eye. Her frantic efforts often strike others as rather pathetic, but few people have the courage to say so in her presence.

The merry widow is a natural target for the numerous fortune hunters who stalk their prey on cruises and in the resorts favored by the rich. She enjoys their flattery, however insincere it may be, but is shrewdly aware of their motives. She likes to bed presentable men of all ages but is wary of marriage proposals: she doesn't want to lose her newfound freedom.

THE FORTUNE HUNTER

The fortune hunter knows that his or her best, and perhaps only, chance of getting hold of some real cash is to trap someone who is blessed with more than enough of it.

In many families, fortune hunting is regarded as a duty. Sons and daughters are expected to go after suitable marriage partners, not merely to ensure their own future comfort but for the sake of the whole tribe. Much time and effort is devoted to preparing them for the task. They are taught the social graces and they are equipped with all the things necessary for elegant seduction: stylish clothes, a substantial expense account, and a year off for the chase. The age of the victim is immaterial, and so are looks. All that matters is that their prey should have a large bank balance and an even larger investment portfolio. Failure is unthinkable, though hunters occasionally find themselves ensnared along the way by more attractive but infinitely poorer men or women.

The biggest problem is that fortunes often look better on paper than they do in reality. They may be based on assets which are of doubtful value—such as a factory which has lost money for years— or consist of shares that cannot be sold without wrecking the owner's business. A lot of young ladies who claim to be rich haven't a clue what they are really worth—or if they have, they manage to conceal the truth until after the wedding.

Genuine fortunes may be beyond the hunter's reach. Wealthy families have a disconcerting habit, in the 1980s, of devising fancy financial schemes that keep what remains of their capital out of the hands of the Internal Revenue (which is just), and prospective husbands, (which is manifestly unjust). Trust funds were designed chiefly to dodge the tax collector, but they are also a handy way of making sure that reckless offspring do not dissipate the wealth which hardworking fathers have built up so painstakingly over the years. Trust funds may become available once Daddy has finally departed to that great Boardroom in the Sky, but the government will certainly try to claim a substantial share. Meanwhile, there is a very real risk that Daddy will regard his daughter's suitor not as an entertaining companion for his darling, born to practice the art of living, but as the son he never had. Before the honeymoon is over her husband will be installed in the executive suite and compelled to work as hard as Daddy does—which means that he will, at best, get two or three days off a year. Most millionaires, alas, are much more interested in protecting fortunes than in spending them.

The fortune-huntress is on somewhat firmer ground. Providing, that is, she tries to ensnare an older man who has already made his millions rather than a capricious youth who may, or may not, get his share of the family pile at some future date.

There are some ways of improving the odds, and it may be helpful to list them. If you are a woman, learn to make great martinis, go where the rich are—Palm Beach, Dallas, Aspen—and always arrive at cocktail parties with a handsome escort. Millionaires *love* a challenge. If you are a man, start by hiring a private detective. It is essential to investigate a prospect's financial status before you spend money on flowers, gifts, telegrams, expensive dinners and other gallantries. Next, get some well-paid but undemanding job that leaves you plenty of time to pursue your quarry. Porfirio Rubiroso, who married Doris Duke and then Barbara Hutton, called himself a "diplomat." He served for a time in the Berlin and Paris embassies of Santo Domingo, but never took the job seriously. It gave him status and allowed him to meet rich and influential people. The diplomatic service may be less glamorous than it used to be, and salaries may leave much to be desired, but it is still a useful stepping-stone.

The same is true of titles. You don't have to be a marquis or a lord these days, but it helps. Mothers everywhere are incorrigible snobs and so are their daughters, despite women's lib. The nouveaux riches cling stubbornly to the illusion that a title of any kind not only makes a man superior but ensures that he will behave with decorum—so they warmly embrace the endless stream of conniving, penniless knights, counts and princes. If you don't have a title, do what the Italians do: invent one. In his delightful book *Bring on the Empty Horses*, David Niven tells of a Chicago friend, Harry F. Ferguson, who decided that he would rather be known as his Imperial Highness Michael Alexandrovitch Dmitri Obolensky Romanoff. He became a rich man—naturally.

Another useful ploy is to call yourself a banker. It can mean almost anything (some of the biggest crooks of the postwar years have been bankers), but you will almost certainly be regarded as the kind of shrewd, respectable, well-connected gentleman wealthy families love to add to their family tree. Daddy may invite you to join his board of directors, but he is unlikely to ask you to dirty your hands with such mundane tasks as business transactions or negotiating with labor union leaders.

The key to successful fortune-hunting, as I hope I have made clear, is to mix with the right people. Be seen in the best nightclubs, not in the local bar. Join a prestigious golf club. Avoid Coney Island. Cultivate men and women who can introduce you to the rich. Dally with young working-class women if you must, but for God's sake don't encourage them to think that you might marry them. Love is a wonderful thing, but as one wealthy heiress told an interviewer not long ago: "Love doesn't last. Love is passion and this—I now know for sure—is no reason to marry."

CHAPTER 13

THE POWER OF MONEY

Every man who is worth thirty million and is not wedded to them is dangerous to the government.

NAPOLEON I

Napoleon was quite right, of course. Wealthy men and women who use their money to influence the course of history can be formidable enemies; governments have much more to fear from people who are interested in political power than from those who are content to devote their lives to protecting and increasing their fortunes. Throughout history the rich have sought to make and unmake political leaders. They have done so for a variety of reasons: to secure new territories or conditions favorable to their enterprises; to gain personal advancement; or just for the hell of it. The rules of the game have changed a great deal, as we shall see, but the basic aim has remained the same: to make the world the kind of place *they* want to live in.

For centuries, rich men would either buy their own armies or finance those of ambitious people who shared, or claimed to share, their ideas of what their particular corner of the world should be like. Some gloried in the public display of power; others shrewdly decided that it was just as satisfying, and usually a lot safer, to pull the strings quietly.

Monarchs could be extremely capricious when they felt that they were being upstaged. They didn't mind rewarding financiers who helped them to deal with their perennial money problems, but they

185

appreciated discretion. Anyone who appeared to be getting too big for his boots was swiftly cut down to size—not only because rulers felt the need to reestablish their supreme authority, but also because it gave them the opportunity to forget about awkward debts and, more often than not, to seize the offender's possessions. Biting the hand that fed them was their prerogative and, if it was done at the right moment, one of their greatest pleasures. But there were usually other rich men who thought that the potential benefits were worth the risk. Napoleon, that opportunistic soldier of fortune, was no one's puppet but he was realistic enough to acknowledge the power of money. Many over-confident leaders, before him and since, did not.

Mind you, the wealthy backers of charismatic politicians often get more than they bargained for. Adolf Hitler is a classic example. When this penniless adventurer joined the DAP in 1919 the party's entire resources consisted of seven marks and fifty pfennigs. His early efforts to raise cash met with little success, but when the party started to make headway at the polls a number of industrialists donated considerable sums. Hitler cleverly exploited their fears of Communism. They didn't think much of this excitable ex-corporal with his funny moustache, but they were impressed by his following and had no doubt that they would be able to control him. It didn't work out that way, as we all know. When Fritz Thyssen, one of his biggest backers, protested against the invasion of Poland he was expelled from the party and his fortune was confiscated. Thyssen went into exile in France, but the Vichy regime handed him over to the Gestapo and he was sent to a concentration camp.

Lenin's fateful return to Russia was financed by the German Kaiser, who badly wanted peace and thought that by giving millions to the Bolsheviks he would be able to get an "honorable settlement." He seems to have had no conception of the forces he was about to unleash. Stalin, meanwhile, was busy raising funds by robbing banks, threatening to murder wealthy Russians unless they handed over large sums, and running bordellos. Mussolini took the same route as Hitler—he persuaded industrialists that he was the right man to deal with the "red menace." In numerous meetings with business leaders he talked at length about the need to restore discipline in the factories. Years later the Duce adopted Hitler's racist views and forced his early Jewish backers, like Gino Olivetti, into exile.

The United States, which at times has seemed just as obsessed with the Communist threat, has had the good fortune (or perhaps it would be fairer to say good sense) to escape the fate of older countries such as Germany and Italy. But the rich have been just as eager to involve themselves in the political power game, either by supplying campaign funds to candidates representing their interests or by running for office themselves.

George Washington, the first president, was one of the wealthiest men of his day. When he ran for the Virginia House of Burgesses from Fairfax County in 1757, he provided his friends with "the customary way of winning votes": twenty-eight gallons of rum, fifty gallons of rum punch, thirty-four gallons of wine, forty-six gallons of beer, and two gallons of cider. Even then it was considered a large campaign expenditure, because there were only 391 voters in his district. (Washington could reasonably argue that he was simply following the example of the English; parliamentary campaign practices in Britain during the seventeenth and eighteenth centuries were notoriously corrupt. "Rotten boroughs," in which voters were either bribed or told how to vote by their masters, were a common political phenomenon. So was the buying of appointive office.)

Many other presidents have come from wealthy backgrounds, or have made it to the White House with the help of rich friends. Money can't guarantee success (Nelson Rockefeller and Barry Goldwater failed to get there despite impressive financial support), but it can certainly smooth the way.

Perhaps the best-known example is that of John F. Kennedy, whose father spent lavishly to promote his career. The amount has never been made public, but it has been estimated that Jack's 1952 campaign for a Senate seat cost him $500,000, his reelection in 1958 another $1.5 million, and his campaign for the presidential nomination at least $3 million. The old man is said to have spent $6 million more on his other two sons, Robert and Edward.

Lyndon Johnson relied heavily on Texas oilmen. His usual method, during his days as Senate majority leader, was to call a potential contributor into his office and tell him exactly how much he was to give, and to whom. If there were any hesitation, he would remind the Fat Cat of pending bills affecting him or his business. His wheeling and dealing, and his establishment of the highly profitable Austin broadcasting network, made him worth about $14 million by the time he reached the Oval Office. But his pursuit of money continued unabated. Arms were squeezed and sometimes twisted, sums were demanded and usually given, hostile legislation was threatened for recalcitrants, and jobs and favors were given in return for promised contributions.

Richard Nixon did not have a rich Daddy, but he too was an expert fund raiser who knew how to make maximum use of the presidency. His organization (headed by men like Maurice Stans and John Mitchell, who later fell from grace as a result of their associations with the Watergate scandal) milked every business in the country.

The rewards took many different forms. Favorable laws (or the suppression of proposals for *unfavorable* laws) were high on the list, but there were many others—access to the White House and the federal government, presidential backing for efforts to secure lucrative contracts, ambassadorships and other appointments. One of the advantages of the American system, as far as the rich are concerned, is that you don't actually have to go through the tiresome business of winning elections in order to get your hands on the levers of power. A president can nominate anyone he likes for the great offices of state. This is why so many millionaires have, over the years, become secretary of the treasury and secretary of commerce.

But the power of money is by no means confined to the White House or to Congress; it is just as much at work in state and local government. A rich man can make his presence felt in dozens of different ways. Public pressure (mostly from the media, but also from politicians who were either too idealistic or too poor to join in the game) produced some long-overdue reforms in 1971. President Nixon (of all people!) was compelled to sign a Federal Election Campaign Act which provided that henceforth all contributions in excess of $100 must be disclosed from the moment a candidate announces his candidacy for office. It also placed limits on the amounts a candidate, his family, or his supporters can spend on an election campaign. Contributions by companies who held government contracts were banned altogether, and there were various other provisions designed to prevent abuse. But it is one thing to pass legislation and another to enforce it; lawyers and tax consultants are expert at finding loopholes. And although the Watergate affair has had the enormously beneficial effect of making politicians at all levels think twice about the things they do, there is still plenty of scope for discreet manipulation on behalf of those who are willing to pay the price.

In Britain, the direct influence of the rich is much more limited. This is partly because it has a different system—one contributes to a party rather than an individual—but also because the Civil Service is both more determined and in a better position to preserve its independence. Britain is a comparatively small country and scandals that would rate only a few paragraphs in American newspapers often get national attention for week after week. John Poulson would have had a much easier run in the U.S. than he did in the U.K.; so would Lord Kagan. For the British, the power of the trade unions has long been a more important issue than the power of the rich. It may simply reflect the prejudices of the media (of which more later) and I have no doubt that it will change if and when the left-wing militants take over the government, but this is the way things are for the time being. Few—very few—rich men and women have gained high office in Britain (the House of Lords no longer counts), and it is hard to think of any who have managed, in recent years, to use their office to enlarge their fortunes. Socialists wouldn't agree, of course, but by and large Britain runs a fairly honest ship. The parliamentary system deserves much of the credit; it may be extremely irritating at times but others are, in many ways, a good deal worse.

THE CORPORATE RICH

This book is chiefly concerned with rich individuals and their families, but one can hardly ignore the fact that, in the modern economy, great corporations are the main units of wealth, to which individuals of property are variously attached. One certainly cannot ignore it if one looks at the power of money—it is the corporation which nowadays tends to have the biggest clout. It may be state-owned, in which case its actions may get the blessing of politicians because they are deemed to be in the national interest, or it may be a privately owned enterprise (i.e., a company with hundreds and sometimes thousands of individual shareholders) which has grown so big that its affairs have an important bearing on a country's economic prosperity. The lone entrepreneur can be taxed out of existence or be allowed to go under; the giant corporation merits special attention. The people who run it are in a much better position to squeeze concessions out of governments. In Britain, successive administrations have used billions of pounds of taxpayers' money to prop up enterprises that might well have gone bankrupt without such assistance. It gives them a distinctive kind of power—let's call it the power of the corporate rich.

Companies have long played an important role on the international as well as national scene. The British East India Company—to take one famous example—virtually ruled the vast Indian sub-continent before the crown took over; Cecil Rhodes, that great imperialist, used his companies to create a new country, Rhodesia. But it is the twentieth century which has seen the biggest growth of corporate influence. The chief executives of large corporations may not, as noted in an earlier chapter, be rich men themselves. They are, for the most part, stewards for a plurality of economic interests. But they can, and do, make just as much use of the millions entrusted to their care. Indeed they are often more ruthless: unlike people who have inherited fortunes they have had to struggle to get to the top and they are determined to stay there. Their daily business decisions collectively have more impact than those of most sovereign governments on where people live; what work they will do; what they will eat, drink and wear; even on how they will behave.

Some corporations are more like states within states than simply businesses, with their own "laws" and tribal rituals, and their own armies of corporate warriors to defend their privileges and, wherever possible, to enhance them. They can afford to hire the best lawyers, accountants, lobbyists and public relations men. Their patronage is extensive: they not only "sponsor" politicians but also secure the help of well-placed bureaucrats by discreetly promising them lucrative consultancies or directorships when they retire. Criticism tends to be countered with the reminder that corporations are the creators of wealth: the attitude of most chief executives is accurately reflected in the much-quoted remark, "What is good for General Motors is good for America."

But their interests nowadays extend well beyond national frontiers. We live in the age of the multinational corporation, with its unique capacity to use finance capital, technology, organizational skills and mass communications to integrate production on a worldwide scale. It not only tries to mold public moods and appetites but also does its best to influence economic policies. Sometimes it even attempts to destroy governments of which it disapproves: ITT's campaign, in the early 1970s to bring down the Marxist president of Chile, Salvador Allende, is one of the most widely publicized examples.

The people who work for these mammoth enterprises increasingly tend to think alike, talk alike and act alike. This is particularly true of America and Japan (where they even have their own anthems), but it is also happening elsewhere. Governments have become very much aware of the dangers: even in Britain the big corporation is nowadays viewed with much less enthusiasm than it was in the 1960s and 1970s. Anti-monopoly legislation is being more vigorously enforced on both sides of the Atlantic. In countries where socialist governments have taken office, such as France, many big companies, including banks, have been acquired by the state. But the corporate rich are here to stay: they may not rule, but they will continue to govern at many of the vital points of everyday life.

THE CORPORATE RICH

The world's twenty biggest companies and their assets, in
U.S. $ billions

Royal Dutch Shell Group	U.K., The Netherlands	59.5
Exxon	U.S.	56.6
British Petroleum	U.K.	34.6
General Motors	U.S.	34.5
Mobil	U.S.	32.7
IBM	U.S.	26.7
Texaco	U.S.	26.4
Ford Motors	U.S.	24.3
Standard Oil of California	U.S.	22.2
ENI	Italy	19.7
Gulf Oil	U.S.	18.6
General Electric	U.S.	18.5
Philips	The Netherlands	18.5
Shell Oil	U.S.	17.6
Atlantic Richfield	U.S.	16.6
Nippon Steel	Japan	16.4
Elf Aquitaine	France	15.8
ITT	U.S.	15.4
Mitsubishi Heavy Industries	Japan	15.4
Siemens	West Germany	15.1

THE EXECUTIVE RICH

American corporations tend to be much more generous in their treatment of top executives than British and other European enterprises, and although Americans complain about taxes like everyone else, they generally manage to keep a higher proportion of their incomes. If one takes into account bonuses, stock options and other forms of compensation, sixteen Americans earned in excess of a million dollars last year. No Briton can match this, although many have extra income in the form of dividends. Here is a list of the most highly paid U.S. executives and their companies, compiled by *Business Week*.

Roland Genin, Schlumberger	$5,658,000
Frank G. Hickey, Gen. Instrument	5,261,000
John W. Kluge, Metromedia	4,231,000
Jean Riboud, Schlumberger	3,029,000
Harry J. Gray, United Technologies	2,971,000
Ray C. Adam, NL Industries	2,904,000
Robert Cizik, Cooper Industries	2,761,000
David Tendler, Phibro	2,669,000
August A. Busch II, Anheuser-Busch	2,617,000
Fred L. Hartley, Union Oil	2,339,000
V. R. MacLean, NL Industries	2,247,000
Hal H. Beretz, Phibro	2,221,000
Robert Anderson, Rockwell International	2,170,000
David S. Lewis, General Dynamics	2,119,000
Daniel G. Schuman, Bausch and Lomb	1,846,000
James R. Lesch, Hughes Tool	1,835,000

CHAPTER 14

PUBLISH AND BE PRAISED

What the proprietorship of these papers is aiming at is power, and power without responsibility—the prerogative of the harlot down the ages.

STANLEY BALDWIN

The press, and more recently, television, have always fascinated the very rich, not just because they represent a chance to make money but also because they offer so much scope for self-aggrandizement and for shaping public opinion.

The late Lord Beaverbrook was quite blunt about his motives. He told a royal commission on the press in 1948 that he ran his papers "purely for the purpose of making propaganda, and no other object." Politics and power were his life, and the *Daily Express*, the *Sunday Express* and the *Evening Standard* were the means by which he tried to influence the one and gain the other. I worked for him for five years, as financial editor of two of his papers and as editor of a financial newsletter, so I had ample opportunity to watch him in action. Beaverbrook, then plain Max Aitken, came to Britain from Canada in 1910 as a rich man intent on taking up a political career. He entered Parliament as M.P. for Ashton-under-Lyne, and six years later bought the ailing *Daily Express* so that it could continue its campaign to bring down Asquith and replace him with Lloyd George. He confidently expected in return a senior appointment from Lloyd George, but was fobbed off with a peerage and the offer of a junior post. He refused office but accepted a peerage, and concentrated on building up his newspaper interests; he bought the *Standard* and, in 1918, launched the *Sunday Express*. Beaverbrook later held office under Churchill in World War II, but he is remembered as a powerful newspaper proprietor rather than as a politician. He loved conspiracy and intrigue, and pursued his various campaigns with relentless vigor. He was concerned not only with major causes—such as the preservation of the British Empire and opposition to the Common Market—but also with individuals who were thought to merit his support or his enmity. He would telephone his editors at all hours of the day and night, "suggesting" headlines and forceful leading articles.

As one of his financial editors, I was frequently summoned to his presence. On some of these occasions, we would take an early morning walk in one of London's parks; Beaverbrook would feed the ducks and talk at length about the business affairs of men he liked or hated and "suggest" that I might care to look into them. He left me in no doubt about the line he wished me to take. He also had a penchant for biblical quotations, which he would work into the conversation whenever he thought them appropriate. "Remember," he said to me on the day we first met, "the Bible says that where your treasure is there your heart will also be." One of his favorite platforms was the *Evening Standard* diary, which was widely read in the London business community. It allowed him to attack people or, if they were in his favor, to bestow fulsome praise, without revealing his identity.

Beaverbrook never hesitated to fire journalists whose work displeased him, but if one stood up to him he often gave way. I had three serious quarrels with him during my five years as financial editor of the *Evening Standard* and one year as financial editor of the *Sunday Express*. The first was over the Common Market: as an ardent European, I declined to write articles condemning the EEC. I won that battle, but lost the second. It concerned another Canadian-born press proprietor, Lord Thomson. Beaverbrook had been kind to him to begin with, but when Thomson bought *The Times* and *Sunday Times* he grew jealous. He telephoned and "suggested" that I should look into Thomson's financial manipulations. I did so, but the resulting article was judged to be too soft. The editor pleaded with him, but the old man was adamant: it could not be published. I kept on arguing but Beaverbrook curtly informed me that, if I didn't shut up, I would have to go. I stayed, but I did resign on the third occasion. I had written a piece in the *Sunday Express* which criticized a new unit trust. The editor insisted on dropping it because, he said, the unit trust had advertised in the same issue. I took the matter to Beaverbrook, saying that a financial editor had a duty to warn his readers against sharp practices. He ruled against me, and I told him that, in that case, I would leave. I later became financial editor of the *Guardian*, where I had a totally free hand.

Much has been said and written about Beaverbrook's success as a propagandist. He clearly failed in his major objectives: the empire collapsed despite his efforts, and Britain joined the Common Market despite his passionate opposition. But he had many successes. He certainly managed to blight the careers of many ambitious people and to secure advancement for others who were close to him. Churchill was among those who owed a great deal to the puckish little press baron.

Beaverbrook was not the only rich man who used his newspapers in this fashion; he wasn't even the first, for William Randolph Hearst and Lord Northcliffe had shown the way. Hearst (the subject of Orson Welles's brilliant film, *Citizen Kane*) walked into the office of his father's ailing *San Francisco Chronicle* one day in 1887 and announced to the staff that he intended to "startle, amaze and stupefy" the world. He then proceeded to do just that. Over the next half-century his newspapers made and destroyed reputations, bought politicians, created stars. Within a few years of becoming proprietor, Hearst turned the papers into vehicles through which he could run successfully for Congress and even put himself forward for the presidency of the United States. Though he never actually made it to the White House, he came close to winning the 1904 presidential nomination. There is a famous and entirely true story, used in *Citizen Kane*, that neatly demonstrates his arrogance. During the Spanish–American War of 1898 Hearst had dispatched the artist Frederic Remington to the Cuban front to make sketches of this, America's first small step into imperialism. Remington complained in a telegram that there wasn't really enough shooting to keep him busy. "You make the pictures," Hearst wired back, "I'll make the war."

Alfred Harmsworth, later Lord Northcliffe, was the son of a barrister. He began his journalistic career as a contributor to *Tit Bits*, at a guinea a column, and in 1894 he bought the staid London *Evening News*. The following year he decided to go into politics, but unlike Beaverbrook he failed to win a seat. He promptly declared that his place was "in the House of Lords, where they don't fight elections." He did not have long to wait.

In 1896 he and his brother Harold launched the *Daily Mail* and seven years later they added the *Daily Mirror*. In 1908 Alfred, now ennobled as Lord Northcliffe, acquired Britain's most prestigious paper, *The Times*. It gave him enormous power (or so he thought) and it went to his head: mounting vanity turned into megalomania and then clinical paranoia. By the time of his death in 1922 he was clearly insane.

Northcliffe was fascinated by Napoleon and delighted in collecting Napoleana, especially furniture, and portraits suggesting physical similarities between himself and the great emperor. He was ecstatic to find that one of Napoleon's hats, which he once tried on, was actually too small for him. (His successors kept the furniture, if not the hat. When I went to see his grandnephew, Vere Harmsworth, at the *Daily Mail* offices a few years ago, I was surprised to find that the imposing desk and cabinets were all marked with the huge, distinctive Napoleonic "N." Poor Vere; he later became Lord Rothermere and the "N" didn't fit in at all.)

Many Fleet Street journalists will tell you that the era of rambunctious, strong-willed proprietors came to an end when Lord Beaverbrook died. I don't agree, but it is easy to see why they should hold that opinion. His own son, Max Aitken, turned out to be a pale shadow of the old man and was eventually forced to sell his birthright. Vere Harmsworth is no Northcliffe. And Lord Thomson, the chubby Canadian who became Beaverbrook's rival in his later years, always insisted that he wasn't interested in the editorial content of his papers—he had bought them to make money. It certainly seemed for a time that in Britain, at least, the newspaper scene had changed for good—the accountants, it appeared, had taken charge. But then new men came along and among them were two flamboyant characters—Rupert Murdoch and Victor Matthews. Both are classic examples of rich men who love playing the role of press tycoon.

Rupert Murdoch is a remarkable fellow, an Australian who built up a chain of newspapers in his own country while still a young man, and then started to look for new fields to conquer. He burst onto Fleet Street in 1969, at the age of thirty-seven, when he took control of the *News of the World*. Shortly afterward he bought the fading *Sun* from Mirror Newspapers for a trifling sum and transformed it into a brash tabloid. His formula—sharply presented stories, racy features and pretty girls—was a tremendous success. He then turned his attention to the United States, where he bought the *New York Post*, *New York Magazine* and the *Star*. In 1981 he took over the London *Times* and *Sunday Times* from Lord Thomson's son, Ken, who had decided that they had become too much of a burden. Murdoch's far-flung interests today include not only newspapers and magazines but also stakes in television stations and Australia's Ansett airline. He has been called "the most powerful newspaperman in the world," and he would no doubt like to think that it is true, although some people would argue that a single newspaper like the *Washington Post*, or a magazine like *Time*, has more real power in the places where it really matters than the whole of his formidable empire. It is hard to think of any big Murdoch campaign in Britain or the United States that has had any significant effect on political events. His *Sun* newspaper supported Mrs. Thatcher in the 1978 election campaign (the editor, not Murdoch, was rewarded with a knighthood), but she would have won without its help.

Murdoch cares deeply about profits (he has to), but he is at heart a journalist, ever ready to sub-edit any story, write any headline, throw aside his coat and work in any part of the paper the unions will allow him to. He is also a gambler. From two-up (Australia's national pastime, played with a couple of coins) to horse-racing and backgammon, Murdoch has always been there with his money, and more often than not he emerges with other people's money. He has been admired, feared, hated and ridiculed. His friends say that wherever he has operated he has created or increased circulation, saved jobs, and fought existing establishments. His critics say that he has managed to degrade the standards of journalism in Britain, America and Australia.

Murdoch is ruthless, but doesn't like to admit it. He once told a television interviewer that he hated firing people: "The first person I ever fired," he said, "I went and walked him round the park and I think I ended up in tears instead of him." He must have shed a lot of tears since then; in true Beaverbrook tradition editors have been fired, long-term companions have been discarded, and his closest friends have had to take that symbolic walk around the park.

Victor Matthews knew nothing about newspapers when he decided that he could do a better job of running Beaverbrook newspapers than Max Aitken. He was a plain-talking Cockney who had been schooled in the tough world of the building site. Some years earlier he had sold his own building company to the Trafalgar House conglomerate, a deal which had made him a millionaire, and he had become a close associate of Trafalgar's founder, Nigel Broackes. The two men had embarked on a series of spectacular takeover deals, including the acquisition of Cunard Lines and the Ritz Hotel. But Victor Matthews had become restless: he wanted more. So when they heard that the Beaverbrook group was for sale they made an offer of $30 million, which was accepted. Broackes says in his autobiography (*A Growing Concern*) that at the forefront of his mind was "the desire to see Victor once again engrossed in a challenge."

Not long after the deal, Broackes invited me to lunch. Would I like to join them as editorial director? I said that I was in the process of forming my own publishing firm. No problem, he replied. "I want you to meet Victor." I went to the Trafalgar offices and, to my surprise, found myself at the receiving end of my first takeover bid. "We would like to buy your company," Broackes declared. "I thought," he added grandly, "we'd offer two."

Broackes, it appeared, was accustomed to leaving off noughts when he made deals. I paused before answering, wondering what he had in mind. Two pounds was clearly absurd. So, alas, was two million. So it must be two hundred thousand ($400,000). Matthews said nothing, but watched me carefully. I thought for a moment and then replied: "No thanks." But, I added, I would be glad to join them on a part-time basis. "In that case," Victor chipped in, "I would like you to become my personal assistant."

I spent the next three years with Victor and had ample opportunity to see him in action. I don't think he had any idea, when he embarked on his venture into the seductive world of the press, what he was getting into. He thought he could handle the unions better than anyone else, but he did not really know what to do with the papers themselves. He said that his chief reading material, up to now, had been the racing-form guide and he had little interest in politics. When a T.V. interviewer asked him what political line the group would take, he said, "We haven't got an Empire any more, but we have got Britain . . . if believing in Britain means being Conservative, then that's what we will be." He added: "We want good news. The newspapers of today always seem to be looking for bad news. I would not discount the Nixon/Watergate story if it had happened here, but it would have been a dilemma for me." And finally: "By and large the editors will have complete freedom as long as they agree with the policy I have laid down."

He was gratified to discover, within weeks of taking over, that his new status brought him invitations to visit the Prime Minister, the Chancellor of the Exchequer and other powerful figures who solicited his opinion on a wide variety of topics, especially the economy. He quickly began to involve himself personally in the editorial affairs of the *Daily Express*. The editor would be summoned at all hours of the day to hear long monologues, full of homespun wisdom, which then had to be turned into leading articles. Victor was no Beaverbrook, but he was clearly just as eager to make use of his new toy. The editor was replaced, after a while, by someone more to his liking — a *Daily Mirror* journalist with the same working-class background as himself.

When I became his personal assistant I wrote a long memo suggesting that we should work out a five-year plan for the *Express* and the other papers. It was ignored. Matthews said he wasn't interested in five-year plans; he wanted results *tomorrow*. Instead, I was asked to help him with the speeches he was increasingly being invited to make. Everyone, it seemed, wanted to hear what the new proprietor had to say. He had no public speaking experience, but he was flattered that so many important people were interested in his views. I also prepared a paper on another acquisition which had been urged upon him by Nigel Broackes, who wanted to create a whole communications division. Victor didn't think much of the idea, but went along with it. The Morgan Grampian magazine group was bought for just over "two" — this time it meant twenty million pounds ($40 million) — and I was put on the board as his watchdog. Morgan Grampian, which had been built up by a brilliant young publisher, Graham Sherren, went on to make a good deal of money for Trafalgar, but Victor never managed to work up any enthusiasm for it. Professional and technical magazines were not exciting enough for him.

Victor duly went into battle with Fleet Street's unions and for a time he had considerable success. He was emboldened to launch a new daily paper, the *Star*, and the *Financial Weekly*. But the *Daily Express* remained his pride and joy. It had made him a figure to be reckoned with and he loved it. There was only one problem: it continued to lose a terrifying amount of money. The *Star* proved an even more expensive venture. As Victor's dreams of making vast profits out of newspapers began to fade, he grew morose. He was, it seemed, surrounded by fools. "At my time of life," he told us at a board meeting of the holding company that controlled Trafalgar's publishing interests, "I could just as well be playing golf or sitting on a beach in the Bahamas." He perked up when Mrs. Thatcher gave him a peerage, but the pleasure was short-lived. His newspapers had become a burden.

I left after three years because he insisted that I should choose between a full-time involvement (I would, he said, "make a good editor of the *Daily Express*") and my own company, which was doing much better than I had hoped or expected. I told him that I would rather do my own thing, but there was another consideration: three years with the mercurial Victor Matthews had been quite enough.

My purpose in telling the Matthews story in this book is to give the reader a first-hand account of the kind of thing that can happen when a rich businessman is seduced by the glamour of the press. Plenty of others have been similarly tempted. Sir James Goldsmith tried to buy the Beaverbrook group at the same time as Trafalgar, but lost. He later launched a British version of *L'Express* which proved to be an expensive failure. More recently another entrepreneur, Tiny Rowland, has succeeded in getting control of the *Observer*, but the journalists on that paper enlisted the government's help in securing guarantees of editorial independence. Beaverbrook would never have agreed to such conditions, but Rowland had no choice. Fleet Street's future is uncertain, but the unions comfort themselves with the thought that there will always be wealthy tycoons who are eager to play the role of press lords.

Perhaps a final comment is in order. Politicians take the press very seriously, but I doubt if newspapers are as influential as they—and the men who own them—tend to think. Today, television is probably a more powerful medium. The public may be swayed by the occasional leading article, or more likely a bold headline, but in the end people choose the governments *they* want regardless of the wishes of a handful of proprietors.

CHAPTER 15

FEARS OF THE RICH

This is the posture of fortune's slave: one foot in the gravy, one foot in the grave.

JAMES THURBER

Money can buy many things, but immunity from ill-health is not one of them: cancer and other diseases hit millionaires and paupers alike. The rich are aware of this disconcerting fact of life, and like everyone else they are afraid of it. Many consider it unfair: they regard themselves as special and find it hard to come to terms with sudden, unexpected illness. This is particularly true of powerful business tycoons. They are so sure of themselves, and so used to controlling every aspect of their lives, that they tend to take good health very much for granted. They work long hours, eat and drink too much, and take little exercise. The possibility that all this may be cut short seldom occurs to them, or if it does they brush it aside. ("I don't have ulcers, I give them," movie mogul Harry Cohn once told an interviewer.) God gave them talents denied to others; surely he isn't going to take it all away, while allowing ignorant peasants to enjoy glowing health right into old age?

He can, and he does. God is not impressed by a man's bank balance. But doctors are, and the rich can have at least one consolation: they know that money *can* buy the very best treatment.

Private medical services are among the growth industries of the 1980s, and many doctors are themselves millionaires. This is particularly true in America, where one in twenty surgeons is reckoned to earn more than $500,000 a year. But Britain also has a large number of clinics whose cash-conscious owners cater to the rich and their ailments. Harley Street specialists have made fortunes, in recent years, out of people (especially Arabs) who not only demand expert skills but also the kind of luxurious surroundings to which the rich are accustomed. A routine operation can cost thousands of dollars, and the frightened clients gladly pay whatever is asked. Their faith in the powers of expensive doctors is often absurdly naive: they refuse to accept that there are diseases which even the most eminent members of the profession cannot cure. If a specialist tells them that he has run out of answers they call in others. Honest doctors do not hesitate to confirm the verdicts of their colleagues, but there are many who encourage wealthy patients to go on hoping because it is profitable to do so. A man who has terminal cancer will try *anything* that might save him, and there is always someone who will gladly oblige—at a price.

Doctors are often included in wills, and it is common for patients to make them aware of it. Their reasoning may strike you as odd. People seem to think that it will buy them extra attention, but it could just as easily be argued that it gives doctors an incentive to abandon them to their fate. The rich also make substantial donations to hospitals and to medical research. Their motives vary. Some genuinely want to play a part in alleviating human suffering; some redeem promises made during bouts of sickness ("Make me well, God, and I'll be good"); some love the idea of having clinics and hospital wings (as well as colleges and museums) named after them; some simply want to make sure that, if they should fall ill, they will get the care and affection due a generous benefactor. Whatever the reason, the medical profession has cause to be grateful.

One doesn't have to like the rich to understand their fears; we are all human. But it is a great deal easier to sympathize with those who are truly ill than with those who are merely self-indulgent. The idle rich are often dreadful hypochondriacs—they have so much time on their hands that they tend to be obsessively concerned with self. Every minor ailment, even a common cold, is treated as a disaster which requires maximum attention from everyone around. Some people fake illnesses purely to get that attention; bored wives are the worst, but men are often just as childish.

Psychiatrists flourish because of rich patients. The poor tell their troubles to relatives and friends; the wealthy rush off to the well-padded couches of expensive shrinks. In New York and California it is almost *de rigueur* to have one's own psychiatrist; it is as much of a status symbol as a Cadillac or a yacht. Some people really need that kind of help, but many more are simply on an ego trip. It must be awfully boring to listen to their rambling dissertations, but it is undeniably lucrative.

The same is true of that other fad, plastic surgery. Its original purpose was to make up for the horrors of war, when surgeons operated on thousands of badly scarred soldiers. In recent years, however, it has been used mainly to change the appearance of aging socialites. In America, "having one's face done" is now considered only a shade more adventurous than having one's teeth capped. According to *Money* magazine, a million cosmetic surgery patients troop into the country's medical waiting rooms each year. At least one in ten is a man—many surgeons say that men make up 15 to 20 percent of their clients—and the ratio is rising.

On my last trip to Los Angeles, a friend suggested that I should telephone the Medical School at the University of California for more information. Surely, I protested, they were much too busy with serious matters to find time to chat about such trivial things? "Just call," he said. I did, and found myself talking to a recording. "The sands of time affect all of us," it announced. I barely had time to nod before it added: "This [cosmetic surgery] is one effective way of turning back the clock." I shouldn't expect to find a new life, or get rich from my new face, nor should I expect to "look like a movie star," but an operation would improve my appearance and boost my self-confidence. I thanked the recording and asked my friend if he knew how much it would cost. He said it depended on the surgeon; if he were well known, I would probably be charged around $6000 for a facelift; $3000 for a rhinoplasty (nose alteration); and $3000 for an eyelift involving the upper and lower lids of both eyes. I could also have my thighs and buttocks "resculptured," but that would cost more—at least $5000. His own nose job, done by a doctor who has made a splendid career of giving perfect noses to nice Jewish girls and boys, had set him back a mere $2000. Had it been painful? "Not really, I went home on the same day, and felt a bit uncomfortable for a couple of weeks, but it was worth it."

Most cosmetic surgery needs to be done only once. A nose job or eyelid surgery lasts a lifetime. A facelift, however, does not. In five or eight years, a patient's face is likely to look the way it did the day before the surgery. It's not that the lift suddenly falls like a faulty soufflé: it's just that the aging process continues. You can turn back the clock, but you can't stop it. Some people have had three or four facelifts.

California is not the only place where plastic surgery is big business; New Yorkers also spend a great deal of money on this kind of self-improvement. One of New York's best-known surgeons, Dr. Howard Bellin, spends about thirty hours a week in the operating room and makes well over $500,000 a year. It finances a flamboyant life-style; the doctor, who likes to wear lots of gold chains around his neck, is an enthusiastic party-goer and has his own ten-seater aircraft as well as an expensive racing car and a turbo Porsche. A patient once sued him because, she claimed, he had repositioned her belly button off center, destroying her sex life, self-image and career. He was eventually ordered to pay $200,000, but insists that it has not hurt his career. "I've never been busier."

Fear of old age and its manifestations has also led to a growing demand for so-called "youth treatments." The Romanian Tourist Office, of all places, has put a great deal of effort into promoting the "youth drug" developed by Professor Ana Aslan—Gerovital H_3. Eager to earn hard currency, the Romanians claim that it can give patients "non-stop youth." Orthodox medicine is understandably skeptical about such boasts, and the doctors who run the Geriatric Institute in Bucharest are rather more modest about the Professor's achievements. Gerovital, one of them told me when I visited the Institute, slows the *rate* of aging, reverses premature aging and ameliorates old-age diseases. It doesn't give someone who is fifty or sixty the face of a twenty-year-old. "The main effect," said the doctor, "is in the brain—it preserves cheerfulness." Aristotle Onassis was a customer, and so was Konrad Adenauer. General de Gaulle and Charlie Chaplin are also said to have tried it, and numerous rich men and women have used it since. It is available in pill form (though injections are better), and is even included in a hair lotion and face cream.

But one doesn't have to go to Bucharest for cheerfulness. Hundreds of clinics all over the world offer various types of treatment. Most of them are based on the use of cells, or cell extracts, taken from organs or glands and then injected into the body. Once there, it is claimed, these substances improve the functioning of the gland they are aimed at by promoting regeneration, repair and healthy stimulation.

Scientists are constantly experimenting with new techniques. In 1982 a doctor working for the U.S. Institute of Alcoholism and Alcohol Abuse told the London *Daily Mail* that he had achieved dramatic results with a rejuvenation process tried out on rats. He removed their pituitary glands but continued to provide all the pituitary hormones essential to life. When the pituitary was removed the rats appeared to stop aging. He subsequently discovered that, without a pituitary gland, they were freed from the effects of an amino-acid which he identified as a "decreased oxygen consumption hormone"—DECO. Rats injected with DECO aged roughly twice as fast as they would otherwise have done. He is now working on an antidote to DECO which, he says, "should be completely non-toxic to humans if administered correctly, with proper supervision." Given sufficient funds, he thinks he should be ready within five years to experiment on a primate; humans could follow a year later.

I am no medical expert and therefore in no position to say whether the *Daily Mail* was talking nonsense when it concluded, "The secret of eternal youth might be ours within a decade." But I can see why reports like these are eagerly lapped up by the rich and famous. If you are worth millions it is a happy thought that someone, somewhere, may soon be able to offer what many people regard as the most precious thing of all—extra time.

CHAPTER 16

TO GEORGE, MY CÉZANNE

Now read me that part again where I disinherit everybody.

RICH CLIENT TO HIS LAWYER.

One of the inescapable facts of life which greatly irritates many of the rich is that they cannot take their wealth with them when the time comes to leave for that Great Boardroom in the Sky. It strikes them as quite unfair that they should have worked so hard to amass a fortune and *then* have to start all over again, in God knows what circumstances.

The Pharaohs, of course, thought they *could* take it with them and we are all richer as a result: the contents of just one tomb, that of Tutankhamen, are a magnificent reminder of the glories of the ancient world. But the rich have discarded (however reluctantly) that simple belief and have turned to other ways of trying to buy immortality: contributions to churches or to charity, and the financing of museums and other ambitious projects which they hope will at least ensure that we remember them for many years to come.

Many people give away most of their fortunes during their lifetime, in the rather desperate hope that it will buy them a place in heaven. Others make similar provisions in their wills. J. Paul Getty left millions to charity and spent millions on the creation of a Getty Museum in California. There are countless other examples.

Many Americans have benefited from the wills of three foreigners who were eager to leave their mark: Cecil Rhodes, James Smithson, and Alfred Nobel. Rhodes, a British-born financier who was a great believer in the Empire and arranged to have a country named after him (Rhodesia, now Zimbabwe), founded the Rhodes scholarships to Oxford University. He said that he wanted to "encourage and foster an appreciation of the advantages which I implicitly believe will result from the union of the English-speaking people throughout the world." James Smithson, a British scientist who had never visited the United States, left his fortune to a nephew with the stipulation that, should he die without issue, the whole estate would go toward the founding of the Smithsonian Institution. Alfred Nobel, a Swedish engineer who invented dynamite, left the bulk of his fortune in trust to establish five prizes for outstanding work in peace, physics, chemistry, psychology or medicine, and literature. They have since become the most prestigious awards in the world.

But some of the rich refuse even to consider the possibility of death. They not only hang on to every cent but stubbornly reject all suggestions that they should make a will. It tends to cause great confusion and much unseemly wrangling when they go. Take the case of Pablo Picasso, who died intestate leaving an estimated $9 million in bank accounts, investments, and real estate, plus an enormous treasure of his own works stored in his many homes. He must have known what a scramble there would be among his legal heirs and claimants, but he clearly didn't care. Like others before him and since, he apparently feared that once he acknowledged that he was mortal the Grim Reaper would come to get him. The renowned Dr. Samuel Johnson took much the same view in an earlier century; he only agreed to make a will when his doctors managed to convince him that the end was near and that his faithful black servant, Francis Barber, would suffer great hardship if he did not provide for him. More recently there has been the famous case of Howard Hughes. He made several wills during his lifetime, but when he died none could be found. It was never established what happened to them, but it is quite possible that he tore them up. As he left no direct heirs, a bizarre legal battle followed in the years after he died. Crooks, forgers, mystics and crackpots all got in on the act. Women declared themselves bigamists in a bid for a slice of the golden cake; men crossed the barriers of mental stability in passions of all-consuming greed.

The judge who presided over the incredibly complex litigation said he had "never come across anything like this." Forty forged wills emerged, including the so-called "Mormon will," which was allegedly pushed under the door of the headquarters of the Mormon Church in Salt Lake City and named garage attendant Melvin Dummar as a beneficiary. Dummar told the court that a disheveled Hughes walked out of the desert and borrowed 25 cents from him. The court threw out his claim. Many women claimed that Hughes married them. Actress Terry Moore said the tycoon married her aboard a yacht in international waters off California, and that they had a child who died in 1952. This claim was also dismissed. Counterevidence suggested that Miss Moore was married to someone else at the time. Dozens of people insisted that Hughes was their father. The poor judge was besieged by crackpots. "Three men," he recalls, "came through my door declaring 'I'm Howard Hughes— can I have a check?' Two of them were black."

There is no telling what goes through a man's mind when he has to decide what to do with his possessions. The norm is to express love and gratitude for those close to him by leaving them legacies. But sometimes due to senility, vindictiveness, momentary anger, helplessness, or even a sense of humor, the bequests take unforeseen and unlikely turns. It is not unusual for a will that has been drawn up in the testator's prime of life to be changed in the last days of his illness. Wealthy people are often remarkably spiteful toward their offspring, either because of some real or imagined slight or because they disapprove of their behavior. Wives may not fare any better. Shakespeare left Ann Hathaway nothing but his "second-best bed." And I have always liked the eloquent bitchiness of the Englishman who wrote in his will:

Seeing that I have had the misfortune to be married to the aforesaid Elisabeth, who, ever since our union, has tormented me in every possible way; that was not content with making game of all my remonstrances, she has done all she could to render my life miserable; that Heaven seems to have sent her into the world solely to drive me out of it; that the strength of Samson, the genius of

Homer, the prudence of Augustus, the skill of Pyrrhus, the patience of Job, the philosophy of Socrates, the subtlety of Hannibal, the vigilance of Hermogenes, would not suffice to subdue the perversity of her character; that no power on earth can change, seeing we have lived apart during the past eight years, and that the only result has been the ruin of my son, whom she has corrupted and estranged from me; weighing maturely and seriously all these considerations, I have bequeathed, and I bequeath, to my said wife Elisabeth the sum of one shilling.

Similar thoughts inspired the wealthy American banker who said:

To my wife I leave her lover and the knowledge that I wasn't the fool she thought I was. To my son I leave the pleasure of earning a living. For twenty-five years he thought the pleasure was mine, but he was mistaken. To my valet I leave the clothes he has been stealing from me regularly for ten years, also the fur coat he wore last winter while I was in Palm Beach. To my chauffeur I leave my cars. He has almost ruined them and I want him to have the satisfaction of finishing the job.

Both men at least had a sense of humor. It is, alas, comparatively rare; far more wills are grim denunciations of relatives who have failed to live up to expectations. Some are written a few hours before death, in a sad attempt to get revenge from the grave. In Munich, Germany, some years ago, relatives were asked to hold the wake in an upper floor of the dead man's house. When they were all gathered around the coffin, the floor collapsed and most of the mourners were killed. It was later discovered that he had sawed through the supporting beams.

Some people express their hate not just for one person but for a whole race. There was, for example, the Englishman who died in what he considered was exile in Tipperary and left a handsome sum:

. . . to be spent annually on the purchase of a certain quantity of the liquor vulgarly called whisky. It shall be publicly given out that a certain number of persons, Irish only, not to exceed twenty, who may choose to assemble in the cemetery in which I shall be interred, on the anniversary of my death, shall have the same distributed to them. Further, it is my desire that each shall receive it by half-a-pint at a time till the whole is consumed, each being likewise provided with a stout oaken stick and a knife, and that they shall drink it on the spot. Knowing what I know of the Irish character, my conviction is that, with these materials given, they will not fail to destroy each other, and when in the course of time the race comes to be exterminated, this neighborhood at least may, perhaps, be colonized by civilized and respectable Englishmen.

If large sums are involved, wills often lead to bitter family feuds. The law is much more generous than it was in Shakespeare's day, so Ann Hathaway would be entitled to the best bed, and much else besides. But there is often scope for argument. In some cases, relatives who feel that they have been unjustly treated try to establish that the deceased was insane at the time he drew up his will. This is what happened when Cornelius Vanderbilt—the "Commodore"—left a fortune estimated at over $100 million. The basis for the claim that Vanderbilt was out of his mind was the fact that he believed in messages from the dead and in supernatural visions. A variety of mediums and spiritualists testified that he had indeed relied on the spirit world to deal with disturbing visions, and a medium confirmed that she had put the eighty-three year old Vanderbilt in touch with his dead wife Sophie. The widow of another spiritualist testified that the Commodore's son William had paid her husband to give the sick old man a phony message from Sophie, requesting him to will everything to William. Despite all this, the judge ruled that such belief in spiritualism did not in itself establish proof of insanity. Other challengers have been more successful. A retired British judge who went rather senile left his fortune "to pay the national debt." A worthy cause, but one of his former colleagues set aside the terms of the will "on the grounds of imbecility."

A woman-hating American had better luck. He stipulated that his estate should go into a trust fund for seventy-five years. At that time the accumulated interest would bring it up to $3 million, to be used for building a womanless library which would bear his name. The words "No Women Admitted" must be cut in stone over the main entrance of the library; only books by men would be allowed; magazines would be censored to eliminate articles by women. Nothing in the design, decoration or appointments must suggest feminine influence. His daughter, who had been left a mere $5, contested the will but failed.

A surprisingly large number of rich people leave fortunes to pets. Dogs and cats come in for the highest share of these bequests, but parrots, canaries, a dove, and even a donkey have lived like royalty after the deaths of their masters. One of the biggest settlements in history is that made by a widow in Fort Lauderdale in the late 1960s; she left her entire estate, then worth $4.5 million, to her 150 stray dogs. By the time the will had been contested by relatives and was finally settled in 1973, the assets had grown to $14 million, and only 73 of the 150 dogs were still living. In the final settlement the dogs were awarded $9 million. Tattooed to prove their membership in the original 150, the dogs were separated by sex so as to prevent propagation. They were provided with the best food, had weekly medical checkups, and were treated by top doctors when they fell ill.

Jonathan Jackson of Columbus, Ohio, a nineteenth-century cat lover, left orders for a cat's home to be built, with instructions for how it was to be laid out. There were to be dormitories, a dining hall, areas for conversation, grounds for exercise, gently sloping roofs for climbing, rat-holes for sport, an auditorium where the cats were to meet every day and listen to an accordion for one hour (that instrument was the nearest approximation he could think of to a cat's voice), and an infirmary. A surgeon and a nurse were to be employed to look after the cats.

Allen Foster of Little Rock, Arkansas, was really hard up for companionship. For more than two years before his death his only friend was a large Rhode Island hen. Foster willed that after his death the hen should be maintained in the manner to which she had become accustomed. The local legend is that the hen was so arrogant after becoming an heiress that she was ostracized by her barnyard companions and died a lonely death at an advanced age.

I don't feel sorry for the hen, but I do feel sorry for people who are so lonely that they are driven to this kind of nonsense. Even those with plenty of relatives (all of whom naturally claim to have been "very close" when the will is read) are often sadly neglected while alive. No wonder so many rich old people try to buy affection.

Families can be extraordinarily callous. It is not unusual for sons and daughters to squabble quite openly about the estate of an aging relative while he is still alive. Everyone not only feels entitled to a major share, but also makes plans for spending it long before the poor soul has decided to give up. Anyone who tries to be nice to him is regarded as a threat and has to be dissuaded from saying a kind word—let alone performing some service—in case the old boy goes berserk and changes his will. I have actually heard people arguing bitterly in front of their prospective benefactor, as if his views and feelings were unimportant.

There are several ways of dealing with such insensitivity. The first is to unsettle everyone by living to ninety-eight and developing sudden enthusiasms for round-the-world trips and other luxuries. It is worth hanging on just to see their faces when you announce yet another expensive plan. The second is to get married again, even if you're eighty-five, and do your best to produce an unexpected heir. The third is to keep threatening to do both these things— and for good measure, to hint at other madcap schemes that you might just get around to in the coming year. It is an interesting way of passing the time, and an almost foolproof way of getting some attention.

Some of the rich amuse themselves, in their last years, by changing their wills at frequent intervals. It gives them great pleasure to say to their lawyers: "Now read me that part again where I disinherit everybody." Many let it be known that they make a habit of doing so, because it gives them a satisfying sense of power and makes at least some of their relatives eager to please.

One Texas multimillionaire rewrote his will when he discovered that his son had fired the top executives in all their various business enterprises, and replaced them with employees of his own choice, while the old man was in the hospital suffering from a bad gall-bladder. The son had assumed that because of his age and serious illness, the old man was about to die. But the father rose from his sickbed and went home. When he learned what had happened, he cut off the son with one dollar and left the bulk of his $400 million estate to charity.

It is not unusual for people to alter their wills in favor of outsiders who have shown them some kindness. Doctors are often left money, and even television newscasters have found themselves mentioned in wills. ("No one else has ever talked to me," a benefactor explained.) One lonely spinster left $50,000 to her "only friend," her bank.

The courts are constantly being asked to decide whether wills have been changed as a result of "undue influence." When Alice B. Atwood, granddaughter of the founder of Texas' King Ranch, died at the age of eighty-five a Chicago policeman who had befriended her was named as her sole beneficiary. She specifically disinherited her two brothers and one sister. They fought a long courtroom battle, but the policeman walked off with millions. The same thing happened in Britain not long ago, though the amount involved—about $400,000—was more modest. An eighty-year old widow left it to a policeman who, as the judge put it, "came roaring up the drive on his motorcycle and into her life." Her relatives said "he made up to her" because he knew she was wealthy, but the judge ruled against them. It might have been a hopeless love, he said, but she was of sound mind when it happened.

I see no reason why eighty-year-old widows shouldn't go bananas over husky policemen. Nor, for that matter, does it bother me that old men so often marry young, attractive women and leave their money to them rather than to uncaring relatives. I would probably do exactly the same. But fortune hunters should take note of that "undue influence" clause. It has wrecked more than one clever scheme.

Because so many rich people die without leaving any known heirs, a new profession has emerged: the bounty hunter. He is usually a trained genealogist, and he specializes in tracking down people who may have a right to unclaimed fortunes. Often the dead man and his heir never knew one another, never met, never even exchanged Christmas cards. Ted Roth, one of the most successful operators in this field, says he has located and restored to more than 100,000 people inheritances or unclaimed sums they did not know existed. Roth, who reckons that one in fifteen Americans has some money awaiting him that he knows nothing about, runs a company called Missing Heirs International. He works by locating an unclaimed sum (lawyers often tip him off), and then finding the people who have a good chance of proving that they are entitled to at least part of it. The process can take years, and he collects a handsome amount—usually 35 to 50 percent—of what they get. He says that if it were not for people like him the money would simply be grabbed by state governments.

In one typical case, a lawyer telephoned Roth to say that an unmarried man had died, leaving $70,000 and no will. The estate had been turned over to a court of probate, and it was the court's duty to decide what to do with the money. The lawyer had been appointed special guardian, and his assignment was to look for missing heirs. "I don't think there are any," he told Roth. "But if you want to try hunting them down, it's your baby." Roth set out to earn his fee. It took nearly four years. He probed the deceased's entire life: the places where he had lived, gone to school, voted, worked. He talked to his teachers, friends, neighbors, employers, anybody who might know something about his family. He eventually found several relatives and prepared all the evidence that would be needed in court to prove their relationship—genealogical charts, statements from witnesses, copies of birth certificates and other corroborating documents. He proved that all other heirs who might have taken precedence were dead. The judge accepted his arguments, but there wasn't much money left by this time. A sizable part of the original $70,000 had been siphoned off by fees which the court had parceled out to lawyers. "My share," he recalls, "was $6,000 and I can fairly say that I sweated for every penny of it." Happily, some of his other quests have involved much larger amounts.

Let me end this chapter by quoting a will which is widely regarded as a classic—an outstanding example of what a will *should* be like. It deserves to be studied by every millionaire. The author is John B. ("Jack") Kelly of Philadelphia, father of the stunning girl who became a Hollywood star and later married Prince Rainier of Monaco. This is what he dictated to a stenographer two months before he died of cancer in 1960:

> For years I have been reading Last Wills and Testaments, and I have never been able to clearly understand any of them at one reading. Therefore, I will attempt to write my Will with the hope that it will be understandable and legal. Kids will be called "kids" and not

"issue," and it will not be cluttered with the "parties of the first part," "per stirpes," "perpetuities," "quasijudicial," "to wit" and a lot of other terms that I am sure are only used to confuse those for whose benefit it is written.

This is my Last Will and Testament and I believe I am of sound mind. (Some lawyers will question this when they read my Will, however, I have my opinion of some of them, so that makes it even.) I revoke any and all previous Wills made before by me.

I give to my wife, Margaret, any interest I may own in any real estate I am using as a residence, either as a home or for vacations, at the time of my death, together with any insurance thereon. I also give to my wife any automobiles, furniture, silverware, chinaware, books, pictures, jewelry, clothing and other articles of household or personal use owned by me at my death, together with any insurance thereon. I would like my wife, Margaret, to give my son John Brendan Kelly, who will be known hereinafter by his rowing title of "Kell," all my personal belongings, such as trophies, rings, jewelry, watches, clothing and athletic equipment, except the ties, shirts, sweaters and socks, as it seems unnecessary to give him something of which he has already taken possession. If however, any special trophy, such as medals, watches, etc., should be desired for a keepsake by Baba, Grace or Liz, this is to be decided by my wife, who is to be the sole judge.

Godfrey Ford has been with me over forty-five years, and has been a faithful and loyal servant. Therefore I want him to be kept in employment as long as he behaves himself well, making due allowances for minor errors of the flesh, if being slightly on the Casanova side is an error. I want my survivors to feel an obligation regarding his comfort and employment. In addition, I give him $1,000 outright. I have already turned over to him the bonds I bought for him at Christmas each year.

I give to Mary Trenwith, if she survives me, $1,000 as a reward for her faithful service while I was in training during my rowing days.

I wish to take full advantage of the marital deduction allowed with respect to the federal estate tax. If my wife, Margaret, survives me, therefore, I give my trustees, as a separate trust for her, a one-third share of the residue of my estate.

217

I give the balance of the residue of my estate in equal shares to my son Kell (John Brendan Kelly), my daughter Baba (Margaret Kelly Davis), and my daughter Grace (Her Serene Highness, Princess Grace) and my daughter Liz (Elizabeth Anne LeVine). If any of my daughters does not survive me, her share shall pass equally to her children who survive me.

In the case of my daughters' husbands, they do not share and if any of my daughters die, her share goes to her children, or if there are no children, then that share goes back into my own children's fund. I don't want to give the impression that I am against sons-in-law—if they are the right type, they will provide for themselves and their families and what I am able to give my daughters will help pay the dress shop bills, which, if they continue as they started out, under the able tutelage of their mother, will be quite considerable.

I can think of nothing more ghastly than the heirs sitting around listening to some representative reading a Will. They always remind me of buzzards awaiting the last breath of the stricken. Therefore I will try to spare you that ordeal and let you read the Will before I go to my reward—whatever it will be. I do hope that it will never be necessary to go into Court over spoils, for to me the all-time low in family affairs is a court fight, in which I have seen some families engage. If you cannot agree, I direct that the executor or trustees, as the case may be, shall decide all questions of administration or distribution, as the executor and trustees will be of my choosing or yours.

I will try to give each of you all I can during my life so that you will have money in your own right—in that way, you will not be wholly dependent on my bequest. I want you all to understand that U.S. Government Bonds are the best investment even if the return is small, and then comes Commonwealths and Municipals, that have never failed to meet their interest charges. As the years gather you will meet some pretty good salesmen who will try to sell you everything from stock in a copper or gold mine to some patent that they will tell you will bring you millions, but remember, that for every dollar made that way, millions have been lost. I have been taken by this same gentry but that was perhaps because I had to learn from experience—when my father died, my hopes were high, but the exchequer low, and the stock market was on the other side of the railroad tracks, as far as I was concerned.

To Kell, I want to say that if there is anything to this Mendelian theory, you will probably like to bet on a horse or indulge in other forms of gambling—so if you do, never bet what you cannot afford to lose and if you are a loser, don't plunge to try to recoup. That is wherein the danger lies. "There will be another deal, my son, and after that, another one." Just be moderate in all things and don't deal in excesses. (The girls can also take that advice.) I am not going to try to regulate your lives, as nothing is quite as boring as too many "don'ts." I am merely setting down the benefit of my experience, which most people will admit was rather broad, since it runs from Port Said to Hawaii, Miami Beach to South America.

I hereby nominate, constitute and appoint my son, John Brendan Kelly, and Provident Tradesmens Bank and Trust Company, as co-executors of this, my Last Will and Testament...I appoint my friend, John Morgan Davis, my wife, Margaret M. Kelly, and my son, John Brendan Kelly, to be the trustees under this, my Will. I direct that John Edward Sheridan, Esquire, shall be retained as counsel for my estate.

I have written this Will in a lighter vein because I have always felt that Wills were so dreary that they might have been written by the author of "Inner Sanctum" and I can see no reason for it, particularly in my case. My family is raised and I am leaving enough so they can face life with a better than average start, financially.

As for me, just shed a respectful tear if you think I merit it, but I am sure that you are all intelligent enough not to weep all over the place. I have watched a few emotional acts at graves, such as trying to jump into it, fainting, etc., but the thoroughbreds grieve in the heart.

Not that my passing should occasion any "scenes" for the simple reason that life owes me nothing. I have ranged far and wide, have really run the gamut of life. I have known great sorrow and great joy. I had more than my share of success. Up to this writing my wife and children have not given me any heartaches, but on the contrary, have given me much happiness and a pardonable pride, and I want them to know I appreciate that. I worked hard in my early life, but I was well paid for that effort.

In this document I can only give you things, but if I had the choice to give you worldly goods or character, I would give you character. The reason I say that, is with character you will get worldly goods because character is loyalty, honesty, ability, sportsmanship and, I hope, a sense of humor.

If I don't stop soon, this will be as long as *Gone with the Wind*, so just remember, when I shove off for greener pastures or whatever it is on the other side of the curtain, that I do it unafraid and if you must know, a little curious.

CHAPTER 17

THE PERILS OF FAME

Fame is the stepmother of death.

PIETRO ARETINO

On a summer's day in 1977, Hanns-Martin Schleyer, president of West Germany's Federation of Industries, attended a memorial service for his good friend Jürgen Ponto, who had been gunned down during an attempt to kidnap him. Ponto had been chairman of the country's second largest bank and a lot of people were there to pay their last respects. As they were leaving, Schleyer turned to one of them and said: "The next victim is almost certainly standing in this room."

He himself was that victim. Two months later, in a one-way street near his home in Cologne, a white Volkswagen minibus followed his car round a corner. At the same time a blonde girl pushed a pram into the road in front of the car and a yellow Mercedes started coming down the road the wrong way toward them. His driver slammed on the brakes to avoid the pram. The escort car, which the state had provided after the Ponto murder, ran into the back of them. Almost simultaneously, five men stepped from the Volkswagen and fired more than a hundred rounds into the two stopped cars, killing the driver and the armed police guards. Schleyer disappeared. A few days later the kidnappers stated their price: the release of eleven remaining members of the Baader-Meinhof gang, with $50,000 each and a plane to freedom.

221

The Rich: A Study of the Species

The German government went through the motions of opening negotiations, to buy time for the biggest manhunt in the country's history. Schleyer's eldest son pleaded with the Chancellor to save his father's life, but Helmut Schmidt had no intention of meeting the gang's demands. Schleyer remained in captivity for forty-four days: in mid-October his body was discovered squashed into the trunk of a car over the French border at Mulhouse.

The Schleyer affair, and the almost identical kidnapping of former Italian Premier Aldo Moro in Rome six months later, underlined what the rich and the famous had known for quite some time: that their wealth would not necessarily save them. One could hire body-guards, but bodyguards had been no match for the professionals who had gone after Schleyer and Moro. One could offer to pay a huge ransom, but the kidnappers' demands might well include concessions which only governments could make. Wealth was more of a liability than an asset — it attracted both would-be revolution-aries, who hated the rich and wanted to make an example of some of them, and criminal gangs who regarded kidnapping as a quick way to a fortune.

Kidnapping is as old as history, though the word "kidnap" itself goes back only to the seventeenth century — it was first used to describe "the trade of decoying and spiriting away young children to ship them to foreign plantations." Julius Caesar was kidnapped by pirates in 78 B.C.; they collected a ransom but Caesar, set free, pursued them and saw to it that they were executed. Richard I, Coeur de Lion, was kidnapped on his way home from the Crusades in 1192 and held captive for more than a year. In medieval England the abduction of wealthy heiresses was commonplace. In America, the early 1930s saw what the newspapers described as an "epidemic" of the crime; the most famous case was the kidnapping of the Lindberghs' baby, which produced such a public furor that it played a key role in the creation of the FBI and gave its name to a new law, the Lindbergh Law. But the racket has acquired a new di-mension in the last decade or so: today's victims include not only political leaders, children and heiresses, but also a wide range of others who rarely had to worry about such things in the past — industrialists, diplomats, managers, lawyers, doctors. And the aim of many kidnappers is not merely to secure the largest possible ransom but to get worldwide publicity for their cause. Television has helped to turn kidnapping into a tremendous propaganda weapon. The Red Brigade didn't make a penny out of the Moro affair, but they held the attention of the Italian public for several weeks. The photographs they took of the former prime minister under their lopsided five-pointed star appeared on T.V. screens and in newspapers all over the world, and the details they chose to reveal of their secret "trial" were eagerly snapped up by the Italian press. They succeeded both in demonstrating the vulnerability of the nation's leaders and in undermining still further its already shaky foundation.

On the other side of the Atlantic, an outfit calling itself the Symbionese Liberation Army gained vast publicity when it abducted Patty Hearst, the attractive nineteen-year-old granddaughter of newspaper millionaire William Randolph Hearst. She would be released, they said, in exchange for a food distribution program to the poor of San Francisco. Her father did his best to oblige. He offered to set up a $4 million trust fund at the Wells Fargo Bank and signed a legally binding agreement to release $2 million worth of food if Patty were set free within a month, and a further $2 million nine months later. But then he received an astonishing message, on tape. In it, Patty accused her parents of "playing games" and said that she had been given a choice of, one, being released in a safe area or, two, joining the forces of the Symbionese Liberation Army "and fighting for my freedom and the freedom of all oppressed people. I have chosen to stay and fight." A few weeks later the gang held up the Hibernia Bank in San Francisco, and photographs taken by the bank's camera showed Patty Hearst, wearing a black wig, brandishing a gun. A "wanted" poster went up for her arrest. She was eventually captured and sent to jail for seven years. President Carter pardoned her after twenty-two months, and she married her bodyguard.

The Hearst case shocked America's rich families even more than the kidnapping of J. Paul Getty's grandson (whose captors cut off his right ear to strengthen their bargaining position) had done a year earlier. It had never occurred to them that crackpot revolutionaries might be able to brainwash their little darlings into joining their ranks. Where would it all end?

One predictable outcome was a sharp increase in the amount of money spent on personal security. People hired bodyguards (including female agents who could pose as their children's nursemaids or governesses), bought guns and Doberman pinschers, and installed expensive alarm systems. Companies specializing in security hardware did splendid business: they found ready buyers for every kind of gadget, including fountain pens that squirted tear gas and a "bionic briefcase" which, it was claimed, would enable one to sweep telephone systems to detect wire taps and phone bugs, flash a high-powered beam that would temporarily blind and stun an attacker, and even activate an electronic transmitter which would enable the police to track down a kidnapper. There was also a rush to take out ransom insurance: Lloyd's had been offering this kind of policy for years, but now a number of American firms joined the act. A considerable part of the insurance was carried by corporations because they could deduct the high premiums as a business expense and cover a number of board members and senior executives on the same policy.

Security has remained a thriving industry in the 1980s. Most millionaires are uneasily aware that nothing guarantees complete protection; if a gang wants to kidnap someone, it will. There have even been stories of teams of security men being one and the same as the gangs of kidnappers and armed robbers who went after the people they were protecting. It is the professionalism of present-day kidnappers which is so frightening. The notion that they would not only allow a victim to keep his bionic briefcase (to take one example), but also neglect to examine its contents, is so absurd that it is hard to understand why anyone should take it seriously. But one can hardly blame the rich for doing their best; at the very least, such devices buy a little peace of mind.

Reputable security companies generally start by doing a "vulnerability" test which takes account of various factors such as the client's ability to pay and his behavior patterns. Potential victims, they say, are most vulnerable at home and when they are driving. Homes can be protected by security systems which may include jimmy-proof, pick-resistant locks, bullet-resistant glass, high-intensity floodlights, alarms, and a "safe room" with emergency lights, a metal reinforced door, food, medical and perhaps even oxygen supplies. But four out of five kidnapping attempts take place when the victim is entering, traveling in, or getting out of, a car. You can turn your Rolls Royce or Cadillac into a mobile fortress, but you are still exposed at the beginning and end of a journey. President Reagan, the most heavily guarded man in the world, was shot and wounded as he was about to enter his armor-plated car outside the Washington Hilton. A more effective ploy is to take a different route to the office each day (Schleyer was urged to do this, but slipped into his old habits after a few days), and to learn the art of evasive driving.

The rich and prominent are also vulnerable when they travel abroad on holiday or business, especially if they go to countries like Italy and Ireland, or to one of the poor and politically unstable South American countries. One tends to be more relaxed on holiday (that, after all, is the whole idea), and hotel security generally leaves much to be desired. British businessman Rolf Schild was kidnapped with his family while on holiday in Sardinia; the gang, unfamiliar with English, apparently thought he was a member of the Rothschild clan.

Millionaires—especially Arab millionaires—sometimes book the entire top floor of a hotel, station their bodyguards near the elevators and emergency staircase, and rarely venture out. But it isn't much fun to spend one's holiday in an air-conditioned hotel suite. It makes more sense to buy an estate of one's own, install a security system, and build separate quarters for the staff; many Arabs nowadays own such estates in Britain and France. There are also a number of well-protected luxury resort developments, such as Lyford Cay in the Bahamas, which cater almost exclusively to the very rich. But that still leaves the problem of getting there and back—not every millionaire can afford a private plane.

Cruises are popular because it is assumed that kidnappers would have little chance of getting their victims off a ship. I think this is a fallacy: professionals would not find it at all difficult to abduct someone in the last days of a voyage and smuggle him or her ashore.

Easily the best protection against kidnapping for ransom is to be poor, or at least *seem* to be poor. A tourist on a package holiday may not be able to afford champagne for breakfast but at least he can walk around freely. This is why some of the smarter rich make a point of behaving like ordinary tourists; they avoid ostentatious symbols of wealth like yachts and Rolls Royces, dress casually, leave their jewelry at home or in hotel safes, eat in good but modest restaurants, and never, but *never*, boast about their money at the dinner table. Some even check into hotels under an assumed name: Mr. and Mrs. Smith is a lot safer than Mr. and Mrs. Rothschild.

Another useful protective measure, at home and abroad, is to make every effort to keep one's name out of newspapers and magazines. Publicity has always been a mixed blessing: it can be very helpful in the early stages of a man's career, but once he has made his millions it can have all kinds of unpleasant consequences. Schleyer would probably be alive today if his picture had not appeared so often in the German press.

The late Paul Getty used to say that loss of privacy was the biggest liability of being rich: "One feels one is a target." But it was largely his own fault that he became so well known: he wrote books with titles like *How to be Rich* (he was even, for a time, a regular contributor to *Playboy*), and he seldom refused to pose for photographs or talk to journalists. He seemed to enjoy being called "the richest man in the world." The man who inherited the title after his death (and who, reputedly, had a greater claim to it during Getty's lifetime) took a very different view: Daniel K. Ludwig turned down all requests for interviews and made strenuous efforts to avoid being photographed.

The ever-present risk of kidnapping attempts has made many other millionaires much more wary of press attention. Some can't avoid it; if you are a Rockefeller or an Agnelli, journalists will write about you whether you like it or not. (Agnelli, the president of Fiat, is one of Italy's best-known businessmen. His sister Susanna once barely escaped a kidnapping attempt, and his daughter's mother-in-law spent thirty-five days in the hands of a gang. But Agnelli himself is heavily guarded wherever he goes. He changes his cars all the time and never reveals his travel plans to anyone.) Other millionaires are more fortunate; journalists are either not aware of the extent of their wealth or consider them too dull to merit more than the occasional brief mention. At one time some of these faceless men would have been tempted to hire a public relations man who could get their names and pictures into the papers; today they are more likely to hire public relations men to keep their names *out* of the press. (Not long ago, the personal aide of one of Britain's richest industrialists took me to lunch at the Savoy. We talked about this and that, but it wasn't until the brandy stage that he got around to the real purpose of the lunch: he begged me not to write about his boss.)

Wives often find it hard to adjust to this new-found urge to keep a low profile. They want to flaunt their possessions; give lavish parties; be featured in magazines like *Vogue* and *House and Garden*. What's the point of having millions if you can't impress the neighbors with your wealth? But even the most ambitious socialite has become uncomfortably aware that this kind of approach has drawbacks.

I can't speak from personal experience, but I have talked to people whose lives have been dramatically affected by kidnapping and I am very much aware of what a shattering business it can be. For the victim the act itself is, of course, a tremendous shock, but the ordeal has only just begun: he or she may spend weeks, if not months, in deep uncertainty. Will one's family be able to raise the money? Will it *want* to make the great sacrifices which may be called for? And even if the answer to both those questions is yes, will it be allowed to pay the ransom? What will the gang do if it doesn't get the cash? Cut off an ear or a finger, or kill you and dump you in some wood? Imagine having to sit there day after day—lonely, disoriented, perhaps chained to your bed, with nothing to think about except your chances of survival. You know nothing about your captors except that they are determined and ruthless people who, if pushed too far, are likely to murder you in anger or frustration, or because they fear that you will identify them if they are tracked down. Every move, every sound, could signal the end.

Even if relatives are desperately anxious to help they may not have the means to do so. An Italian friend of mine is an economics professor who, some years ago, was appointed head of a bank. His name appeared in the papers from time to time, and a gang of kidnappers concluded, wrongly, that any man who was head of a bank must be extremely wealthy. They abducted his young grandson and demanded an enormous ransom. My friend was frantic. He loved the child but he simply did not have the money. He sold his house; so did the boy's parents. It wasn't nearly enough. He borrowed as much as he could, but the kidnappers were still not satisfied. He eventually managed to convince them that they had squeezed him dry. The child was released, unharmed. On the day the little boy came home he solemnly said to my friend: "Grandfather, I'm not going back to school. I'm going to start work so I can pay you back." I had a long talk with him a few months later and was glad to find that he had regained his natural exuberance; his harrowing experience had not, apparently, left any permanent scar. His parents and grandparents, though, will never forget what they went through.

One of the first and often most difficult decisions that relatives have to make is whether to call in the authorities. If the victim is kidnapped in broad daylight, and ransom demands involve freeing prisoners, they have no choice. The state steps in automatically and, indeed, generally determines the outcome of the case. But if there are no witnesses, and the sole motive is money, the situation is different. The kidnappers' instructions are always explicit: keep quiet or else. The family has to consider the risks. For the police this is just another job; there is no emotional commitment. An incompetent or over-zealous officer may make a mess of it. It is tempting, especially if one is rich, to conduct secret negotiations, hand over the ransom, and get the victim back without any fuss.

There are many examples on both sides of the Atlantic of angry clashes between the families of kidnap victims and the authorities. In Ireland recently, a gang with IRA connections kidnapped the thirty-four-year-old heir to a chain store fortune; he was on his way to open a new store in the north when he was dragged from his car by four masked gunmen. The gang demanded a million dollars, and his wife decided at once that she would pay the ransom. "I will do whatever the kidnappers want," she said. "My husband's release is my only priority; I don't care what the authorities' view of the situation is." But the police were equally determined to stop her, chiefly because they thought the money would be used to finance terrorist activities. They foiled three attempts to hand over the money. The case had a happy ending: the victim was set free after six days. But you can imagine how his wife would have felt if the gang had carried out its threat to shoot him.

In Italy there was an outcry when a magistrate announced that henceforth he would block all the assets belonging to the family of someone who had been kidnapped. For a while the move seemed quite effective, but then it was found that people had simply stopped going to the police. When the authorities did get to hear of cases, they found families totally uncooperative. Ransom money continued to be paid; families who had their assets blocked borrowed it from wealthy friends. The magistrate abandoned his hard line.

In France, many people are unhappy about the police's habit of intervening at the moment a ransom is handed over. They feel that it puts the victims at maximum risk just when they should be able to look forward to their release.

There are bound to be other occasions when the families of kidnap victims behave as if the authorities rather than the kidnappers are the villains. The police are better at handling this kind of crime than they used to be—like everyone else, they have learned from experience—and they have an impressive array of modern technology at their disposal. But things can and do go wrong, and it is not really surprising that anxious families should sometimes see the authorities as the enemy. The rich still tend to think that they know best. Not long ago, a group of wealthy Italians formed a cooperative which they decided to call the Organization for Solidarity Against Kidnaps. They raised $50 million, which they intend to use to pay bounty for information leading to the freeing of victims, arrests and convictions. Money, they say, not only talks — it persuades others to open their mouths, too.

CHAPTER 18

ROOM AT THE TOP

Successful people are just ordinary folks who have developed belief in themselves and what they can do.

DR. DAVID J. SCHWARTZ

You may feel by now that being rich is not such a good thing after all. Indeed, you may well have held that view all along: this book may merely have helped to convince you that you were right. But there *are* a great many people who would dearly love to be rich, and who would be disappointed if I did not make some attempt to tell them how this desirable state can be achieved. We have looked at the careers of a number of fortune-builders, past and present, and they should have provided some clues. But most people want to be given a magic formula—a simple recipe, with no ifs and buts, for making millions.

Over the years, many authors have tried to oblige them. There have been dozens of books with titles like the *Success Trip* and the *Success System that Never Fails*. A few have been written by people who have actually made fortunes—Paul Getty and W. Clement Stone are outstanding examples—but most of the authors were (and are) journalists and sociologists who have spent most of their lives struggling to make ends meet. I am no Getty myself and never shall be, but after spending thirty years writing about the business world I decided five years ago to start my own company and I suppose some people would call me rich, though I certainly do not, yet, come into any of the classifications set out in Chapter 1. I have homes in the South of France, Sicily, and in the Bahamas, which my friends regard as sufficient proof that I have made it (they may simply prove that I am a spendthrift!), but they are modest places which I bought because life is short and I would rather invest my money in property that I can enjoy than in boring stock certificates. I have no desire to make $50 million or $100 million. Money, to me, means one thing and one thing only: the freedom to do what I like, in comfort, for the rest of my life.

I hate to be a spoilsport, but if there is one thing I have learned— from personal experience as well as observation—it is that *there is no magic formula*. Success in business is the result of many different things or a combination of all of them: luck, timing, knowing the right people, single-mindedness, an understanding of human nature, the ability to think big, and the courage to take *calculated risks*. Ray Kroc, the hamburger king, instinctively recognized his opportunity when he saw it and, in his own words, "decided to go for broke." But there was no *guarantee* of success. Hugh Hefner desperately wanted to have his own magazine, but if his timing had been wrong he would almost certainly have been a failure. Nigel Broackes realized, when his early efforts flopped, that the key lay not only in getting to know the property business but also in persuading people who controlled substantial funds that it was in their interest to back him.

Lord Beaverbrook once said, "A man must feel those early deals right down to the pit of his stomach if he is going to be a great man of business. They must shake the very fiber of his being as the conception of a great picture shakes the artist." I am sure that most self-made men would agree with him. They have all had their share of sleepless nights. There is a point in every deal when you wonder whether you have pulled off a coup or committed yourself to the biggest disaster of your life. As in military battles, the dividing line between victory and inglorious defeat is often uncomfortably thin. All of us have moments of doubt when we are faced with the need to make major decisions; the only difference is that in business the stakes are higher.

Some of the writers who have tried to assess what Getty called "the millionaire mentality" have drawn weighty conclusions from the fact that so many self-made men come from poor families. It is easy to find evidence to support the argument that the sense of insecurity produced by this kind of background is a powerful driving force, but it is just as easy to show that many successful people come from prosperous homes. Hardship cannot be measured in financial terms alone: lack of parental love in one's formative years can be an even more important factor.

The only safe generalization, it seems to me, is that one should always mistrust generalizations. Horatio Alger, the author of one of the most widely read self-help books of all time, maintained that the key to riches was hard work and more hard work. But there are millions of people around the world who have worked like demons all their lives without getting anywhere at all. There are also a great many people who have made fortunes from financial deals with the minimum of effort. Alger himself died flat broke.

Schoolteachers and parents have a vested interest in persuading the young to accept another myth: that academic accomplishments will automatically lead to financial success. It doesn't follow at all. Many academically brilliant young men and women make very little money, however hard they try. School dropouts often do a great deal better.

Soichiro Honda, the founder of the motor company that bears his name, told me in Tokyo a few years ago that he went to a technical high school but was dismissed. "Other students memorized the lessons, but I compared them with my practical experience. My marks were not as good as those of others, and the principal said I had to leave." Honda, of course, went on to become one of the most successful engineers of his generation. He told me that if he had to take the current entrance examination of his own company he would probably fail.

In America Jeno Paulucci, a college dropout who had built up a large food distribution business, actually applied for a job in his firm under an assumed name. He took the psychology test usually given to applicants and was rejected as "unfit for a responsible position." Soon afterward he sold his shares in the company for $60 million.

History is full of people who, in their youth, seemed unlikely candidates for fame. Hitler left school at sixteen, failed the entrance examination at the Academy of Arts in Vienna, and only made it to corporal during World War I. Cornelius Vanderbilt, the most astonishing of the parvenus who made great fortunes in America during the nineteenth century, never went to school at all (he was tutored in the rough world of New York's docks), and although he later learned to read and write he was, right to the end of his life, unable to spell correctly. There are umpteen examples like these, and the only thing they prove is that there are no hard and fast rules. The best one can do is to consider attitudes and patterns of behavior which, if channeled in the right direction and backed by luck, *can* produce handsome rewards.

The vast majority of people are quite content to work for others: they are conscientious and reliable workers who are satisfied with a steady job and the security of a regular paycheck. They don't want to make the effort required to be rich, and because they don't want to make the effort it is highly improbable that they ever will be rich.

Then there are the people who like to be their own bosses but whose ambition does not extend beyond having their own small business—a bar, a restaurant or a shop. They don't care for the hassle involved in building something bigger. The McDonald brothers who sold Ray Kroc the rights to their name were quite happy with the one restaurant they already owned; as one of them told Kroc: "See that house up there? That's home to me, and I like it there. If we opened a chain, I'd never be home."

Next there are the bright and often extremely able people whose sole aim is to rise to the top of a large corporation. Some grow rich through stock ownership in the company they help to run, but most of them devote their working lives to making money for someone else.

Finally, there are the men and women for whom none of this is enough—who have their eyes on the main chance. They are opportunists who are constantly on the lookout for new worlds to conquer. They tend to be strong, individualistic personalities (which is why so many of them are, or would be, judged unsuitable for executive roles in a big corporation), and they thrive on challenges. Rupert Murdoch is a classic example of this type.

Many opportunists fail: if you botch an important deal, it may take years to recover. Some have impressive success in the early stages and then fall at some hurdle. Jim Slater, hailed as Britain's greatest whizkid in the late 1960s and early 1970s, started from scratch and built up a banking group valued at $600 million within a few years, but he over-reached himself and his empire collapsed. The possibility of failure exists for all of us; the difference between people like Slater or Murdoch and the man in the street is that they take bigger, bolder risks.

I said earlier that success in business is a combination of many things. Let us now take a closer look at some of the ingredients I mentioned.

LUCK

There is no doubt that some people are luckier than others. We all know people who, through no fault of their own, stagger from one misfortune to the next. You probably also know at least one person for whom, it seems, nothing can go wrong. He is lucky at the gaming tables, lucky in love, lucky in health, lucky in business. Some experts put it all down to fate: they maintain that our life is mapped out for us in advance. Perhaps there is some truth in that, but personally I don't believe it. Appearances can be deceptive. Men and women who are lucky in some respects are often unlucky in others—it's just that they don't advertise their setbacks. What we call "luck" generally turns out to be ability (so common in successful people) to recognize opportunities when they arise and make the most of them. Life, and especially business life, offers many opportunities, but most of us manage to find some reason for ignoring or rejecting them. We tell ourselves that the risks are too great, or that "this is the wrong time to do it," or that "I am too busy doing something else." When another man grabs the opportunity and makes a go of it we call him a "lucky devil" when all he has really done is to exploit the opening which we chose to miss. Nothing irritates a self-made millionaire more than to be told that he has been lucky. He knows that it takes a lot more than luck to achieve success.

You can't win a game without entering it. A man who shuns the gaming tables is never going to win a fortune in Las Vegas. A man who doesn't like to play the stock market is never going to make a killing in some speculative investment. A man who hates the thought of getting involved in a business venture is never going to have the pleasure of seeing it grow and make millions. To attract lucky chances you must put yourself in a position to receive them, and when you have been given the signal you must take your courage in both hands and plunge in. Faint heart never won fair lady—or control of a lucrative business.

A highly successful tycoon once told me that he made his own luck. His technique was to keep thinking up bright ideas and selling them to people who could play a major part in making them work. A lot were turned down, but he also had some big winners. I have tried to use the same approach myself. There are times when one gets awfully discouraged, but the important thing is to keep on trying. You are bound to get lucky sooner or later.

KNOWING THE RIGHT PEOPLE

Having the right sort of contacts is of crucial importance to anyone who believes in making his own luck. A factory worker who spends his entire life in the company of other factory workers may have a lot of fun, but he is not going to meet people who can help him to make a fortune. They will listen to his ideas, and tell him what a clever chap he is, but they are not in a position to offer the kind of financial backing he needs. The local bank manager may lend him money, but bank managers are cautious people with limited room for maneuver and they tend to be highly skeptical of anything that departs from conventional thought. They go by the manual; if they were entrepreneurs they would be running businesses themselves. The only way to get substantial support from a bank is to deal directly with the top men at the head office—the people who are accustomed to deal with millions. But in Britain even that road often leads to a dead end: British banks are traditionally much more concerned with short-term lending than with long-term investment. Most of them have dabbled in "venture capital" during the last decade, and it is always worth finding out if one can get a commitment from one of their offshoots or associates, but by and large the commercial banks are only willing to provide a large sum of money if (a) you don't really need it, (b) you operate in a field such as property, which they understand, (c) you have substantial assets which you can pledge as security.

Merchant bankers tend to be more daring—they have to be. They are, essentially, middlemen who prosper through deals, and over the years they have established a close relationship with the people who handle institutional funds and earn their salaries by making shrewd investments. But it is rare for a beginner to walk into the office of a merchant bank and leave with a check for a million dollars in his pocket. He is much more likely to get to first base if he has met the chairman at a dinner party and impressed him with his entrepreneurial flair and financial acumen.

The people most likely to succeed in the art of fund-raising are those who already have a good track record. If you can prove that you know what it takes to run a profitable business you can get capital for all kinds of hare-brained schemes which would be rejected out of hand if you were merely an ambitious young man with an interesting idea. The message others want to hear is that you need capital for *expansion* and that you might be willing to consider letting them in on the action. An entrepreneur who is "hot" may actually have to fight off people who are eager to put money into his company. Nothing succeeds like success, and it is a well-known dictum among the rich that it's much easier to make your second or third million than it is to make your first.

Merchant bankers, investment managers and stockbrokers are clearly among the "right people" to know. But opportunity can knock in the oddest places, and on the most unexpected occasions. I know a businessman who made his biggest deal at a funeral. He started talking to one of the relatives, who happened to be an extremely powerful figure in the financial community, and they reached agreement there and then. Some of the biggest mergers of the past few decades have started with a casual remark on the golf course, and many a profitable partnership has begun with a chat between two complete strangers at an otherwise boring lunch. Opportunists always meet—and recognize—even bigger opportunists. All they have to do is to mention the prospect of substantial profits and, bingo, the fish is hooked.

CONCENTRATION

Although they are always ready to explore every opportunity, successful tycoons tend to have strong powers of concentration. They may rush from project to project, but each one is tackled with single-minded determination. While the rest of us fuss over detail, and allow ourselves to get sidetracked by the things which happen outside work, the empire builder tends to focus on essentials.

I say "tends to" because there are exceptions: some businessmen involve themselves in so many different activities that they cannot possibly do justice to them all. But that generally happens *after* they have been successful; most entrepreneurs have few, if any, interests outside their business while they are still on the way up. Ask their families.

This ability to discipline the mind and channel all one's energies in one direction can clearly be a useful asset. It can also make a man a dreadful bore—but that, of course, is another matter.

TIMING

Good timing is a much underrated factor in business success. This is particularly true of the stock market, but it also applies to just about everything else. An investor who buys shares at the peak of the market may have to wait months—sometimes years—before he shows a profit, even though the company he has invested in is perfectly sound. A property developer who puts all his capital into an office building, and then finds that he has hit a period when demand is flat, may have to sell at a loss because he cannot afford to sit tight until conditions improve. An innovator who spends large sums on the premature launch of a new product may find, to his intense annoyance, that competitors who wait until the idea has caught on make far more money.

There has always been a great deal of argument about the subject of timing, and you will no doubt have your own views. Paul Getty used to say that the best time to buy or invest is when everyone else is gloomy; he regarded economic recessions as periods of great opportunity. I am inclined to agree with him, *but* it requires nerve and a lot of financial elbow room.

THINKING BIG

Of all the factors I have mentioned, the ability to "think big" is probably the most important; it is the one ingredient of the millionaire mentality which is absolutely essential. You can get to know all the right people, concentrate like mad, and develop perfect timing, but if your horizon is small you will never join the ranks of the very rich. You will do well, but you will not do spectacularly well.

Let's try a little test:

When you think about money, do you think about the things it can buy— a new car, perhaps, or a home in the sun?

If you do, you are not thinking big. The people who make great fortunes regard money as something you use to expand a business or as a sort of gambling chip: it is an abstract thing, a means of making still more.

Does the thought of borrowing a million dollars frighten you?

If it does, you are not thinking big. The very rich—and those who hope to join them—are experts at using O.P.M. (other people's money) to achieve their objectives. They know that most successful companies have been built with borrowed cash. You have to do your homework, of course, but you should never be afraid of borrowing large sums.

What figure comes into your head when you hear the word "fortune?" Two hundred thousand? A million? A hundred million?

If you consider two hundred thousand a fortune, you are not thinking big. Even a million is considered a modest figure in the league you are hoping to play in.

If you had a chance to buy a promising business for $10 million, but knew that you couldn't raise anything like that amount, would you say "too bad" and let the opportunity slip?

If you did, you wouldn't be thinking big. How can you be sure that you couldn't raise $10 million? Have you explored all the possibilities? Have you considered forming a syndicate, as Conrad Hilton did when he set out to buy his first hotel? Have you thought of asking a supplier for help, as Charles Forte did when he made his first takeover bid?

I know, it's all very well telling you to think big, but how on earth does one do that when one only has a few thousand dollars in savings? The short answer is that, unless someone leaves you a fortune, you will almost certainly have to start small. The point I am making is that once you get under way, you must not allow yourself to get bogged down. You have to believe that you can do just about anything if you really try. It does *not* mean that you should be reckless, or that you should press on even if there are clear signs that your venture is likely to fail. Most millionaires are good at cutting their losses: if an idea isn't working out they accept defeat and move on to the next one. One can't be right all the time. What it does mean is that, if you want to be truly rich, you cannot afford to have the attitude of a small-time grocer.

THE FIRST MILLION

Launching a company, either alone or in association with others, is still the most popular route toward the first million. It is the one my partners and I chose ourselves when we resigned from well-paid jobs to go into business five years ago. During my years at *Punch* I had started an in-flight magazine for British Airways called

High Life. It was making profits (which we shared with the airline), and when I was offered a contract to publish *High Life* myself, I had to decide whether I really wanted to be a businessman. I knew a great deal about editing publications, but I wasn't sure whether I would be happy with the business side of things. I concluded that I needed good associates. Fortunately they were available: Bob Forrester and Peter Hymans had been taking care of the advertising side for some time past (and making a great success of it), and they were eager to join me. I retained 51 percent of the shares, and divided the rest between them. We also agreed that, for the time being, we would all take the same salary. It would be modest; our aim was to plough back as much as possible so that we could embark on new ventures. It is terribly important, in these early stages, not to get into arguments over money or to grab too much of the profit: many small companies go to the wall because their owners are too greedy. The printers of *High Life* guaranteed our bank loan in return for a three-year contract, and we found a modest office in Soho. We were a bit apprehensive at first, but we needn't have worried; we never actually had to take up that loan. Five years later we have a number of magazines and our turnover is rapidly approaching the $7 million mark. I am glad we rejected that early takeover bid from Nigel Broackes and Victor Matthews. It is difficult to say what our company is worth, but it is certainly a lot more than the $400,000 we were offered.

At this stage, several options are open to a business like ours. We can continue to plough back most of our earnings, and use the cash for further expansion. We can raise funds by going to a City institution—once you have a good track record, it isn't difficult to do so. We can "go public," which involves selling some of our shares to outside investors. Or we can sell the company to a larger group for the maximum amount of cash and spend the rest of our lives in the sun.

We want to expand, because we enjoy the kind of work we do and have reached the stage where we can allow ourselves to "think big." You would not, I am sure, expect me to reveal our plans for the future, but let me dwell briefly on the merits and drawbacks of the cash-raising technique which is widely favored by entrepreneurs—going public.

A stock market quote inevitably deprives the people who run a business of some of their freedom. One has to consider the interests of others as well as of oneself. But it also has considerable advantages: it provides funds, and it adds prestige to a company. It also opens the door to the paper game.

Many of today's organizations have been built up by using paper to finance both organic growth and growth by acquisition. The paper has taken many forms—debentures, loan stock, convertible stocks, preference shares, non-voting ordinary shares and so on. Public companies have used one or the other (and sometimes a combination of several) to get cash and to make offers for businesses which they felt would fit neatly into their existing set-up.

The stock market value of a company's shares depends not only on what it owns at any given moment but also on what investors consider to be its growth potential. When one buys ordinary shares, one takes a chance on what the management will do *tomorrow* rather than today. If we sold our business, the price would be based to a large extent on what the buyer reckons we might earn in the next few years. It is a useful plus. A public company that is expanding rapidly can generally count on a high growth rating, which means that its shares command a substantial premium over its assets value. By issuing more and more shares, it can exploit that rating. That is the technique used by conglomerateurs to create their enterprises. Investors are more wary of high-flyers than they used to be (they have had some bad experiences), but growth stocks continue to have wide appeal.

Sounds great? Well, let us assume that you have made up your mind to do your own thing. Various options are open to you. You may acquire a franchise, or you may join several other people in that increasingly popular gambit, the management buy-out. Put simply, this is a transaction whereby the executive managers of a business join with financial institutions to buy that business from its present owners. The institutions put up most of the money in the form of debt and preferred capital, and are content to take a modest part of the equity. The managers put all the cash they can raise into equity. It means that for a relatively small outlay—often under 20 percent—they are left with a large shareholding in the company. Often they have control. The risks and rewards which

241

come with the ownership of equity capital are concentrated in their hands. If you can't find a suitable opportunity of this sort, you can start a company from scratch. I would urge you most strongly to stick to a field you know well. The people best placed to succeed are those who have spent a few years working for someone else in their chosen field and are thoroughly familiar with the pitfalls as well as the opportunities. (A common error is to assume that one can run, say, a restaurant because one has been a customer for many years and watched the proprietor making money. The reality comes as a shock.) It is also advisable to choose partners you'll enjoy being with, and who possess management qualities that you may lack. Last, but certainly not least, you should try to ensure that your future is not tied to one product, however good it may be. There is safety in numbers.

Our own company is in what is loosely called the "service industry," and this is the area which continues to attract more newcomers than any other because less capital is needed than for manufacturing, and because people are willing to pay for personal attention. Like all industrialized societies, Britain is in a period of transition: old industries are declining and new ones are taking their place. We are in the early stages of a revolution which is largely based on high technology: the silicon chip is transforming life at home and at work. Though today's leaders are computer-based products, other technologies will also move into the limelight between now and the year 2000. The life sciences may well be to the 1990s—and beyond—what computers have been since the 1960s. Given time and money, biotechnology may revolutionize medicine and agriculture, take over from many existing processes in the chemical industry, and help to solve the energy problem. It will also be applied to food processing, pollution control, waste utilization and mineral extraction. Many other changes offer fascinating possibilities: for example, new developments in photovoltaic cells, which turn sunlight directly into electricity, could sharply reduce the need for oil and coal by the late 1990s.

There are two ways of responding to all this. One can either complain about the disruptive effect of these changes (as so many politicians do) and try to resist them (as so many trade unions do), or one can view them as challenging new areas which will produce considerable benefits.

There is also good reason to believe that services of all kinds will play an increasingly important role in the years to come. Medical care, especially geriatric care, is likely to be one of the major growth areas. Communications is another.

Some of the new business ventures in these and other fields are bound to fail, while others will have a hard struggle in their first few years. Many entrepreneurs will be tempted to give up. But there will also be companies that will make fortunes equal to those which were made in the Industrial Revolution. It is a comforting thought that, despite the economic recession which has troubled so many countries for so long, new millionaires continue to emerge on both sides of the Atlantic every year. Sometime in the 1980s one of them could be you.

ADVICE FROM THE RICH

When you want something from a person, think first of what you can give him in return. Let him think that it's *he* who is coming off best. But all the time make sure it is you in the end.

Sir Ernest Oppenheimer, talking to his son Harry

Success is a combination of lucky breaks, the ability to seize them as they arise, and a great deal of hard work and determination.

Lord Thomson

Keep looking tanned, live in an elegant building (even if you're in the cellar), be seen in smart restaurants (even if you nurse one drink), and if you borrow, borrow big.

Aristotle Onassis

Never give up, and never under any circumstances deceive anybody. Have your word good.

Conrad Hilton

The Rich: A Study of the Species

Don't be a conformist. A businessman who wants to be successful cannot afford to imitate others or to squeeze his thoughts and actions into trite and shopworn molds. He must be an original, imaginative, resourceful and entirely self-reliant entrepreneur.

J. Paul Getty

How did I make my fortune? By always selling too soon. Sell, regret—and grow rich.

Nathan Rothschild

I sometimes say that success just happens, but it's not true. You have to *make* it happen. When I make up my mind to do something, I make sure it happens. You can't wait for the phone to ring. You have to ring *them*.

Lord (Lew) Grade

Think big, and take calculated risks.

Charles Clore

The man who gets ahead in business is the man who knows what he wants—and what he is willing to give up in order to get it.

Lord Beaverbrook

It pays to be ignorant. If you're smart, you already know it can't be done.

Jeno Paulucci

It's better, I think, not to remember how much money you have, so you still have to work hard.

Y. K. Pao

Life is based on seeing, listening, and experimenting. But experimenting is the most important.

Soichiro Honda

Nothing in the world can take the place of persistence. Talent will not; nothing is more common than unsuccessful men with talent. Genius will not; unrewarded genius is almost a proverb. Education

244

will not; the world is full of educated derelicts. Persistence and determination alone are omnipotent.

Ray Kroc

Life is not a battle except with our own tendency to sag with the downpull of "getting settled." If to petrify is success, all one has to do is to humor the lazy side of the mind; but if to grow is success, then one must wake up anew every morning and keep awake all day.

Henry Ford

Pioneering don't pay.

Andrew Carnegie

The true speculator is one who observes the future and acts before it occurs. Like a surgeon, he must be able to search through a mass of complex and contradictory details to the significant facts. Then, still like a surgeon, he must be able to operate coldly, clearly, and skillfully on the basis of the facts before him.

Bernard Baruch

CHAPTER 19

WEALTH AND SOCIETY

When all candles be out, all cats be gray.

PROVERB

Socialists seldom bother to acknowledge the risk element in private enterprise, or the role it plays in the creation of wealth: it suits their argument to portray the rich as parasites who live on the hard work of others. There are, as we have seen, people who qualify for the label—it would be foolish to deny it. I would not wish to excuse or defend the vulgar spending habits of some of the Arab sheiks and princes—so sharply at odds with the poverty in much of the Arab world—or for that matter, the cynical gamesmanship of the Hunts. Nor would I wish to excuse or defend the destructive greed of the millionaire dealers in drugs and the viciousness of Mafia godfathers. The world of the rich has its ugly side. But there are also a great many people whose drive and creative enthusiasm have been of great benefit to the rest of us, and I am not among those who seek to deny others the opportunity to do the same. I have no time for the self-appointed levelers who want to reduce everyone, and everything, to the lowest common denominator.

I am sometimes asked to name my favorite businessman. It is the kind of question fellow guests tend to come up with at dinner parties and one is tempted to give a frivolous reply. But let me try to be serious, for once, and nominate a candidate: the late Walt Disney. He not only gave enormous pleasure to millions of people all over the world; the treasures he left will endure to entertain and enlighten generations to come.

Disney came from a poor family and took a part-time job while still at school, delivering newspapers. His parents needed the money. He did not hang around street corners, or experiment with drugs, or blame a cruel world for depriving him of an easy life, as so many young people do today. He did not join the Communist Party so that he could go to meetings and denounce the rich. When he left school, he took whatever work he could get. At sixteen he worked a fourteen-hour day at the local post office, sorting the mail and making special deliveries. He then went into the army (this was 1918) and was sent to France, where he became an ambulance driver. When he got back, he made up his mind to become a cartoonist— he had always been interested in drawing—but had to settle for an apprenticeship with two commercial artists who were doing work for an advertising agency. A year later he joined the Kansas City Film Ad Company which was producing one-minute advertising films to appear in movie theaters. The animation was primitive; human and animal figures were cut out of paper and pinned to sheets; the joints of the figures were moved and photographed, creating the illusion of movement. Disney, not content with such crude methods, persuaded his employers to substitute drawn cartoons. He also rigged up a makeshift studio in his brother's garage and spent hours each night working on cartoon films of his own, based on traditional fairy tales. His first production was *Little Red Riding Hood*, and he was so pleased with it that he gave up his job at Film Ad and started a company called Laugh-O-Gram Films, with $15,000 from local investors who each contributed between $250 and $500. The president of the new company was twenty years old. Other young animators joined him and they put additional subjects into production including *Alice's Wonderland*. But the money ran out when *Alice* was half finished and the investors refused to put up any more. A year after embarking on his bold business venture, Disney had to resign himself to bankruptcy.

He left Kansas City to try his luck in Hollywood, with just $40 in his pocket. An uncle who had retired to Los Angeles gave him a room and he was soon at work in *his* garage. He finished *Alice*, sent it to a New York distributor, and was commissioned to do a series of six *Alice* comedies. He talked his elder brother Roy into joining him, and he in turn persuaded the uncle to invest $500 in the new enterprise. The Disney Bros. Studio was born. But they remained desperately short of money and eagerly accepted an offer to make another series, to be called *Oswald the Lucky Rabbit*. The distributors were happy with it—so happy that they stole away the Disney animators and did the job themselves. For the second time in his young life Walt Disney had to accept defeat. He went back to Kansas City, and on the train journey thought up the character that was to change everything—Mickey Mouse. The rest, as they say, is history. Mickey Mouse became a national craze and brought in badly needed income. Walt worked so hard that he had a nervous breakdown, but Roy stayed with him and together they built up Walt Disney Productions—a company which later went on to make great films like *Snow White and the Seven Dwarfs*, *Pinocchio*, *Fantasia*, *Bambi*, *Dumbo*, *Peter Pan*, *Cinderella*, *Lady and The Tramp*, *Twenty Thousand Leagues under the Sea*, *Davy Crockett*, *The Living Desert*, and *Mary Poppins*. Walt also created Disneyland and, toward the end of his life, Florida's marvellous Disneyworld.

His story underlines several points made in this book: a humble background is no barrier to success; a really determined man is not put off by initial failures; and it pays to give one's imagination a free rein. Disney had the courage and vision to try bold new ideas, often against the advice of his colleagues and financial backers (he frequently staked everything on his next project), and he knew how to bring out the best in other creative people. He was fortunate to have the help of a capable brother, but it was his talent and sunny optimism that made the company what it was. He said in his later years:

> I've always been bored with just making money. I've wanted to *do* things, I wanted to build things. Get something *going*. People look at me in different ways. Some say "The guy has no regard for money." That is not true. I *have* had regard for money. But I'm not like some people who worship money as something you've got to have piled up in a big pile somewhere. I've only thought of money in one way, and that is to do something with it, you see? I don't think there is a thing that I own that I will ever get the benefit of, except through doing things with it.

What I particularly admire about Disney is that, throughout, he managed to remain a child at heart. He bought his first electric train when he was forty-six, and set it up in a room next to his office so that he could play with it in his spare moments. He also had the ability to act out his concepts and dialogues; it must have been a splendid sight to see him at work in the boardroom, playing all the parts in a Mickey Mouse or Donald Duck scenario. When he died, at the age of sixty-five, Eric Sevareid paid him a moving tribute on the *CBS Evening News*. Disney, he said,

> . . . was an original; not just an American original, but an original, period. He was a happy accident; one of the happiest this century has experienced; and judging by the way it's been behaving in spite of all Disney tried to tell it about laughter, love, children, puppies, and sunrises, the century hardly deserved him . . . he probably did more to heal or at least to soothe troubled human spirits than all the psychiatrists in the world.

Disney's career, like that of so many other self-made millionaires, also underlined the absurdity of the widely held view that one can only grow rich at the expense of others—that if someone gains, someone else loses. Business can, and sometimes does, involve exploitation. But this isn't necessarily so, or even frequently so. More often than not, *both* sides gain. Disney made millions, but he also gave people a great deal of pleasure. Edwin Land, the inventor of the Polaroid camera, made millions but he also gave people something they found useful. Picasso was the richest painter in history, but the collectors who bought his paintings did not feel exploited. The Beatles piled up enormous wealth, but their countless followers throughout the world gladly paid for their records.

Let us, while we are about it, try to dispose of some other fallacies. One of the Left's articles of faith is that society can be made perfect by confiscating all private wealth and handing it over to the state. When Georges Marchais, the leader of the French Communist Party, was asked during an election campaign how he proposed to finance his grandiose schemes he waved the catalog of a high-class Paris jeweler at his audience. "You see," he said. "There is money. There are rich people. And the rich can pay." The socialists later echoed his comments and, of course, the same view has frequently been aired in Britain and America. But now that it has won power, the Left in France has discovered (if it did not know already) that life isn't that simple. The number of truly wealthy people is comparatively small, and even if the government were to grab everything they had, there would not be any significant or lasting improvement in the living standards of 50 million people. The major problems of the day—low production, unemployment and so on—would not go away. Only the *creation* of wealth, through greater effort, can secure that desirable objective.

The Soviets seized the assets of the rich many years ago, but not even the Kremlin propaganda machine would claim that they have managed to build a perfect society. What they have built is a joyless bureaucratic empire without grace or style, in which individuality is ruthlessly suppressed. Its cities are drab (Soviet architecture is functional rather than aesthetically pleasing), and so are most of the inhabitants. Moscow frequently suffers serious food shortages (meat and butter had to be rationed in the winter of 1981–82) and homes are notoriously overcrowded. It is common for two or three families to share one modest apartment. Much the same is true of satellite countries like Romania, Poland and Czechoslovakia. The rich have been replaced by a gray elite that talks about equality but enjoys special privileges (see Chapter 8) and keeps the workers firmly in their place. One doesn't expect Georges Marchais to acknowledge all this, but there is no reason why the rest of us should be fooled by Communist claptrap.

I do not object to the principle that the rich in Western societies should be taxed more heavily than those who are less fortunate. They can afford it. But I do object to moves that are chiefly inspired by envy. I believe in equality of *opportunity*, but not in enforced equality.

The French have introduced a wealth tax, and socialist politicians in Britain intend to bring in a similar tax if and when they regain office. There is nothing wrong with the idea as such, but it is absurd to pretend that it can be some kind of magic cure. There is a thick file at the Treasury which contains the results of several lengthy investigations made by the Inland Revenue and others during the last few decades. A wealth tax, Whitehall insists, is difficult to operate because there are considerable problems in measuring wealth (one cannot be sure what a property is worth until it is sold). Non-income-producing assets such as works of art and family homes would have to be exempt, and the administrative cost would be so high that the net gain to the Exchequer would be very modest. Labor Chancellors like Denis Healey (who, you will recall, was determined to "soak the rich") accepted these findings. But the party hates to be confronted with reality; it prefers to put its faith in slogans.

The plain fact (generally ignored) is that we already tax wealth, though we don't actually call it a wealth tax. Governments have been hammering away at the rich for years through a high tax on investment income, a capital gains tax and a capital transfer tax. But these forms of taxation don't have the same emotional appeal as a "wealth tax," and therefore tend to be brushed aside.

The impact of increased taxation on inherited wealth has been much greater than is generally realized. Inheritance tax has sharply reduced many fortunes. Owners of large estates have been forced to sell land and other assets, stately homes have passed into the hands of national trusts and foundations, and many family firms have either vanished or have been absorbed by big corporations. You may well approve: inheritors do not, on the whole, command much sympathy from their fellow men. But there *is* a case for inherited wealth, apart from the obvious argument that a man—or a woman—should have the right to pass the benefits of his labors on to his children. It is based chiefly on the unfashionable view that society gains by having *individuals* who have both the freedom and the means to make their own judgments on a wide variety of issues, including conservation and patronage of the arts. It is in the area of personal (as opposed to group) liberty that the rich are important. The existence of an independent class provides a useful counterweight to the tyranny not only of the state but also to that of popular opinion. Darwin, who possessed what the Victorians called an "independence," wrote, "The presence of a body of well-instructed men who have not to labor for their daily bread is important to a degree that cannot be over-estimated." If he had been a university teacher, dependent on salary, could he in the atmosphere of the time have published the results of his researches? Even Marx had reason to be grateful for the support of wealthy friends like Engels.

One of the greatest fallacies of the 1980s is that the state is best qualified to judge what is in the public interest—that politicians, civil servants and committees are the people who deserve the right to decide how we should live. We have seen what this kind of folly has led to in the Communist world; it seems to me vital that we should not make the same mistake. The rich have over the centuries devoted much time and care to beautiful things: magnificent houses, splendid gardens, great paintings. We have all benefited from their enthusiasm. Walk around any museum and look at the treasures they have left us, and ask yourself what there would be to see if Communism had arrived a few centuries earlier. Medici money financed the work of some of the greatest artists in history; Rockefeller money has financed some of the finest work in the twentieth century *and* paid for the restoration of places like Colonial Williamsburg.

The whims of the rich have often been delightfully impractical. Who would build the Taj Mahal in India today? Who in Britain would construct a Hampton Court or a Blenheim? The existence of the rich still provides the best chance for the truly original, the completely unorthodox. Instead of having one, two or three possibilities of finding support, the artist has one, two or three hundred. The disappearance of private patronage would be a disaster for writers, painters, musicians and architects.

Much has been written about the use of foundations and charitable trusts as a way of keeping large sums out of the tax collector's ever-growing net, and nearly all of the comment has been critical. There is no doubt that many of the rich see them mainly as a means of preserving their wealth—or at least their control of it—and that the system is open to abuse. But few of the critics bother to distinguish between tax evasion and tax avoidance. Evasion is deliberate fraud; avoidance means making full use of allowances and loopholes. It is, of course, appalling that so much time and effort are devoted to this complex game, but there is nothing immoral about tax avoidance. Taxation is an Act of Government, not an Act of God. It has no morals; it may not even claim to be fair. If governments want to close loopholes, let them do so. Until then everyone is entitled to arrange his affairs to suit himself rather than the Internal Revenue Service. The rich have the advantage of being able to enlist the help of expensive accountants and lawyers, but the principle is the same for all.

It is also quite obviously unfair not to acknowledge that many foundations have a genuine philanthropic purpose. Many rich people give generously to causes that are close to their heart: hospitals, colleges, museums, libraries, research, churches and so on. The fact that they can get tax concessions does not make the donations less valuable. As the rich see it, *they* created the wealth which makes these payments possible—not the tax collector or some politician. They are therefore entitled to decide who should benefit. It is, of course, an argument which has been heard ever since taxation was invented. Carried to its logical conclusion it leaves no room for governments at all, which is clearly unrealistic. But one can see why the rich should feel the way they do, and why they should consider themselves to be at least as capable of deciding which cause deserves support as any group of officials. There are, to be sure, times when they spend their money foolishly. But that is just as true of the politicians and bureaucrats who spend *our* money.

Millionaires who devote their later years to philanthropy are often said to have a guilty conscience. There may be something in that, but a far more powerful reason, I think, is that it gives them pleasure. They get the same kind of satisfaction out of watching a new college or museum grow as they used to get out of the acquisition of another company. It is nice to have one's name emblazoned over the portal, or to collect an honorary degree, but what really turns them on is the feeling that they have made things *happen*. One should not sneer at it; the beneficiaries certainly don't.

THE FUTURE OF THE RICH

How will the rich fare in the next few decades? I said in the previous chapter that there will be ample opportunity for the creation of new millionaires. But how will society deal with them?

The twentieth century has seen tremendous political and social upheavals. The Russian Revolution wiped out some of Europe's wealthiest aristocrats; World War II finished off many others. More recently we have seen a revolution in Iran. Who can tell what the future holds for countries like South Africa?

The Rich: A Study of the Species

Even in Britain the rich are not what they were in Victorian or Edwardian days, partly due to high taxation but also because so much of their wealth and power has passed into the hands of the people who run nationalized industries and large corporations. The Thatcher government has helped small businesses, but it can hardly be said to have gone out of its way to restore the rich to their former position. A future socialist government would deal more harshly with them than any of its predecessors. The Tories take comfort from the fact that the Labor party is bitterly divided, and even Michael Foot assures us that Tony Benn will never be Prime Minister. But it seems likely that the left will gain power *some time* in the next decade—and when it does, it will certainly restore high marginal tax rates and make it still harder to pass on wealth. Landowners may be faced with confiscation of their land; businesmen will see more companies pass into state ownership (despite the disastrous record of so many nationalized industries); and the rest of us will face a relentless assault on our freedom of choice. Men like Andrei Sakharov and Alexander Solzhenitsyn have warned us not to be taken in by the surface simplicity of socialist dogma, but there are plenty of people who seem stubbornly determined to ignore what has been happening in Eastern Europe.

The Left's program calls, among other things, for the abolition of the House of Lords and of all titles. Some people think that even the monarchy will vanish by the end of the century. I do not share that view, but I have no doubt that the power of what remains of the aristocracy will continue to decline. There will be other changes, even if the Left fails to get into office. The rich will have to come to terms with growing hostility, and increased crime. The ostentatious display of wealth will be even more dangerous in the 1990s than it is in the 1980s. We are also likely to see more dilution of ownership, even under a middle-of-the-road government, with institutions like pension funds and insurance companies accounting for a still larger share of wealth. I am sure the rich will manage to survive somehow, but we shall probably see fewer Rockefeller-sized fortunes. More family-owned firms will be swallowed up by the corporate rich; power in the private sector will continue to pass to the paid meritocrat-director.

Much of this is already happening in countries like Italy and

France, and even the oil-rich Arabs have reason to worry about the future. They may have enough oil to last for another century, but for how long can they continue their feudal rule? It is an anachronism which seems unlikely to survive for another fifty years, let alone a hundred, and I can't say I blame them for building up comforting hoards in foreign banks.

It will also be fascinating to watch developments in the Soviet Union and its satellite states. Marxism is already dead, as we have seen, and although the Kremlin will go on paying lip service to the idea of equality there could well be an even stronger move toward *inequality*. It would be ironic, you will agree, if the rich were to stage a vigorous comeback in the East at a time when their power and influence is declining in many parts of the West.

If I were one of the super-rich, I would feel safest in Switzerland or North America. The Swiss worry endlessly (and, it seems to me, needlessly) about the prospect of invasion, but they have great respect for private property. The Americans still believe in the individual's right to do his own thing, and continue to have great regard for private enterprise. They have their share of would-be revolutionaries, but I firmly believe that the U.S. is likely to remain a capitalist society for longer than any other industrialized country in the non-Communist world. Many of my rich friends in Britain feel the same, which is why they have taken advantage of exchange control freedom to invest heavily in American stocks and property.

It may be that, as the doomsayers predict, the coming decades will see major financial upheavals. It is by no means inconceivable that we shall one day see a repetition of the Great Crash of 1929, which turned millionaires into paupers overnight. Paper wealth, represented by stocks and bonds, can quickly vanish if there is a serious and prolonged loss of confidence. Business enterprises that depend heavily on borrowed money can easily collapse if the flow of credit suddenly dries up. Western economies are less stable than they were in the 1960s and early 1970s, and although I am an optimist by nature I am also enough of a realist to accept that the *possibility* of a crash exists. But America, like other Western countries, recovered from the 1929 debacle and went on to greater prosperity. For entrepreneurs like Paul Getty and Conrad Hilton the setback was a period of opportunity; they were able to acquire solid assets which later soared in value. History could well repeat itself: great fortunes are invariably made when rapid economic changes occur, in either direction.

I have tried to show how much in life depends on one's own attitude. If there is a message in this book it is that you don't get rich by being fainthearted. I have emphasized the positive aspects and I make no apology for doing so: there are plenty of authors who have been all too eager to deal with the negative side. I admire people with a spirit of adventure and I strongly defend the individual's right to do his own thing within the framework of the law. The world would be a poorer place if the rich ceased to exist.

FURTHER READING

Although I interviewed many people for this book, it clearly would not have been possible to write it without a large number of other sources, including newspapers, magazines, autobiographies and biographies, speeches and academic studies. I warmly thank all those whose diligent efforts over the years made my task easier.

If you want to stay in touch with the activities of the rich I urge you to keep your eye on newspapers like the *Financial Times* and the *Wall Street Journal*, and on magazines like *Fortune*, *Forbes*, *Time*, *Town and Country*, *Vogue*, *High Life*, and *Harper's and Queen*. I also recommend this short list of books which I have found not only informative but also a pleasure to read.

Broackes, Nigel. *A Growing Concern*. London: Weidenfeld and Nicolson, n.d.

Carr, Albert Z. *Business as a Game*. New York: New American Library, 1969.

Churchill, Allen. *The Splendor Seekers*. New York: Grosset and Dunlap, n.d.

Collier, Peter, and Horowitz, David. *The Rockefellers*. New York: Holt, Rinehart and Winston, 1976.

Duncan, Andrew. *Money Rush*. New York: Doubleday, 1979.

Fay, Stephen. *The Great Silver Bubble*. Kent, England: Hodder and Stoughton, n.d.

Galbraith, John Kenneth. *The Affluent Society*. New York: New American Library, 1978.

———. *The Great Crash*. Boston: Houghton Mifflin, 1979.

Getty, J. Paul. *As I See It*. Englewood Cliffs, N.J.: Prentice-Hall, 1976.

Handy, Charles. *Gods of Management*. London: Souvenir Press, n.d.

Heller, Robert. *The Common Millionaire*. New York: Delacorte, 1974.

Hilton, Conrad. *Be My Guest*. Englewood Cliffs, N.J.: Prentice-Hall, n.d.

Huber, Richard M. *The American Idea of Success*. New York: The Free Press, n.d.

Hurt, Harry, III. *The Texas Rich*. New York: Norton, 1980.

Josephson, Matthew. *The Money Lords*. New York: New American Library, n.d.

———. *The Robber Barons*. New York: Harcourt, Brace, Jovanovich, 1962.

Lacey, Robert. *The Kingdom*. New York: Harcourt, Brace, Jovanovich, 1982.

Lucie-Smith, Edward, and Dars, Celestine. *How the Rich Lived*. New York: Paddington Press, n.d.

Lundberg, Ferdinand. *The Rich and the Super-Rich*. Secaucus, N.J.: Lyle Stuart, 1968.

Marriott, Oliver. *The Property Boom*. London: Hamish Hamilton, n.d.

Mills, C. Wright. *The Power Elite*. New York: Oxford University Press, 1956.

Morton, Frederic. *Rothschilds: A Family Portrait*. New York: Atheneum, 1962.

Raw, Charles; Page, Bruce; and Hodgson, Godfrey. *Do You Sincerely Want to Be Rich?* London: André Deutsch, n.d.

Sampson, Anthony. *The Sovereign State*. Briarcliff Manor, N.Y.: Stein and Day, 1980.

Schumacher, E. F. *Small Is Beautiful*. New York: Harper & Row, 1973.

Smith, Adam. *The Money Game*. New York: Random House, 1968.

———. *Supermoney*. New York: Random House, 1972.

Sobel, Robert. *Panic on Wall Street*. New York: Macmillan, 1972.

Thorndike, Joseph J., Jr. *The Very Rich: A History of Wealth*. New York: Crown, 1976.

Toffler, Alvin. *The Third Wave*. New York: William Morrow, 1980.

Winchester, Simon. *Their Noble Lordships*. New York: Random House, 1982.

Wiseman, Thomas. *The Money Motive*. London: Hutchinson, n.d.

INDEX

Index

Index

Index

Index

Index

Index

Index

Index